FLYING TIGER ACE

THE STORY OF BILL REED, CHINA'S SHINING MARK

FLYING TIGER ACE

THE STORY OF BILL REED, CHINA'S SHINING MARK

CARL MOLESWORTH

OSPREY PUBLISHING
Bloomsbury Publishing Plc
PO Box 883, Oxford, OX1 9PL, UK
1385 Broadway, 5th Floor, New York, NY 10018, USA
E-mail: info@ospreypublishing.com
www.ospreypublishing.com

OSPREY is a trademark of Osprey Publishing Ltd

First published in Great Britain in 2020

ISBN: HB 978 1 4728 4003 5; PB 978 1 4728 4004 2; eBook 978 1 4728 4002 8; ePDF 978 1 4728 4000 4; XML 978 1 4728 4001 1

20 21 22 23 24   10 9 8 7 6 5 4 3 2 1

Edited by Tony Holmes
Maps by Bounford.com
Index by Zoe Ross

Typeset by Deanta Global Publishing Services, Chennai, India
Printed and bound in Great Britain by CPI (Group) UK Ltd, Croydon CR0 4YY

Front cover: Bill Reed, by then a seasoned combat veteran with the AVG's 3rd PS, is seen at Yunnanyi, China, in May 1942. The "Hell's Angel" cartoon painted on his flight jacket replicates the one that adorned his P-40 "No. 75." (*Photograph by R. T. Smith, © Brad Smith*)

Osprey Publishing supports the Woodland Trust, the UK's leading woodland conservation charity.

To find out more about our authors and books visit www.ospreypublishing.com. Here you will find extracts, author interviews, details of forthcoming events and the option to sign up for our newsletter.

MIX
Paper from
responsible sources
FSC® C020471

Contents

Preface

I remember well the night nearly 35 years ago when "Bill Reed" become more to me than simply a name on various military reports I had been studying for a book I intended to write. I was in a banquet room of Trader Vic's restaurant in Seattle to attend a reunion of the Chinese-American Composite Wing (CACW), a little-known military unit that had seen air combat in China during the final two years of World War II. American veterans of the CACW had held banquets before, but this was the first time that Chinese pilots had come from Taiwan to take part.

Thirty-seven years earlier, these men had fought together against the Japanese before saying goodbye at the end of the war. Now, 28 aging Chinese pilots had traveled across the Pacific to rekindle old friendships with their American comrades and hoist a few drinks in honor of those from both countries who did not survive the war. As a 30-something writer just starting to flesh out the CACW's history for my first book, I felt very fortunate to have been invited.

They were a reserved group as the banquet opened, but the conversation soon warmed up as memories stripped away the years. A few men told stories of air combat during the evening, but most of the reminiscences concerned their lives together on the ground – a Jeep wreck, a rare USO show, their celebrations on V-J Day. Later, a movie projector was wheeled into the room, and the lights went down. As a surprise, the Chinese had brought along a film that had been pieced together from footage held in the

Republic of China Air Force archives. The film revealed scenes of several CACW squadrons training at Malir, in India, in 1943, and it quickly brought even more memories rolling back.

"That's me!" called out one American from the darkness on seeing the face of a young pilot in the cockpit of a P-40 Warhawk fighter.

The scene switched to the Chinese and American leaders of one squadron as the two men stood chatting on a dusty airfield. Retired Maj Gen Hsu Hua-chiang sat quietly watching the movie and nodded in affirmation when someone asked if he was the Chinese officer in the scene. Then, in a voice of deep reverence, former pilot Wilbur Walton identified the American aviator in the scene as his squadron commander, Lt Col Bill Reed. A murmur rippled through the crowd as others recognized Reed's handsome face, and then someone proposed a toast to him. I realized that this must have been a very special man to elicit such a reaction. Though dead for many years, Reed still held a place in the hearts of these men. I knew I had to write about him.

Since then, pieces of the Bill Reed story have appeared in five of my books. Now, as the centennial of his birth passes, I finally have the opportunity to tell the full story of Bill Reed's life. In doing so, I hope to add flesh, bones and heart onto the grim statistics of World War II.

Bill Reed never had a wife. He never had children. He missed many of the joyful experiences that most of us take for granted. Perhaps by telling what he did experience during his short life, this book will help us appreciate our good fortune as Americans that Bill Reed and many thousands like him made the ultimate sacrifice so that we could live in freedom and prosperity.

Carl Molesworth
Mount Vernon
Washington
USA

Introduction

Advanced Flying School
US Army Air Corps
Selma, Alabama

Saturday – June 21, 1941

Dear Mom,
Finally getting around to a letter, and I don't relish the task of writing this one. A week ago Thursday I signed the contract to go to Burma as a check or test pilot. The contract calls for a year, but one paragraph states that I can quit any time during the year. I signed for $8,000.00 a year, the same as my room-mate and three other fellows in the squadron. There is no reason for you to worry about the work being any more dangerous, because it's not. And the pay is going to enable us to get out of debt and financial worry for good.

I will be home sometime next week. I've written Izzy and will write Leota today. I want to have sort of a family reunion or get-together so I can see them all without too much traveling around. Don't know just when I'll get there, but it will probably be late in the week.

Please don't worry too much about this until I get there to talk to you.

Love, Bill

Hotel Pennsylvania

August 8, 1943

Dear Mom,

Well, here's the letter I promised you over the phone last night, and there isn't a great deal I can add to what I told you then. I have a plane reservation tomorrow to Miami Beach. Should move out very shortly though, and am flying wherever I go – so my baggage is restricted pretty much.

I know how you feel about my going back, Mom, and I can't blame you – I think I can take care of myself all right, though, and do more good there than here.

I'm certainly glad I was able to get more news of this two or three weeks in advance of orders (through the Army grapevine) because it enabled me to take a swell vacation.

Seems funny that just 11 months ago I was sitting in this very same hotel phoning you to tell you I was back from China, and now I'm headed off again. I'll phone or write again before I leave – got quite a few letters to write.

Don't worry about me, Mom, because I will be all right. Write me as often as you can.

Love, Bill

Headquarters Fourteenth Air Force
A.P.O. 627, C/O Postmaster
New York City, New York
December 28, 1944

Dear Mrs. Reed,
With deep regret and a keen sense of personal loss, I must inform you that your son, Lt Col William N. Reed, was killed in action December 19, 1944. No doubt you have already been informed by the War Department.

I can appreciate your feelings only too well. Your son and I had been together since the old AVG days and shared the kinship granted to those who struggle against difficulties together. Bill had successfully coped with danger for so long that he was considered well-nigh indestructible. Indeed, in the highest sense he will always be indestructible, for the unique record he created serving his country will live forever. He flew 75 missions with the AVG and 66 missions thereafter, selecting for himself the more difficult assignments, rather than those likely to result in headlines. With characteristic modesty, he was never concerned with credit for himself, but always was interested in credit for his men. His achievements were recognized by awards of the Silver Star, the Distinguished Flying Cross and Oak Leaf Cluster, the Air Medal, the British Distinguished Flying Cross, and the Fifth and Sixth Order of the Chinese Cloud Banner. Bill Reed will always be cherished in our hearts and memories.

Please accept this as the expression of the heartfelt sympathy of the officers and men of the Fourteenth Air Force.

Sincerely yours,
C. L. Chennault
Major General, U.S.
Commanding

People come and go in your life, especially during wartime. Some you know for just a short time; others for much longer. A few you never forget.

PART ONE

The Making of a Man

I

"Everything anyone would ever want to be"

Maj Bill Reed may have paused to think about his father as he was settling into the cockpit of his Warhawk fighter plane in the predawn twilight of June 7, 1944. Yesterday would have been Edward Reed's 78th birthday. Was it possible that eight years had passed since Pop had died? So much had happened, and yet life was continuing to throw challenges at the 27-year-old pilot as the brutal war he was fighting dragged on.

Soon Reed got down to the business at hand, a dive-bombing raid by eight P-40N Warhawks that he would lead from the remote airfield at Ankang, China, against a Japanese-held railroad yard at Chenghsien (now Zhengzhou). The yard was a key facility on the rail line connecting Peking (Beijing) up north with the Japanese stronghold at Hankow (Wuhan). Damaging it would help to relieve pressure on hard-pressed Chinese troops fighting in the Hsiang (Xiang) River valley southwest of Hankow by delaying deliveries of supplies and ammunition for the Japanese forces advancing in the valley. The air raid would amount to a pinprick compared to the scope of the war in China, but it was better than nothing.

Reed's crew chief, SSgt Homer "Jug" Nunley, stood on the wing and helped the pilot fasten his safety harness, then jumped down to stand by for the engine start. Once he had completed the cockpit checks, Reed fired up the P-40's big 12-cylinder Allison engine. Blue flames and smoke gushed from the exhaust stubs for a few seconds as the propeller began to turn and the engine coughed to life. Soon, the engine note smoothed out to a deafening roar – as always, Nunley had it tuned to perfection.

Nunley had a few minutes to admire his P-40 while the engine warmed up. It was a handsome bird, with dark olive drab over gray camouflage setting the background for blue-and-white Chinese Air Force insignia on the fuselage and wings. Twelve alternating horizontal stripes, also blue and white, adorned the rudder. A large rendition of a leering shark's face was painted on the radiator cowling below the engine, and its white propeller spinner identified this P-40 as the 7th Fighter Squadron (FS) commander's aircraft. The name *BOSS'S HOSS* in large block letters on the left side of the nose played on Reed's nickname in the squadron. Nunley laid claim to the other side, where he had painted the name *JUG'S PLUG*. Hanging from the rack underneath the P-40's belly was a plump 500lb bomb.

From the cockpit, Reed looked down the Ankang flightline and observed that all seven of the Warhawks accompanying him on the mission were running smoothly and ready to go. They were organized into two flights, with three American pilots joining Reed and four Chinese pilots led by Capt Yang Yun Kuang in the second flight. Reed gave a wave to Nunley, released the P-40's parking brake and taxied out for takeoff, with the others close behind.

At 0440hrs Reed shoved the throttle forward, and *BOSS'S HOSS* began to roll down the runway. The tail rose as he gained speed, giving him a clear view of the dark runway in front of him. He fed in some right rudder to counteract the engine torque trying to push the P-40's nose to the left. He could feel the crunch of the gravel surface under his wheels, but then the crunching stopped as the P-40 lifted off the runway. Reed retracted the landing gear and made a slow, climbing turn to the left to give the others time to form up. Soon, the eight P-40s set out on a northeasterly heading toward Chenghsien, some 300 miles away.

The mountainous landscape of Honan (Henan) Province rolled by below the eight P-40s for the next two hours, but the pilots had little time for sightseeing. This was disputed airspace, and it was all too likely that Japanese fighters could jump Reed's boys at any moment if they did not keep a sharp lookout. No enemy planes happened to be aloft, so the strike force reached the target area unopposed. From two miles up, Reed could clearly see the marshalling yards at Chenghsien – the same target he had bombed just four days earlier. A train was stopped next to the station, with smoke chugging out of the locomotive's stack.

In accordance with the mission plan, the two flights split up. The American pilots would bomb first, while the Chinese remained at altitude to provide top cover in case enemy fighters should attack. After their bomb runs, the Americans would climb up to cover the Chinese pilots while they made their drops.

The attack began at 0645hrs, when Reed peeled off and started his dive toward the target. Feeling his plane begin to roll as it gained speed in the dive, he added some port trim to keep his nose pointed at the target. *BOSS'S HOSS* was screaming down at nearly 400 mph when Reed released his bomb and then pulled back hard on the control stick. His vision grayed as the gravitational pull forced blood from his head. In a few seconds he was seeing clearly again as the P-40 zoomed back up into the sky. He watched from above as one by one the other Warhawks made their runs, but was disappointed to see that only two of the eight 500-pounders hit in the target area, causing little if any damage.

This would never do. Reed was not about to return to Ankang with nothing accomplished. The train was still puffing away down in the yard, so Reed radioed to Capt Yang to cover him while he led the American flight back down to strafe it. Reed's four P-40s flew off, out of sight of the railroad yard, and let down to treetop altitude. Then they came roaring back, headed directly for the train. Moving at more than 300mph, Reed took careful aim at the locomotive and opened fire at about a quarter-mile out from the target. The six machine guns in his wings spat out a long burst of 0.50-caliber slugs that tore into the boiler of the locomotive, setting off an eruption of steam and twisted metal when it exploded. Reed's three wingmen – Capt A. W. "Bill" Lewis and Lts Don Burch and Ed Mulholland – proceeded to riddle the rest of the train.

Having flown more than 100 combat missions since the beginning of the war, Reed might have been satisfied to call it a day at this point. The element of surprise was gone, which meant Japanese troops on the ground would be shooting back if the P-40s returned. But Reed's fighting blood was up. He figured a second strafing run would finish off the train, so he circled for another attack. Down he went, picking up speed, with the other three P-40s right behind. The train was burning by now as Reed's machine guns ripped into it again. However, as he pulled up from the strafing run he felt a jolt, and his engine cut out for a second or two, then restarted. This was not good.

Reed turned the fighters westward and began watching his fuel gauge. Before long he could see that the fuel tanks in *BOSS'S HOSS* were draining rapidly. He would never make it back to Ankang. Then the engine quit for good. The plane had run out of fuel over a valley in mountainous terrain. A stream ran down the valley, and Reed could see that it provided his best – and perhaps only – chance for surviving a landing. There was no time to determine the wind direction. He would have to take his chances with a straight-in approach, wheels up.

Reed dropped full flaps at an altitude of 500ft and the P-40 mushed rapidly toward the shallow river. The only sound was the rush of the wind past his open cockpit canopy. Then the fighter hit the river, and he could hear the splash of water before the rocks and sand of the river bottom began tearing away at the P-40's aluminum belly, which was beginning to burn. The fire was spreading as the plane ground to a halt, and Reed jumped out with no injuries beyond singed hair on an eyelash and the back of one hand. He had managed to fly *BOSS'S HOSS* about 100 miles away from the target area before they went down 15 miles southeast of Sunghsien (Songxian). But he was not out of the woods yet. This was disputed territory, where he was just as likely to be captured by a Japanese infantry patrol as he was to reach friendly Chinese guerrilla troops who could escort him to safety.

Capt Bill Lewis, Reed's close friend and second-in-command, recalled the mission in a letter to this author many years later:

A visual observation by me showed a lot of liquid streaming back from his ship. I kept telling him to bail out if his ship conked out completely, which it did about that time, and he decided to belly it in on a sandbar. I circled him a few times and saw that he was out of the cockpit and apparently okay. I don't believe Bill had ever bailed out, and he seemed to have an inordinate fear of doing so, since bailing out would have been far safer than trying to belly in in that area. He was absolutely fearless in all other aspects, so maybe I am imagining that he had a fear of bailing out. We will never know.[1]

The remaining seven P-40s returned to Ankang to deliver the bad news about the boss. June 7, 1944 ended with this apprehensive note in the 7th FS's daily operations log:

The entire squadron is concerned over Maj Reed's safety. It would be a demoralizing blow to the entire outfit if he should be captured by the Japs.

STONE CITY

There is not much left of Stone City, Iowa. The dolomite limestone quarries that once gave economic life to the settlement on the Wapsipinicon River have been dormant for more than half a century, replaced by more efficient underground mining. The railroad is gone, too, as are many of the buildings, including the Columbia Hall opera house/hotel and the Green Mansion, once famous as the site of Grant Wood's Stone City Art Colony. A population estimated at more than 1,000 people in the 1890s has dwindled to fewer than 200 today.

What does remain among Stone City residents is a strong sense of their community's past, with a commitment to historic preservation of the remaining stone structures there. Two of the most prominent of those buildings are the general store – since transformed into a destination restaurant – and the handsome three-story house at 12623 Stone City Road, both built by Stone City co-founder and pioneer quarry owner Henry Dearborn. It was in the Dearborn home that William Norman Reed, Henry's last grandson, was born on January 8, 1917.

Henry Dearborn, born in New Hampshire in 1828, was a stone cutter, mason and entrepreneur when he opened his first limestone quarry at Stone City in 1859. An ambitious young man, he had left his parents' farm at age 18 to pursue his fortune in a series of jobs as he moved westward from Vermont to Pennsylvania, before settling in eastern Iowa in 1856. Dearborn's quarry prospered, employing inmates from the penitentiary in nearby Anamosa, but he foresaw greater opportunity at another site not far away. He sold the first quarry and opened a new one half a mile down the river. There, over the next half-century, Dearborn would make his fortune.

Henry Dearborn and his wife Martha, a native of England with the wonderful nickname "Merry Isle," would produce eight children, including three who died in infancy. As might be expected, the three surviving sons followed their father into the quarry business. The second son, William Norman "Will" Dearborn, proved the most successful, eventually expanding into banking and construction contracting.

The Dearborns' general store stood on the banks of the Wapsipinicon next to the railroad bridge that crossed the river. By the early 1890s, a train would arrive in Stone City each morning from Marion, Iowa, bringing in quarry workers who lived in communities along the 25-mile stretch of track. The train would be loaded with limestone and then carry its load and the workers back westward at the end of the day. From 1859 through to 1895, an estimated 225,000 carloads of stone were shipped out of the Stone City quarries.

The youngest Dearborn child was Mary Ellen, born in 1873. Nicknamed "Mayme" (pronounced "Mame"), she grew up in the family's big Stone City home and went to work in the general store when she finished her schooling. A serious girl, Mayme had an attractive face with a straight nose, a strong chin and brown eyes. She might have been considered pretty when she smiled, but smiles rarely crossed her face.

A water tank serving the steam locomotives of the Milwaukee Road stood next to the general store, so the train stopped there every day on the Stone City run (Chicago, Milwaukee, St. Paul and Pacific Railroad). It is likely that Mayme met her future husband, railroader Edward Joseph Reed, one day when he went in the store during a water stop. Reed, another native of New Hampshire, was born in 1867 and moved to Iowa with his family at the age of four. A husky man of medium height, he went to work for the railroad in 1892 as a fireman, shoveling coal into the engine.

Edward and Mayme were married in Stone City on Christmas Day, 1893. Some may have looked askance at the daughter of a prominent family marrying a railroad worker, but that was not the Dearborn family's way. The young couple initially lived in Maquoketa, Iowa, and welcomed their first two children – Leota, born 1895, and George, 1897 – into life there. When their third child was on the way, the Reed family moved to Marion, Henry Dearborn buying them a home there on Irish Hill. Marion was a relatively compact community of about 4,500 citizens located just a few miles northeast of Cedar Rapids. When their second daughter arrived in 1899, the Reeds named her Marion. Two more daughters were born in that community, Dorothy in 1901 and Isabelle in 1904.

Frank and Will Dearborn took over operation of the Stone City quarry from their father in 1903. By this time, however, Portland cement was beginning to supplant limestone as a primary building material for roadbeds, bridges and buildings. The boom town that Stone City once was began to decline. When Henry Dearborn died in 1907, only "Merry Isle," now 73, remained in the family's big house. The Reed family left Marion to move in with "Merry Isle" in Stone City so that Mayme could care for her mother in her declining years.

"Merry Isle" died in 1913. By that time Mayme had given birth to three more children. Josephine Reed arrived in 1908 but died in her infancy. Sons Edward (1909) and Kenneth (1912) followed and, finally, five years later, Mayme delivered her last child, William, on a cold day in early January 1917. The Reeds named him for his Uncle Will Dearborn and hoped Billy would grow up as successful and honorable as his namesake was at the time.[2]

The next addition to the Reed family came on November 18, 1918, when Billy's sister Marion, now 19 years old and living with her aunt in Akron, Iowa, near Sioux City, gave birth to a son. She named the baby William Raymond Reed, as the boy's father was not in the picture. Thus, two Bill Reeds – uncle and nephew – arrived just 22 months apart in age. Somehow, the younger boy came to be called Dick, and later his schoolmates would nickname him "Junior." Marion's second son, Laurence, would come along in 1923 after she had married Lawrence "Stub" Martin, another railroader.

QUAKER OATS ENGINEER

With the turn of the calendar to 1919, a tumultuous year began for the Reed family. Edward, after 27 years as a fireman and engineer on short-run train routes throughout eastern Iowa, left the Milwaukee Road to take a job in Cedar Rapids. In his new position as an engineer, Edward shuttled grain cars around the yard at the big Quaker Oats plant. The family lived for a short time in Cedar Rapids and then moved back to the Dearborns' two-story, wood-framed house at 386 16th Street in Marion. There, Edward could ride the streetcar about six miles to work at Quaker Oats, while the younger children took advantage of Marion's excellent public-school system.

When the Reeds returned to Marion, they found it little changed from the town they had left some 12 years before. Although now a suburb of Cedar Rapids, the community still had a distinct identity as a railroad town – the Iowa Division First District headquarters of the mighty Milwaukee Road. Attached to the handsome railroad station on what is now 6th Avenue was an office building for railroad administration, and the railroad also had a roundhouse on the eastern edge of town. The rail line ran through Marion, with the main line running westward toward Omaha, Sioux City and beyond. Residents of Marion lived with the rumble and smoke of steam locomotives and the scream of their whistles at all hours of the day and night.

They also lived with its weather. Winter winds out of the upper Midwest and Canada brought bitter cold and the occasional blizzard. Summers were just the opposite – blazing hot and muggy. But the "shoulder" seasons were delightful. Years later, Bill Reed would mention this in a letter to his mother from half a world away:

> There's something about spring in Marion that I've never found anywhere else.

Most of Marion's downtown businesses were located along brick-paved 7th Avenue, just a block north of the tracks. Banks, retail shops, pharmacies, barber shops, grocery stores and restaurants, plus a department store, a bakery, a pool hall, a Case farm implement dealer and the library provided all the goods and services needed by Marion's residents.

The residential neighborhoods were overhung by elm, oak and maple trees, and vegetable gardens filled many vacant lots. The homes of Marion's more prominent citizens lined the streets north of 7th Avenue, and most of the churches were there, too. A large percentage of the railroad families, including the Reeds, lived in the Irish Hill neighborhood, a gentle bump in the landscape on the south side of the tracks and within walking distance of the Milwaukee Road facilities.

City Square Park, facing 7th Avenue and bounded by 10th and 11th streets, was the social center of town, with tall trees and a handsome statue of an unknown Civil War soldier. Indian Creek ran though Thomas Park, 50 tree-lined acres on the road to Cedar

Rapids that was established in 1917 to provide campgrounds for overnight visitors. The Carnegie Library had opened in 1905. Farm fields stretched away from the north and east sides of town on rolling hills, and Indian Creek ran along the west side as it wandered its way southward to join the Cedar River just east of Cedar Rapids.

Between the railroad and the agriculture industry, jobs were plentiful. If any town in America could claim to be an ideal place for raising a family in those days, that town was Marion.

Bill Reed's eldest brother George would not survive to see the arrival of the 1920s. In Cedar Rapids on a cold Thanksgiving Day (November 27, 1919), 22-year-old George was having trouble getting his motorcycle to start. Repeated jumps onto the kick starter proved unsuccessful, so George caught his breath and then gave it one more try. The engine did not catch, but George fell to the ground with a heart attack and died on the spot. Mayme grieved for her second lost child and leaned on her Episcopalian faith for comfort. But with two teenage daughters and three rambunctious boys in the household, there was little time for mourning before her motherly responsibilities drew Mayme back into her daily routine.

Although Billy was still a toddler when the Reeds arrived back in Marion, brothers Eddie and Kenneth were both in elementary school and big sister Isabelle ("Izzy") was a high-school student. Dorothy ("Dort"), now age 18, may still have been living with the family at this time as well. With Edward the only wage earner, it must have been tough for the Reeds to make ends meet, even though they owned their home. The average annual wage of a railroad worker at this time was $1,476, but the US Bureau of Labor Statistics estimated that a family of five living in the Midwest needed to spend $1,500 to $2,100 per year in order to live at "a fairly decent and healthful standard." Edward's job at Quaker Oats may have paid a little better than railroad wages, but then again it may not have.[3] Either way, with a family of seven or eight to support, Edward's paycheck would have barely covered the basics.

Although the Reed family finances were thin, the children did not know it. Kenny wore clothes handed down from Eddie, and would pass along the ones that survived to Billy when he got older. Style was unimportant to the young boys, but food was plentiful, and that is what mattered. Sisters Izzy and Dort both married in 1923, within a month of each other, and moved out. This made room available in the Irish Hill home, so Marion and her husband moved back from western Iowa with their young sons Dick and Larry. Because of their closeness in age, Billy and Dick soon became the best of friends, and Larry would look up to both of them as big brothers while he was growing up.

The Reed boys were town kids, so they did not have the crushing schedule of chores like the farm boys in the surrounding countryside. Occasionally, the family would travel north to the lakes of Wisconsin on fishing trips – joyful outings that instilled a lifelong love of fishing in the boys. Years later, Billy would write nostalgically about those fishing trips in letters to his mother from far-off corners of the world.

The area around Marion offered endless opportunities for boys with imagination and a sense of adventure to have fun, especially in the summertime when school was not in session. Billy's neighborhood friend Ed Ferreter recalled carefree afternoons hiking on the bluffs outside town and swimming in the holes of Indian Creek, including Fry's, Granger's pasture and the Wiggens place. They also played a lot of sandlot baseball, with Billy pitching and Ferreter covering third base in most games. Ferreter recalled:

> During early fall, a bunch of us would enjoy a watermelon from a nearby farm. Just one melon. We never destroyed a patch or took a bunch of melons to throw in the streets. We always had good, clean fun.

PLANESPOTTING

The rare sight of an airplane flying over Marion in the 1920s and '30s was sure to trigger a jolt of excitement among the kids of the town. In those days, aviation was still considered an exotic new frontier – an industry in the making. Pilots were heroes, from local barnstormers to World War I aces like Eddie Rickenbacker and racers such as Speed Holman, Roscoe Turner and Jimmy Doolittle. Then there was Charles Lindbergh, the "Lone Eagle," who made the first solo flight across the Atlantic Ocean in 1927 to become America's most renowned aviator. In Marion, it did not hurt that Lindbergh's Ryan NYP plane was named after the nearby city of St. Louis.

When a plane did fly over Marion in those days, the man in the cockpit was most likely Dan Hunter. A military pilot during World War I, Hunter returned home to Cedar Rapids in the early 1920s with big plans to establish a career for himself in civil aviation. His first step was buying a war-surplus JN-4 Canuck biplane, which was a Canadian-built version of the famous Curtiss Jenny trainer. Rugged, maneuverable and relatively dependable, the JN-4 was just the plane Hunter needed to launch his first venture, an air "show" he called Hunter's Flying Circus.

In 1924 Hunter rented a parcel of farmland just south of Cedar Rapids off Highway 30 and established an airport. At the same time, he started a company he called Cedar Rapids Airways Inc. With a grass landing strip lined by trees, Hunter Field was only usable during daylight hours on dry days. But it was enough to get Hunter started. He established a flight school to train future pilots and a charter service carrying cargo and people to distant locations. In 1928, Boeing Air Transport (later United Airlines) made a deal with Hunter to establish air mail service for Cedar Rapids at Hunter Field. Later, Hunter went on to become a leader in the Civil Air Patrol and continued to operate Hunter Field until he retired in 1960, by which time the current Cedar Rapids Airport had been built several miles south.

In Dan Hunter, local youngsters smitten with airplanes and flying had a real-life example of what the coming years could hold for them. Two such youngsters were Billy and Dick Reed, as future events would confirm.

SCHOOL

Billy Reed had started first grade in 1923, the same time Eddie began eighth grade and Kenneth the sixth grade. Learning came easily to the Reed boys, and they earned good grades without spending excessive amounts of time hitting the books. In fact, when Kenneth graduated from high school in 1930, his yearbook prophecy noted humorously that his ambition for senior year was, "To sleep through a class without pedagogical interruption."

All of the Reed boys were athletic, so first Kenneth and then Billy followed big brother Eddie's path into high school sports. Dick, perhaps the best athlete among them, came a year behind Billy. Eddie's demeanor, both on the playing field and off, earned him the nickname "Toughie." When Kenneth got to Marion High School (MHS), he played on the football team for three years but made his mark on the baseball field. Playing second base during his senior year, he led the team in batting with a .415 average. The Indians finished the 1930 season with a record of seven wins and two losses, including a tough 7-2 loss to Center Point in the county championship game.

Billy arrived at MHS in the fall of 1931, just over a year after Kenneth graduated. In that period, a new MHS had opened at the site of the current Vernon Middle School, and the Reeds had moved to a two-story, five-bedroom house at 1314 Fifth Avenue, directly across the street from the school. Mayme, Ed and their two youngest sons lived downstairs, while Marion, Lawrence, Dick and Larry lived upstairs. Reed sister Dorothy, who had married Joe Dumbolton in 1923, lived with her growing family in the house on Irish Hill.

Billy quickly established himself at MHS as the quintessential student athlete. Good grades earned him a place on the honor roll, and his fellow students elected him as the treasurer of the freshman class. When spring came, Billy turned out for baseball and made the team. Playing third base on a fairly regular basis, he was the only freshman who completed enough innings to earn a letter, and thus membership to the school's M Club. Sophomore year was much the same, except that Billy lettered in basketball and was joined on the team by freshman Dick. Students now started calling Dick by the nickname "Junior" to differentiate him from Billy, the older William Reed who preceded him onto most of the school's sports teams. Though not yet a particularly big fellow, Dick also lettered on the football team that year. But he was growing.

Then, as now, football was a big deal at MHS. Each game garnered front-page coverage in the town's weekly newspaper, the *Marion Sentinel*. The Indians played in the Tri-Valley Conference, which included schools of similar size to MHS from the east-central Iowa area, with Marion roughly in the middle. All but one of the schools were within about 30 miles of Marion – Independence and Manchester to the north, Belle Plaine to the west and Tipton to the south. DeWitt, to the east, was about 60 miles away, making for long road trips when the Indians played the DeHawks.

Football coach Don Wolfe was a devotee of the single-wing offensive formation, invented by the famed coach Glenn "Pop" Warner. The single wing used an unbalanced line, with both tackles on the same side of the center and four players in the backfield. This concentrated strength on one side of the line for the run-oriented offense. The center would snap the ball shotgun-style to the tailback, who would then follow the other three backs into – and hopefully through – the opposing line for a gain. The tailback also had the option to pass the ball to an end or one of the other backs, and trick plays such as the end-around reversal were used on occasion.

The 1933 MHS football season featured Billy, now a junior, and sophomore Dick in the Indians' backfield. The uncle and nephew shone, both earning letters. Billy usually played quarterback, being one of the blockers. Dick backed up starting tailback Garth Hunter and earned this poetic mention in the 1934 yearbook – "Reed, too, was fast and small – when Hunter was out he carried the ball." That year's team was very successful, going undefeated with eight wins and one tie.

When tryouts for the 1934 football season took place at Thomas Park Field on September 6, 48 potential players turned out. That means nearly half the boys attending MHS, with an enrollment of perhaps 250 students that year, had dreams of gridiron glory. Coach Wolfe ran the boys through a series of blocking and tackling drills, plus general conditioning, while he tried to figure out how to replace Hunter and the other seniors in last year's outstanding backfield. Two of his choices were obvious – Billy and Junior Reed.

The opening game of the season, on September 28 at Tipton, marked a change in routine for the Tri-Valley Conference. Before then, all games had been played on Friday afternoons, but floodlights had been installed at the Tipton field, so the game could start at 1945hrs. That way, students could watch the game without a disruption in Friday afternoon classes. In a few years, night games would become common.

The Tipton game was a disappointing start for the Indians. Billy played halfback, Junior was the fullback and punter, while Ed Ferreter played one of the end positions. On a muddy field, neither team could generate any offense. Time after time, the MHS possessions would end with Junior punting the ball away. He did well, averaging kicks of 40 yards, with the longest at 65 including its roll. But the Tipton team managed to block one of Dick's punts, recover the ball and run it into the end zone for the only score of the game. Marion lost, 6-0. The team made the long road trip to Clinton County the following Friday and came away with a 13-0 win over the DeWitt DeHawks.

The first home game for Marion was against Manchester on October 12. With a large hometown crowd cheering them on, the Indians started strong. Early in the game Junior Reed got the ball at his own 25 and ran off tackle for a 35-yard gain. After three more short gains, Junior completed a pass to fellow junior Dale Luwe, who carried it across the goal line for a touchdown. Junior then ran off tackle for the extra point, and Marion led 7-0. The Indians scored again on their next possession, but Junior slipped on the extra point try, so the lead became 13-0. That ended the scoring.

Billy and Junior both ran the ball, and Billy attempted a pass to Junior that fell incomplete. The defense held Manchester scoreless, and MHS won its second game.

Marion played another home game on October 19 against Independence, and again muddy field conditions hampered the offenses. Independence tried a lot of complex plays that did not work. Marion's strong defensive line blocked a punt in the first quarter, and Dale Luwe recovered it in the end zone for a touchdown. Billy intercepted two passes while playing defense, and Junior picked off another. Marion did not attempt a pass until the fourth quarter, when Junior threw to Billy incomplete. The game ended with MHS winning again, 6-0. That was the high-water mark for the season.

The Indians lost the next two games when they traveled to Vinton on October 26 and Belle Plaine one week later. Then they played Mount Vernon at home on November 9 and tied 13-13.

There was high excitement leading up to the Homecoming game on November 16, as the two remaining players from Marion's first football team in 1896 who still lived in town were introduced before the game. That was the high point of the afternoon, however, as Monticello's outstanding halfback Matthieson carried, passed or kicked on 90 percent of his team's plays on the way to a 20-6 victory. The season ended with a 15-0 loss to Anamosa in the annual Thanksgiving Day game, the first time Marion had lost to Anamosa in seven years. Bill played halfback for most of the game, but Junior had been injured in a previous contest and did not play.

Although the season had been a disappointment following the success of the previous year, about 200 people turned out at American Legion Post 298 on December 12 for Marion's annual football banquet. Billy and Junior were among the 17 Indian lettermen honored that night. Many of them would return for the 1935 football season, when Junior Reed led the team to an undefeated season and earned himself a place in the Marion High School Athletic Hall of Fame. Junior scored 112 of the 1935 team's total 198 points, including 22 successful extra-point kicks. The MHS *Quill* yearbook his senior year contained this joke:

> Jr. Reed, a champion athlete, in bed with a cold, was told he had
>   a temperature.
> "How high is it, Doc?," he wanted to know.
> "A hundred and one."
> "What's the record?"

The 1935 basketball season followed quickly, but none of the players from the football team were available for the first game of the season. Only three returning lettermen – Billy, Junior and Dale Luwe – were on the team. Billy, wearing No. 6 on his crimson-and-gold jersey, played guard and was team captain, while Junior, No. 12, was a forward and also played center. The young team showed promise, but it could not seem to maintain momentum for a full game, losing 16 straight to open the season. Finally, on February 28, 1935, the Indians tipped off against Anamosa. Typical of basketball games of the period, it was a low-scoring affair. Billy and Junior led the team with seven points each in the 27-16 victory. Two more losses rounded out one of the worst basketball seasons in MHS history. Billy's MHS athletic career would close with the 1935 track and baseball seasons, but he was far from finished as a student athlete. Sports had given him self-confidence, daring and aggressiveness, along with an appreciation for tactics and strategy. These traits would serve him well for the rest of his life.

If Billy Reed had been simply a top athlete at MHS, he still would have stood out in the crowd. As he grew taller and filled out, he approached his adult size of about 5ft 10in and 165–170lb. His brown hair rolled in waves across his head, and he had the same straight nose, strong chin and brown eyes as his mother.

Mayme was stern, but she did show her softer side occasionally. When the 1934 World Series rolled around, the St. Louis Cardinals were in the fall baseball classic against Detroit. The Cardinals were as close as it came to a home team for Marion, so there was a lot of fan interest in the town – especially at the high school across 5th Avenue from the Reed home. Knowing that, Mayme would listen to the games on the radio and post the scores as they changed on a large board on the front porch, so Billy and the other kids could peek out the windows to keep up with the games. It was rumored that the principal also sneaked a peek at Mayme's scoreboard more than once.

Given his good looks and outgoing personality, it comes as no surprise that Billy developed an eye for the girls, which lasted throughout his life – and they reciprocated. His favorite date during high school was Margaret "Mick" Forbes, a pretty redhead who was a year behind him in school. It would not have been surprising to see them together at the annual MHS wiener roast in Schaeffer Park, at November's all-school dance in the gym or dancing to the jukebox in the back room at the K-V Café in uptown Marion. Their romance would continue well beyond high school, Billy and "Mick" remaining faithful correspondents while he was away at college and then during World War II.

Writing many years later, Ed Ferreter described his friend Billy as "the All-American boy. Handsome, with a contagious smile. Very friendly. He was everything anyone would ever want to be."[4]

Billy Reed's academic career at MHS was, if anything, more successful than his exploits in sports. After two solid years on the honor roll, Billy was elected to membership in Delta Sigma Delta, the national honor society. It says a lot about Billy that the society listed membership qualifications as "scholarship, leadership, character and service." Only three other juniors were elected with him to the 17-member organization. Billy also found time to wedge a part in the school play, "As the Clock Strikes," into his busy schedule during his junior year.

When the 1934–35 school year began, Billy's classmates elected him president of the senior class. He was also chosen to be treasurer of Delta Sigma Delta, and he helped organize the Mathematics Honor Society, along with Ed Ferreter and their friend Don Goodyear.[5] Membership required a "B" average in math classes and a "C" average or better overall, which posed no problem for Billy. In addition, Billy served as the advertising manager for the *Quill* yearbook, where his "boss" was Ferreter, the business manager. In a small high school like MHS, the kids with good brains and leadership abilities had to wear a lot of hats.

Billy Reed's high school career ended on a high note in May 1935. He attended baccalaureate services at the Methodist Church with his class of 55 students and their families, then participated in Class Day at Lincoln Auditorium. The event included songs, skits and other entertainment presented by members of the class. It was Billy's job as class president to present that year's borrowed cap and gown to Betty Hense, representing the junior class.

The MHS Class of '35 went back to the Methodist Church for Commencement on May 24. With the Great Depression now in full effect, the school had no funding to hire a speaker for the event and chose several students to speak instead. Billy Reed was one of them. The *Marion Sentinel* sent a reporter to cover the occasion, and this account appeared on the front page of the May 30, 1935, edition:

> Billy Reed gave a short but thoughtful address on "War Profits." He said that from 1916 to 1918, the US Steel Corporation alone made a profit of $633 million, and the DuPont Company $257 million. Such enormous profits tend to encourage war and should be made impossible by federal taxes. If business was allowed no more than six percent profit during war times, they would not want war, and if they did not want it, the chances are that there would be no war. Future wars, if they must come, should be paid for by the generations doing the fighting and not leave the burden for the future to pay.

As Billy was giving his speech, war was already under way or brewing in such distant places as Ethiopia, Spain and China. In the coming years it would spread and blossom into the largest and most deadly conflict in world history. Billy, Dick and many thousands of other

Americans in his generation would pay in a way they could barely imagine on that warm spring day in 1935.

One of the last items of business at the end of each MHS school year was the distribution of the *Quill* yearbook. Due to the economic squeeze, the 1935 *Quill* was a slim volume with a flimsy cardboard cover. Still, it contained all the standard yearbook fare, including biographies of the seniors, reports on the sports teams and other activities, and a section called "Prophesies," in which members of the senior class predicted what the future would hold for them in the years to come. After Billy Reed's name in the Prophesies was one word – "Aviator."

2

"Justifiable homicide"

On Saturday and Sunday mornings during his senior year in high school, Bill Reed would make his way a mile north from home to Marion Country Club, where he worked as a caddy at the golf course. This was a great situation for the young man, because it not only allowed him to earn some much-needed spending money, but also gave him insight into the game of golf and acquainted him with local players.

As at most golf clubs, Bill worked as an independent contractor, paid by his client players at a set fee per round, plus a tip that depended on the player's satisfaction with Bill's work. An athlete in top condition, Bill had no trouble toting a player's golf bag for two circuits around the nine-hole course. Over time, he developed knowledge of yardages, pin placements and optimum club selections for each hole and lie. He enjoyed helping his players plot strategies for playing the course, and most importantly, his keen eyesight made him good at finding errant balls. Free rounds of golf on slow days were a bonus that allowed him to develop his own game and a love for the sport.

One of Bill's client players at Marion Country Club was Edward J. McPartland, a successful Cedar Rapids lawyer with an office downtown in the landmark Merchants National Bank Building. Bill caddied enough times for McPartland that the two had a chance to get well acquainted, since Bill apparently was not aware or accepting of the "three ups" of caddying – show up, keep up and shut up. The attorney was impressed by Bill's intelligence and outgoing personality. On one pivotal day, McPartland asked Bill what he was planning to do after he graduated from high school.

The truth was, Bill had no plan. This was 1935, the depth of the Great Depression, and the unemployment rate stood at 20.1 percent nationwide. He would be lucky if he could get on as a laborer at Quaker Oats, where his father was still working in the rail yard. Or perhaps he would move to the Chicago area to join his sister Leota and brothers Ed and Kenneth and seek work there. In any case, the Reed family had no money to send Bill to college, he told McPartland. At a cost of $800 to $1,000 per year for tuition, room and board, books and incidentals, college was out of the question.

Don't be so sure, McPartland replied. He was a man of his time, when philanthropy was often a one-on-one proposition – especially where advanced schooling was concerned. It was not unusual in those difficult years for a prosperous person to sponsor the college costs of a promising youngster, and that is precisely what McPartland suggested to Bill. If the Reeds were not in a position to send Bill to college, McPartland was. And he would.

In short order, Bill applied to Columbia College in Dubuque, Iowa's oldest institution of higher learning, and was accepted. His college career would start with freshman orientation and football turnout in August 1935. The bus ride to Dubuque, about 65 miles northeast of Marion, took about two hours, with a stop in Anamosa. On arrival in Dubuque, Bill found a landscape unfamiliar to a boy from the plains of Iowa – hills. The town spread along the west side of the Mississippi River and up a series of steep bluffs to the farmland and woods above. Industrial facilities, warehouses and docks lined the river bank, and the downtown commercial district ran along Main Street at the foot of the bluffs.

From the bus station it was a manageable walk up the 14th Street hill to the campus of Columbia College.[1] Large Victorian homes in the surrounding neighborhood overlooked the river, with

Wisconsin and Illinois visible beyond to the east. Bill enrolled in his classes and was given lodgings in Keane Hall, which was then a dormitory.

College life at Columbia must have come as a shock to Bill, who had enjoyed what might be termed a free-wheeling lifestyle while attending MHS. For starters, Columbia was a Catholic school, operated by the Roman Catholic Diocese of Dubuque. The Reed family attended the Episcopal Church, and Bill was not known as a particularly ardent Episcopalian at that. Attending mandatory chapel and Sunday services would require some flexibility on his part. Even more jarring was the realization that Columbia College was a males-only school, so socializing with the opposite sex – one of Bill's favorite pastimes – would be somewhat limited. This was only partially ameliorated by the fact that the Dubuque Diocese also operated Clarke College, an all-women's school, just a few blocks away. Opportunities for interaction among the students of the two campuses were infrequent and strictly controlled.

Students' behavior at Columbia College was governed by a strict set of rules that current-day college students would find hard to believe. Curfew was 2200hrs, telephone calls were only allowed with the permission of the dean and students could visit relatives just twice a month. The reading of newspapers and magazines was not allowed during study halls. Residents of Keane Hall were also prohibited from having automobiles or motorcycles, although this posed no hardship for cash-strapped Bill, who could not afford a vehicle anyway. Adjusting to the rules at Columbia College apparently posed no problems for him either. He signed up for 15 credit hours of classes and got down to work. His major was Economics. When the first semester honor roll was announced, there was Bill's name with a 3.0 ("B") average.

Bill also turned out for Columbia's football team, the Duhawks, and earned a spot on the roster for the Purple and Gold. Then, as now, the school's teams competed in the Iowa Intercollegiate Athletic Conference. The football team also scheduled several non-conference games each season. It did not take long for the first-year player to make his presence felt. The "As I See It" sports column in *The Lorian* school newspaper included this mention on November 8, 1935:

> "Spider" Reed and "Louie" Nagy, freshman ends, did great work against Winona Teachers, showing that much can be expected from them in coming years and for the remainder of the season.

Bill's nickname seems not to have stuck, but *he* did, anchoring the Duhawks' backfield throughout his four years at Columbia. As the school year progressed, he would compete on the basketball, track and baseball teams as well.

Someone in the Reed family gave Bill a present when he started college – a package of personalized stationery with BILL REED – COLUMBIA – DUBUQUE, IOWA printed across the top. Bill was slow to start corresponding with his parents and the rest of the family, but once he got started he never stopped. He would write hundreds of letters home from locations across the globe over the next nine years. One of his earliest saved letters reported to Mayme and Edward that he had returned safely to the Columbia campus after the Christmas 1935 vacation. It went on:

> We started classes in earnest today and from now on I'm going to burn the midnight oil. I'm taking 20 credit hours this year instead of only 15 and that means more work. I know I'm slow at writing this time, Mom, but I'll try to be more regular from now on, and you write, too, and take care of yourself. There are a lot of colds going around at this time of the year.

In a few sentences Bill introduced topics that he would repeat many times – concern for his mother's health and the desire to receive more mail. He was a great speller, and the lack of markover revisions in his letters reveals a clear writer who composed sentences fully before committing them to paper.

With spring came baseball season, and again Bill rated several mentions in the school newspaper for his exploits on the playing field. In a May 15 story about the Duhawks' game against Platteville Teachers' College, *The Lorian* referred to Bill as, "Reed, mighty purple and gold third baseman."

The school year ended at the beginning of June, and Bill returned to Marion to look for a summer job. He had barely settled into his old bedroom at the house on 5th Avenue when his father was hospitalized with heart trouble. Edward, who had just turned 70 on June 5, was still working in the rail yard at Quaker Oats. This is hardly surprising, as retirement was little more than a dream for working people back then. The federal Social Security Act and the Railroad Retirement Act, two key elements of the Roosevelt Administration's "New Deal" financial legislation, were less than a year old and had not yet built up sufficient equity to provide income for retirees. Like most workers, Edward's plan for old age would have been to work as long as he could and hope for the best after that. If Social Security held any hope for him, he was not counting on it.

Edward Reed was treated at Mercy Hospital in Cedar Rapids, but when he took a turn for the worse he was transferred to the University of Iowa hospital in Iowa City. There he died on July 7, 1936. In the four weeks following Edward's heart attack, the Reed family finances went from difficult to disastrous. Edward did not even have a suit of clothes suitable for burial, so Bill went to Armstrong's Department Store in downtown Cedar Rapids and bought a suit for him. Bill, however, did not have the purchase price (likely around $20). He arranged to make payments on the suit, but nine months later he would admit to his mother in a letter that he had made no payments and the store was threatening to sue him. Somehow, Mayme and Bill managed to pay off the debt.

Edward's funeral brought all of his surviving children together for the first time in several years. He had been a member of the Marion lodge No. 6 of A. F. and A. M., and the Masons took charge of the services. Among the attendees was Bill's benefactor from Cedar Rapids, Edward McPartland. Burial followed in the riverside cemetery at Anamosa, Iowa.

As the Reeds' sad summer of 1936 turned to fall, Bill returned to Dubuque for his sophomore year at Columbia College. This year would be different, because Bill's nephew and best friend Dick was joining him at the school. How the family afforded having two boys in college at the same time is a mystery. Now Bill and Dick would be closer than ever, not only playing on the Duhawks' sports teams but also rooming together in Keane Hall. Dick signed up for the same freshman classes Bill had taken the previous year, and Bill took on a heavy load that included Geology, Meteorology, French II, Psychology, English Literature and Economics. Bill described their dorm room in a letter to his mother:

> Our room is really fixed up swell. We didn't need curtains. They put up a swell set of drapes and curtains and gave us a swell thick rug, modernistic lamp and book shelf.

In addition to their classroom work, both Reeds would be playing an eight-game football schedule. Bill, wearing Number 34 and weighing 155lb, started at quarterback. Dick was ten pounds heavier than Bill and played halfback, with jersey Number 56. The star of the team was John J. Paul, who collected conference honors that year and went on to a distinguished career in the ministry. Paul was inducted into the school's hall of fame in 1983.

Despite the best efforts of the Reeds and their teammates, the Duhawks posted a losing record in 1936. In fact, the Duhawks' gridders won only 12 of the 32 games they played during the four years Bill was on the team. Still, the 1937 Purgold yearbook saw reason for hope that the coming season would be an improvement with Dick's presence on the team:

> Freshman halfback performed credibly throughout the whole of last season. With this year's experience under his belt, Dick will make a formidable foe for opponents of coming years.

Unfortunately, Dick would not live up to the yearbook writer's expectations, as injuries to both shoulders in his second year would hamper his performance on the field. Dick also took time from his studies and football to audition for a part in the Loras Players production of "Columbia's Hollywood" and secured the role of Ross Alexander. No reviews of Dick's performance are known to have survived.

As the 1936 Thanksgiving vacation approached, Bill put a blemish on his heretofore stellar record at Columbia when he was caught breaking curfew. Maybe he had succumbed to the allure of a Clarke College coed or stayed too long at one of the many taverns down the hill from the Columbia campus, but he was an hour late returning to the dormitory. That earned him an indefinite confinement to campus and forced him to miss playing in the football game against Luther College. "I'm so damn sore about it I've got half a notion to quit at the end of the semester and get a job," he wrote to his mother.

By the end of the Christmas vacation Bill's pique had passed, and he wrote on January 6, 1937, that he was determined to get straight As for the second semester after receiving two As and three Bs (3.439 average, which was easily good enough to make the honor roll) on his fall semester report card. Dick's grades were respectable but not quite good enough to make the honor roll.

Basketball season soon got under way, and Bill played guard for the Duhawks, though not as a starter. The Purgold yearbook described his role on the team:

> Does much to bolster up the Duhawk reserve material. A steady, hard-working basketeer, "Bill" can be put in at any time and carry on a good defensive game.

When spring came, Bill returned to the baseball diamond as the Duhawks' starting third baseman. The May 14, 1937, edition of *The Lorian* reported that Bill had a hit in four at-bats and scored a run in the game against Wartburg, and he also got a hit against Buena Vista.

College life agreed with Bill and Dick Reed, despite their constant struggles with money. In one letter home, Bill thanked

Mayme profusely for slipping a dollar bill in with the clean laundry she had sent. "That dollar came in awfully handy. I can use it for good purpose this year."

Late May brought the push toward final exams, and both boys were studying hard when they received shocking news from home. Bill's older brother Kenneth Reed was dead, killed during a labor demonstration in Chicago.

FALLEN BROTHER

At age 25, Kenneth Reed was finally getting some order into his life by 1937. He was married, with a baby daughter and another child on the way, and he had found steady work in the steel industry. He was a slim fellow with a narrow, handsome face and a thick head of dark hair combed straight back. There was an intensity in his brown eyes that fit his personality. Kenneth Reed was a battler. When he saw the little guy getting the worst of a fight, Kenneth was a guy who would jump in to help.

The first years after graduating from MHS in 1930 had been rough for Kenneth. On the plus side, he had a high school diploma – a job qualification that only 29 percent of his contemporaries nationwide could claim. On the minus side, there were few jobs to pursue. In the six months since the stock market crash of October 1929, the Gross National Product of the United States had dropped 13.5 percent, and the unemployment rate had nearly tripled. The Dow Jones Industrial Average was in the 230 range, down from a high of 381.7 the previous September, and was dropping fast. The reality of the Great Depression was just starting to take hold.

For a while, the city of Marion was able to ride the economic momentum of the 1920s to complete civic improvements such as the construction of a large swimming pool in Thomas Park and asphalt paving on the streets in the east part of town. But jobs were scarce and getting scarcer. Kenneth's older brother Ed helped him get on at the Paris Steam Dye Works and Laundry in Marion, driving a delivery truck. But the two young men essentially had to share the job, and that would not support either one of them financially. Kenneth apparently moved to Stone City the following year to work in the Dearborn family's quarry, but that business was fading fast and he soon left for Cedar Rapids. There, he took a job driving a taxicab on the night shift for the Silvertop Cab Company.[2]

Kenneth was making his way around the dark streets of Cedar Rapids one night in 1933 when he stopped the cab to pick up a young woman seeking a ride. He asked her destination and was surprised when she failed to reply, just sitting quietly in the back seat of the cab. After a few moments, she told him she had nowhere to go. She simply wanted to get off the sidewalk and out of the weather. Kenneth turned off the cab's meter as he pulled out into traffic. For the next few hours he drove around the city while Josephine Van Sickle told him a few facts about her life situation from the back seat. Josephine lived with her mother, but it was not a comfortable arrangement. Her mother's lifestyle bothered Josephine, and in the evenings she retreated from the house they shared. It is not known exactly what the mother did during the evenings – perhaps she welcomed gentlemen callers or served illegal alcohol (Prohibition would not be repealed until December 1933) – but Josephine did not feel safe or comfortable in the house. Kenneth dropped her off at the end of his shift and went home pondering her predicament.

Kenneth picked up Josephine again the next night. Soon, she was riding with him every shift. Sometimes on slow nights she would sleep in the back seat, but mostly they drove around and talked while Kenneth carried paying passengers to their destinations. Before long, a romance blossomed, and they decided to get married. When Josephine told Kenneth they were going to have a baby, he realized that he needed a more lucrative and stable job than driving a cab.

By now it was 1934. The eldest Reed sister, Leota, had been living for more than a decade in the Chicago area, where her husband, Ervin "Monk" Shesler, worked as an electrician in a steel plant. Learning of Kenneth and Josephine's situation, the

Sheslers invited the young couple to join them in their home in Indiana Harbor, Indiana, just across the state line from south Chicago. Monk secured Kenneth a job with his own employer, Inland Steel Co., in Chicago Heights, Illinois, and the Reeds made the move. Kenneth went to work for Inland, and some months later he and Josephine became the parents of a baby girl, Jacqueline.[3]

Unlike today, the United States led the world in steel production during the 1930s. Typical steel plants of the time such as Inland were massive operations, with blast furnaces, Bessemer converters, open-hearth furnaces, rolling mills, coke ovens and foundries, plus transportation facilities. The largest ones were operated in the region from Chicago south to St. Louis and east to Baltimore, Philadelphia and Buffalo. Even though the onset of the Great Depression had slowed the industry at first, construction of urban infrastructures, office buildings, factories, railroads, bridges and other items was resuming under the New Deal, and demand for steel was growing. Steel had replaced other commodities – particularly wood – in the manufacture of automobiles and household appliances as well. The mills were hiring again.

Kenneth Reed joined the American steel industry at perhaps the most contentious period to date in its 75-year history. Every day when a steel worker entered the mill he got a hint of the afterlife that might await the sinners among his co-workers. The furnaces and ovens produced stifling heat and sickening fumes. The threat of injury and even death lurked in every corner, where molten iron could burn, and machines could crush. Hours were long and overtime pay was a dream. For putting up with all that, steel mill workers earned an average of 65 cents per hour in 1935, according to the US Bureau of Labor Statistics. That is the equivalent of about $17,500 per year in 2016 dollars. Vacation? Sure, take as much time off as you want as long as you do not expect to be paid for it. And maybe your job will be waiting when you come back. Maybe not. Why would Kenneth Reed choose to take such a job? Well, a steady paycheck, even a meager one, apparently was preferable to the uncertainty of driving a taxicab.

Discontent had been building for decades among steel mill workers, and many of them saw unionization as their best bet for improving working conditions and compensation. The Amalgamated Association of Iron, Steel and Tin Workers had formed way back in 1876 and lost bitter strikes in 1892, 1901 and 1919, when the steel companies employed public relations, strikebreaking and rumor-mongering to demoralize the picketers. The weakened union backed off for nearly 15 years, but by the mid-1930s workers' anger again began rising to a boil. The Steel Workers Organizing Committee (SWOC) was formed by the Congress of Industrial Organizations (CIO) in June 1936 to lead a new organizing effort. The goal of the SWOC was to get signed contracts and union recognition for workers at steel plants across the United States.

Powered by the effectiveness of the sit-down strike, a relatively new tactic in which workers in factories and mills simply shut off their machines and sat down in the plant rather than walking off their jobs, success came quickly for the SWOC. US Steel Corporation, the nation's largest steel company, shocked the nation when it agreed to unionize in March 1937. The agreement, signed in early May, provided for a standard pay scale, an eight-hour work day and time-and-a-half for overtime.

SWOC expanded its efforts to the so-called "Little Steel" manufacturers, a group of companies including Youngstown Sheet & Tube, Republic Steel, Inland Steel, Bethlehem Steel, National Steel, American Rolling Mills and some smaller companies. However, "Little Steel," under the leadership of Tom Girdler, president of Republic Steel in Chicago, refused to recognize the union. Although the "Little Steel" companies adopted the same wage and hour provisions specified in the US Steel Corporation contract, they would not meet any of SWOC's other demands, particularly the call for a formal contract with the union. In response, SWOC opened a large-scale campaign to organize the steel industry. It is not surprising that Kenneth Reed signed up when SWOC began recruiting members, since most of the employees at Inland Steel did the same. And besides, Kenneth had been stepping in to fight for the little guy – and gal – since he was a boy in the school yards and sandlots of Marion. In addition, his family responsibilities were growing. Josephine was pregnant again and would deliver Kenneth Dearborn Reed on May 8.

The union called a national strike in some of the "Little Steel" companies – including Girdler's Republic Steel and Kenneth Reed's employer, Inland Steel – in mid-May. Inland Steel employees struck on the evening of May 21, 1937. The walkout was peaceful as Inland Steel shut down its Chicago Heights plant. Members of SWOC Lodge 1010, Kenneth Reed among them, waited to see what would happen next.

It was a different story at Republic Steel five days later. At the sprawling Burley Avenue facility on the Calumet River, several hundred SWOC members staged a sit-down strike, while others walked out. Some non-union workers stayed on the job, however, and company president Girdler took steps to keep the plant up and running. He had arranged to stock the plant with hundreds of weapons, including clubs, pistols, rifles, shotguns and even four submachine guns. His cache of tear and vomit gas was said to be larger than the city's supply. Girdler also arranged to supplement his 370 plant guards with officers from the Chicago Police Department, which had a long history of working with industries to suppress the organized labor movement in the city.

The trouble started in mid-afternoon of May 26 when the sit-down strikers agreed, at the urging of a SWOC official, to vacate the Republic plant and join a picket line that had formed outside. The police captain, in command of about 150 officers, had assured them that the picket line would not be harassed. However, as soon as the new picketers joined the line, the police attacked with clubs. As the officers tore into the unarmed picketers, the line broke and the strikers retreated along Burley Avenue, with the police in hot pursuit. Chicago Mayor Edward S. Kelly, recognizing that the police had acted in violation of federal labor law as written in the Wagner Act, announced the next day that heretofore peaceful picketing would be allowed. Nevertheless, that very night, police attacked again when a column of about 700 demonstrators advanced toward Republic Steel from the unofficial strike headquarters at

Sam's Place, an old tavern and dance hall several blocks from the plant. In the melee that followed 18 people were injured, including three who required hospitalization.[4]

The *Chicago Tribune* described the weather as "hot and sticky" when more than 1,500 strikers and supporters gathered at Sam's Place on Sunday, May 30, for a Memorial Day outdoor rally and picnic. Their ardor for the strike had only deepened in the two days since their last run-in with the police, so when one of the speakers introduced a resolution to march to the plant and assert the union's right to picket, it was quickly and loudly approved. A day that had started with a light, holiday atmosphere now turned much darker.

Opinions differ as to whether the Memorial Day demonstration was pre-planned by SWOC or not. It is known that medical personnel attended the rally at Sam's Place, and several vehicles were designated to serve as makeshift ambulances. On the other hand, none of the top-ranking local SWOC officials were there to lead the march, and there was no systematic arming of the marchers (although some likely carried weapons). Another unanswered question is whether the marchers planned to enter the Republic plant with the intention of removing non-striking workers inside.

In any case, a crowd estimated at up to 2,000 people – strikers, family members and supporters – set out across an open field that stretched for about three city blocks from Sam's Place to the Burley Avenue gate at Republic Steel. They followed a dirt road that ran diagonally through the field, led by two people carrying American flags. Somewhere near the front of the column marched Kenneth Reed, who had left Josephine at home in Indiana Harbor to care for their children.

As Kenneth made his way across the field, he began to make out a group of perhaps 250 uniformed policemen who had lined up in such a way as to block the marchers from reaching the Republic gate. They obviously had been expecting the marchers, because a movie camera crew from Paramount News was set up behind the police line to film the likely confrontation, and paddy wagons were lined up behind the policemen. The silent newsreel camera captures the scene as the marchers approach through the field and the front of the column reaches the police line. A large group of strikers gathers before the blockade, and heated arguments break out as the marchers' demand to be allowed to pass. At that moment there is a break in the newsreel, reportedly caused when cameraman Orlando Lippert stopped shooting to change the camera's lens.[5]

By the time the film resumes, all hell has broken loose. Clouds of tear gas rise around the marchers, and policemen are seen with guns drawn as they fire into the crowd and then pound the demonstrators with heavy-duty billy clubs manufactured and provided by Republic Steel. The column doubles back on itself in confusion as marchers attempt to flee toward Sam's Place. Some lie crumpled and still on the ground, while others are trying to crawl away from the melee. Police shove injured Mrs. Lupe Marshall, a social worker who marched in support of the strikers, into a paddy wagon already overloaded with wounded men. The film ends with a peaceful shot of the Republic mill gate, showing a mass of people in the yard beyond and a few picketers in the foreground carrying signs as they circle on the far side of Burley Avenue. Nowhere in Orlando Lippert's footage are policemen seen being injured, although several later claimed to have suffered various cuts and bruises.[6]

In all, ten marchers died and 100 to 110 were injured in what came to be known as the Chicago Memorial Day Massacre of 1937. Some 40 marchers (but no policemen) were hit by gunfire that day, and Kenneth Reed was one of those who died of his wounds. Perhaps it is for the best then, considering all the pain and suffering that Mayme Reed and her family endured over the years, that the newsreel film does not show the exact moment when Kenneth Reed was gunned down by the Chicago police. The film initially was suppressed by the latter, but it became available later, and no doubt the Reed family had occasion to watch it.

The last person to see Kenneth alive was Lupe Marshall, who encountered him on the floor of the overloaded paddy wagon as it was carrying her and 16 wounded men toward Burnside Hospital. Several months later, Mrs. Marshall testified in detail before the US Senate committee (known informally as the La Follette Committee for its chair, Senator Robert La Follette of Wisconsin) charged with investigating the incident. Her testimony included this account:

> As soon as the wagon started I started helping these men that were in the wagon. I started straightening out their heads and lifting their arms from underneath, and I noticed that there was one particular fellow there who looked very gaunt and haggard, and he seemed to be in a terrible position. There was a heavy-set man that had fallen on top of him, and this fellow was pinned completely with his head over his knees. I straightened him out, managed to get his head on my lap, but when I did that I noticed that his face was getting cold and was black, turning black, and he was motioning to his pocket, his shirt pocket. He had a package of cigarettes there, and I understood he wanted me to light a cigarette for him, but I had no matches, and when I did get the cigarette out it was stained with blood, and it was cloaked with blood, so he said, "Never mind, kid," he says, "you are all right. You are a good kid." He says, "Never mind. Carry on." And he started to say "mother," but didn't finish, and he stiffened up and I became somewhat hysterical.

That wounded man was Ken Reed, who was pronounced dead after he was delivered to Burnside Hospital.[7]

Kenneth's wife Josephine was called to the city morgue to identify his body. Then Dr. J. J. Kearns performed an autopsy. From the coroner's report it is possible to reach two conclusions. First, to have been hit three times Kenneth must have been close to the front of the column when the shooting started. Second, at least one of the shots – the one that killed him – hit Kenneth in the back, which suggests he had turned to flee and did not pose a threat to the police when he went down. Yet, somehow, the Cook County coroner's inquest exonerated the Chicago police, and by inference blamed the union for Kenneth Reed's death:

> We find that Kenneth Reed came to his death on the 30th of May in the Burnside Hospital from a bullet wound of the abdomen, caused when the deceased was struck by a bullet fired from a gun held by an unknown police officer. From the testimony presented, we believe the occurrence to be justifiable homicide.[8]

The La Follette Committee found that despite vastly differing accounts of who provoked the violence on Memorial Day, the bloody consequences were avoidable on the part of the police. But no one in the police department was ever prosecuted, much less punished, for their actions during the Memorial Day Massacre. The event took the starch out of SWOC's steel strike, and it would be five more years before the union reached agreement with the "Little Steel" companies to represent their workers.

SWOC organized a preliminary memorial service for Kenneth Reed at Indiana Harbor on June 2, and 300 people attended to pay their respects to their fallen union brother. Then his body was shipped to Marion, where his open casket was placed in the family's living room the next day for viewing. A formal funeral service followed at Yocum Chapel, with the Reverend Irving E. Wade of the Christian Church presiding. Six of Kenneth's former teammates on the MHS baseball team served as pallbearers. The *Marion Sentinel* newspaper chose that very week to publish a front-page editorial condemning the "Little Steel" strike as anti-American and suggesting that communists were behind it. A short story about Kenneth's funeral appeared on page five.

Larry Martin, Kenneth's nephew who was 14 at the time, recalled that Mayme and her family handled their grief by resorting to utter silence over the circumstances of his death. All of the Reeds, even the outspoken Bill, simply refused to talk about it. Josephine, left with no source of income, brought her two children to Marion to live briefly with the Reed family before she returned to the

Chicago area and resumed her life. The people of Marion soon forgot about Kenneth Reed. But Kenneth Reed and the other victims of the Memorial Day Massacre have not been forgotten by the steel workers in the Chicago area. They remember the episode as one of the most violent in the history of labor organization in the United States. Today, a plaque is posted outside the United Steelworkers of America Local 1010 office, which stands very near the site of Sam's Place in south Chicago. It lists the ten men who were killed in the Memorial Day Massacre of 1937, including Kenneth Reed, and closes with the following statement:

They died for democracy; their cause can never die.

3

"Three of us passed out of 47"

On the same July 21, 1937, *Chicago Daily Tribune* front page that reported the results of the coroner's inquest into Kenneth Reed's death in the Memorial Day Massacre, there appeared this bold headline: "U.S. TROOPS IN TIENTSIN STAND BY FOR TROUBLE." The opening paragraph of the story below went on to announce, "Fighting between Japanese and Chinese troops along a wide front south of Peiping [Beijing] began yesterday at 2:30 p.m. and continued into the night." This was one of the first reports of the events that followed what came to be known as the Marco Polo Bridge incident, which most historians now consider to be the start of World War II in Asia. It would have profound implications for Bill Reed and the members of his family, although they had no way of knowing this at the time.

Military confrontations between China and Japan were nothing new. They dated back to the late 19th century, when Japan was emerging as a modern nation and its rulers began looking for additional territory in which to assert their power. Nearby China, with its large territory, huge population, rich natural resources and weak dynastic leadership, was the logical target. As a result of its victory in the first Sino-Japanese War (1894–95), Japan occupied the Korean Peninsula and the island of Formosa (Taiwan). That was just the beginning.

The arrival of the 20th century brought more conflict in China. Barely hanging on after nearly 450 years in power, the Manchu

(Qing) Dynasty began to collapse in 1908 after the death of the Dowager Empress Cixi and the Guangxu Emperor. The Wuchang Uprising on October 11, 1911, led to the Xinhai Revolution, which resulted in the abdication of Puyi, the last emperor, four months later. Sun Yat-sen, who had been instrumental in the overthrow of the Manchu Dynasty, was appointed to serve as provisional president of the newly founded Republic of China. The new government soon foundered as competing factions sought control. By 1917, China, lacking a proper central government, had become divided among different military warlords.

Seeking to reunify the country under a modern government, Sun Yat-sen co-founded the Nationalist Party of China (Kuomintang, now Guomindang) and served as its first leader. In 1921 Sun started a self-proclaimed military government in southern China, and with assistance from the Soviet Union he began to develop the armed forces needed for an expedition against the warlords ruling in the north. He established the Whampoa Military Academy near Canton (Guangzhou), with his young protégé Chiang Kai-shek as the commandant of the National Revolutionary Army. He also took steps to establish national capitalism and a banking system.

With Sun's death on March 12, 1925, a power struggle began between Chiang Kai-shek and Sun's old revolutionary comrade Wang Jingwei. Both men sought to lay claim to Sun's legacy. In 1927 Chiang Kai-shek married Soong Mei-ling, a sister of Sun's widow Soong Ching-ling, and subsequently he could claim to be a brother-in-law of Sun. The Communists and the Kuomintang split in 1927, marking the start of the Chinese Civil War. Chiang, now the leader of the Kuomintang, then led Sun's long-postponed Northern Expedition, conquering or reaching accommodations with China's many warlords.

Chiang Kai-shek served as chairman of the National Military Council of the Nationalist Government of the Republic of China. He was socially conservative, promoting traditional Chinese culture and rejecting both western democracy and Sun's nationalist democratic socialism in favor of an authoritarian government. The Western media conferred on him the title "Generalissimo."

However, Chiang's government remained surrounded by the warlords, who remained relatively autonomous within their own regions and were a constant source of unrest. Corruption within the Kuomintang ran rampant as well, and the Chinese Communist Party remained a rival for power.

Throughout this period the Japanese worked to increase their influence and control in Manchuria, the mineral-rich territory in northeastern China abutting the Kwantung Peninsula. Japan viewed Manchuria as an essential source of raw materials for the war machine it would use to conquer Southeast Asia in the years ahead.

On September 18, 1931, Japanese officers of the Kwantung Army created the Mukden Incident, which served as an excuse for the invasion of Manchuria. Blaming an explosion along the Japanese-controlled South Manchurian Railway on the Chinese, Japanese troops occupied the city of Mukden and began shelling a nearby Chinese garrison. Chinese resistance quickly crumbled, and within five months the Japanese had overrun all major towns and cities in Manchuria's three provinces. The conquerors declared Inner Manchuria an "independent state" and appointed the deposed Manchu emperor Puyi as puppet emperor of Manchukuo. The Japanese also began looking south for more areas of China to conquer.

Chiang Kai-shek and his Nationalist army spent the early 1930s in a bitter civil war with the Red Army of the Chinese Communists. With the help of German advisors, Chiang launched the fifth Bandit Suppression campaign in 1934 and nearly succeeded in wiping out the Red Army in southeastern China. The remnants of the Red Army, numbering 90,000 to 100,000 troops, managed to escape to the west and spent the next year in what became known as "The Long March" through the outback of China to eventual refuge in remote northern Shensi (Shaanxi) Province.

The Japanese, meanwhile, used this period to probe northern China from their base in Manchukuo. Forcing political concessions from local warlords and flooding the economy with Japanese goods (including opium), they made steady gains southward. By 1937, there were significant numbers of Japanese troops stationed in areas around Chiang's capital in Peiping, taking advantage of

Chinese policy allowing certain foreign nations to place their own troops along an important railroad leading to the city so that communications could be maintained between the various governments who had an established presence in China.

On July 7, 1937, Japanese troops in the Fengtai District about 15 miles southwest of Peiping reported that one of their number had gone missing during a night exercise. They said they suspected that he was being held at a Chinese army camp in the nearby town of Wanping, and demanded permission to search the camp. Between the Japanese and Wanping stood the Marco Polo Bridge over the Luguo (Yongding) River, an arched granite structure that gained its Western name from its mention in Marco Polo's record of his travels. The 874ft-long bridge, and a railroad bridge next to it, was in a strategic location because it was then the only link between Peiping and an important region to the south controlled by the Chinese Nationalists. Gaining control of the bridge would provide the Japanese with control of the city of Peiping and the surrounding territories.

When negotiations broke down the following morning, the Japanese opened artillery fire on the Marco Polo Bridge and then stormed across it with infantry to surround the walls of Wanping. Gunfire rang out between the Japanese troops and the Chinese defenders, and these are generally considered to be the opening shots of World War II in Asia. The Chinese initially managed to hold Wanping, but the fighting intensified as units of the Kwantung Army poured into China from Manchukuo. This was the situation reported in the July 21 edition of the *Chicago Daily Tribune*. Within a week, Peiping fell to the Japanese, leaving the North China Plain open to Japanese occupation. By the end of the year, the Japanese had taken the strategic cities of Nanking and Shanghai as well. But Chiang's Nationalists refused to surrender, choosing instead a strategy of trading territory for time by moving their capital far inland to the Yangtze River city of Chungking (Chongqing). Perhaps if they could hold out long enough, the Western powers would come to China's aid.[1]

BACK TO SCHOOL

Bill and Dick Reed probably did not give much – if any – thought to the conflict in China during their bus ride from Marion to Dubuque for the start of the 1937–38 school year at Columbia College. Their focus was more likely on class work, football and girls, but not necessarily in that order.

It would not be a good year for either of the Reed boys. The football team was no better than the previous season's squad, and both boys were hurt in the October 1 game against Platteville. Nursing shoulder injuries, they did not start in the backfield again until the October 29 game against Parsons, but even then Dick's contribution was limited due to more damage in both of his shoulders. In addition, their grades suffered. Bill failed to make the mid-semester and semester honor rolls for the first time since starting college. He did, however, join the Drama Club on campus.

As the family finances continued to worsen in late 1937, Bill again considered leaving school. It became a topic of heated disagreement between Bill and his older brother Ed, and Bill applied for a job at the John Deere plant in Dubuque. Although the personnel director at John Deere told Bill he would give the young man a job if anything opened up, apparently nothing did. Besides, spring would bring baseball season, and Bill was looking forward to alternating between the pitcher's mound and third base on the Duhawks team. He stayed in school and played throughout the 1938 season.

As the school year drew to a close, Bill wrote home to Mayme to apologize for not calling her on Mother's Day. The problem, he explained in a letter, was that he did not have enough money to make the telephone call:

> You know darn well that I thought of you, and would have gotten in touch if I hadn't been absolutely flat broke. Whatever I could have done even if I had been "flush" would have been a very small acknowledgement of the never ending debt I owe

you for all the care and worry I've been for the past 21 years plus; but someday, Mom, in the near future I hope, I may start to prove a worthwhile investment for your patience and care in the past.

Meanwhile, Dick Reed decided to call it quits at Columbia College at the end of his sophomore year. His reasons for the decision to leave school are unclear, but finances almost certainly played a big part in it. However, having two years of college on his record would prove extremely important just a few years down the road when he met the Army's requirements for acceptance into flight training.

Bill apparently worked for Colonial Baking Company, the Des Moines-based producer of Rainbo Bread, during the summer of 1938, before returning to Dubuque in the fall for his senior year at Columbia College. By most measures, his last year at the school would be his best. The football team had another forgettable season, but in Bill's final home game as a Duhawk he accomplished a goal that had eluded him for the previous three years. *The Lorian* school newspaper reported this in its coverage of the November 5 game against Western Union College:

Bill Reed waited until his last home game to score a touchdown which was his first tally in his four-year tenure as a Duhawk. The Marion boy was considerably shaken up in the first half, but came back strong to drive over from the three-yard line to count the final Columbia score of the 60 minutes.

Despite the fact that he was an Economics major, Bill's schedule for the fall semester included two education classes and a class in coaching. Perhaps he was widening his options for finding a job after graduation. In any case, his grades improved from a 3.4 average at mid-term to 3.6 for the semester, earning him another spot on the honor roll. He also earned an even bigger honor when he was named to the Who's Who of American Colleges and Universities by combined vote of faculty and students at Columbia College.

With spring 1939 came Bill's last season on the Columbia baseball team. He again alternated between playing the infield and pitching. He also served on the finance committee for the senior prom. And as is the case with many college seniors, his grades suffered as graduation neared, dropping to a straight B 3.0 average to barely hold his place on the honor roll. Finally, on May 29, 1939, in commencement exercises held in the gymnasium, William Norman Reed graduated from college with a bachelor's degree in Economics. But his degree is not from Columbia College. The school had changed its name the previous month to honor its founder and avoid confusion with other schools named Columbia, so Bill Reed's diploma is from Loras College.

With his freshly issued economics degree in hand, Bill Reed set out in the summer of 1939 to find suitable employment. Four years of hard work by him, sacrifices by his family and the financial assistance from lawyer McPartland were behind him. Now Bill would justify those efforts by setting out on a career in business. He worked briefly for the Witwer Grocer Company in Cedar Rapids. Bill's employer was a large food wholesaler that operated 32 farms, various processing plants and a large fleet of red trucks that delivered Witwer products to stores throughout the Midwest. When a better opportunity arose in the office at Quaker Oats, he took it. Receiving a regular paycheck would make it possible for him to start paying off the debts that had accumulated during college. For several months Bill attended to his office duties and played on the company basketball team, but his heart was not in it.

Bill Reed craved adventure, and he was not getting it working in an office at Quaker Oats. His eyes were on the skies, as they had been since high school. Every time he watched an airplane fly overhead, or read in *Air Trails* magazine about the latest hot military ship, Bill's desire to become a pilot grew stronger. World events transpiring that year would make his dream come true.

On September 1, 1939, Europe erupted into war with Germany's invasion of Poland. This tragedy was not unexpected, as Germany had become increasingly aggressive in the years since Adolf Hitler's

Nazi Party had taken power in 1933. Most people in the United States had watched the news of increasing Nazi belligerence with disapproval, but also with determination not to become embroiled in the next war. World War I, the so-called "war to end all wars," had accomplished nothing, and memories of American involvement during 1917–18 were still too painful and too fresh.

American military leaders, while perhaps sharing these views, recognized that they could not ignore what was happening in Europe and the Far East. Their nation's armed forces had grown progressively weaker over the past two decades and would be woefully unprepared to enter combat in their current state if the United States were forced to go to war. The commander of the US Army Air Corps (USAAC), Gen H. H. "Hap" Arnold, pointed out in September 1938 that while Congress had just approved USAAC increases to 2,320 aircraft and 1,600 officers in the latest budget, Germany at that time had an estimated 6,000 aircraft. Arnold told President Franklin D. Roosevelt that he needed 7,500 combat aircraft, 2,500 training planes and the personnel to man them. Ground and naval commanders rolled out similar plans, and Roosevelt bought in. They were making a late start, but at least America's military buildup was getting under way.

After training just 301 new pilots in 1938, the USAAC was tasked with producing 4,500 pilots in the two years commencing July 1, 1939. To accomplish this hefty goal, the plan called for using nine civilian training schools around the country to provide Primary training, with Army instructors taking over for the Basic and Advanced courses. At the same time, the USAAC placed large orders for training and combat aircraft.

This expansion was just what Bill Reed needed. He applied to the USAAC for pilot training, then went back to his desk at Quaker Oats to wait for a reply. His timing was excellent, and before long he was instructed to report to St. Paul, Minnesota, for his physical examination and testing. Bill should have felt confident of success, since he met all of the USAAC's requirements – he had a college degree, was in perfect physical condition with good eye–hand coordination, and his eyesight was 20-20. At 1452hrs on November 16, 1939, Bill sent the following telegram to his mother from St. Paul:

Three of us passed out of 47. Home Saturday.

Bill spent the Christmas season of 1939 at home in Marion, waiting for his induction notice from the USAAC. When it came, he was instructed to travel to Des Moines to sign his enlistment papers on January 28, 1940, and then proceed to the Chicago School of Aeronautics at Glenview, Illinois, to begin his flight training.

It is likely that Bill was impressed by his first view of the airport where the Chicago School of Aeronautics was located. Arriving at Curtiss-Reynolds Airport, Bill would have encountered the huge Hangar One, which faced the street on one side and the flightline on the other, so it could serve as the airport terminal as well as providing aircraft storage and repair facilities. Locals proclaimed it to be the largest, most modern airplane hangar in the world. Once through the terminal's impressive front door, Bill was directed to the second-floor offices of the flight school. From there, he was shown to his quarters, which also were located within the mammoth hangar.

Curtiss-Reynolds Airport – named for the developer, Curtiss Flying Service, and the land owner – was built in 1929 just north of Chicago and near the shores of Lake Michigan. Harold S. Darr, a former military pilot who had served in the US Army Air Service during World War I, established the Chicago School of Aeronautics on the field in 1935. Business was slow at Darr's flight school until he obtained a contract from the US War Department in 1939 to begin training pilots for the USAAC. Darr's first training class for his new customer began on July 1, 1939, and four classes of about 30 cadets apiece had passed through the school by the time Bill Reed and the others in his class arrived to begin learning to fly in February 1940.[2]

At Chicago, as at the other contract training centers around the nation, Darr had a crew of civilian instructors who taught the rudiments of flying to the cadets in Stearman PT-13 trainers. The PT-13 was an open-cockpit, two-seat biplane noted for its robust construction and excellent flight characteristics – an ideal craft for its purpose. Each school had, in addition to its civilian personnel, a small USAAC detachment to supervise the military aspects of aviation cadet training and provide final checks on students' progress.

The Primary Training syllabus called for 60 to 65 hours of airborne flight training plus 225 hours of ground-school instruction. Bill's primary training class had the misfortune to arrive at Chicago during one of the worst Midwest winters in recent memory. Day after day, young men eager to starting flying sat in classrooms absorbing lectures on topics including theory of flight, meteorology, air navigation, aircraft engines, Morse Code and more while they waited for the weather to improve. Outside, low clouds, high winds and the occasional snow storm kept them earthbound for days at a time. Originally, Bill's primary training class was designated part of Class 40-E, which would be the fifth USAAC group to complete training during 1940. However, by the time the weather broke and regular flying could commence, the class had lost so much time that it was moved back to 40-F.

At the start of training, the USAAC issued each cadet a log book in which he would record details of his flights. Bill Reed's log book has not survived, so the details of his progression from earthbound cadet through primary training are not known. He seems to have had little trouble learning to fly, however, likely making his first solo flight after about six hours of dual instruction. That first solo consisted simply of a takeoff, a circle of the field and a landing. Though short in duration, it is a flight that every pilot remembers for a lifetime. From that humble start, primary trainees progressed to practicing steep turns, stalls, spins and dives. The cadets at Chicago faced an added degree of difficulty, for cold weather flying required them to be bundled up in padded leather coats and pants while they wrestled with the controls of their PT-13s. A one-way connection called a Gosport tube extended from the instructor's mouthpiece to an earpiece in the student's helmet, allowing the instructor to give instructions and feedback to the student. The cadet was expected to listen and learn. Not everyone could do it. Occasionally, struggling trainees would be subjected to a "washout ride," which if failed would result in elimination from the school and reassignment to other duties in the USAAC. Bill apparently had little fear of washing out, but he discussed the topic in a letter written to his mother on one of the days when bad weather canceled flying:

> Another rainy and foggy day here at the airport and no flying. A lot of going to classes, though, and that isn't so hot. They keep one doing something incessantly with no chance to take a nap now and then, like I used to in college. There isn't much going on here. The axe is ready to fall, though. By that I mean that they are getting ready to thin our class down again the next day we fly. Probably four or five kids more will get the gate. Certainly hope I am not among them, but one never knows.

Bill and his classmates at the Chicago School of Aeronautics completed their primary flight training during the last week of May and received orders sending them to basic flight training at Randolph Field – the so-called "West Point of the Air" – located about 15 miles northeast of San Antonio, Texas. At Randolph, the trainees of Class 40-F would get their first taste of actual USAAC life. They traded their blue-gray cadet uniforms for USAAC khakis and their former casual lifestyle for strict USAAC discipline. Now they would be subject to spit-and-polish inspections, hazing and more. They would even learn to salute and march.

On arrival, the Class 40-F cadets could see why Randolph Field had such a good reputation among military posts. The place was beautiful. Opened just nine years prior, the base featured modern buildings – many designed in Spanish Colonial Revival style – and lots of trees. The layout placed the buildings in the center of the base, with streets laid out in the fashion of a wheel. Hangars with checkerboard roofs lined the east and west sides of the base, with aircraft ramps and runways beyond them. The signature structure was the Administration Building, nicknamed the "Taj Mahal," with its tall water tower rising out of a two-story office complex in the center and single-story wings on two sides. Several small auxiliary airfields, where pilots could practice takeoffs and landings, were located within ten miles of the main base.

On his first visit to the flightline, Bill got a look at the aircraft he would be flying at Randolph, the North American BT-9. A long line of the trainers, each with yellow wings and tail contrasting a blue fuselage with a large three-digit number on the side, stood waiting. This plane was a major step up from the 200hp PT-13 primary trainers. While the PT-13 resembled nothing so much as a World War I warplane, the BT-9 was a modern low-wing monoplane with a 400hp radial engine and a large Plexiglas canopy over its two-seat tandem cockpit. Although both trainers were fully aerobatic, the BT-9 was considerably faster and much more difficult to fly because of its dangerous stalling characteristics, which made landings tricky. During the time Bill was at Randolph, 15 of the 18 total BT-9 accidents reported took place during landings. Fortunately, no fatalities occurred.

Bill sailed through the basic flight training syllabus with no particular problems. After going up with an instructor for his first BT-9 flights, Bill soon soloed. Then began the process of getting comfortable with his tricky mount, practicing takeoffs, landings and the whole gamut of aerobatic maneuvers. Most the flying was done at 2,000–4,000ft. At each step in the training, cadets would fly with an instructor long enough to learn a particular maneuver and then practice solo until mastering it. The basic course comprised about 70 hours of flight time.

Bill got his first experience in instrument flying during basic training. The BT-9s were fitted with flight instruments that allowed the pilot to fly the plane blind without visual references outside the cockpit. A hood was fitted inside the canopy that closed over the student's seat to block the view and simulate the sensation of flying at night or within a cloud. The instructor would sit in the other seat and tell the student what to do, and the student would attempt to make the maneuvers based entirely on the information he was getting from the instruments – turn, bank, ascent, descent, direction of flight etc. The key to success was learning to trust the information imparted by the instruments, even if the pilot's backside was trying to convince him that something else – usually more sinister such as a spin or stall – was happening. Once a pilot was competent at instrument flying, more of his flights would take place at night.

Ground school classes alternated with flying. The subject matter was more sophisticated, covering topics such as meteorology, communications including Morse Code, navigation, aircraft engines, radio procedures and more. The daily schedule started with reveille at 0530hrs and breakfast at 0615hrs. After two hours of classroom instruction, the cadets moved to the flightline at 0930hrs and flew until lunch time. A rest period followed during the hottest hours in the Texas summer afternoon, and then came an hour of physical education before the evening meal. The evening was free for study and recreation until "Taps" at 2130hrs. Saturday afternoons and Sundays were free time.

Bill was closing in on completing his basic training when he wrote a letter to Mayme in mid-July that gave uncommon detail (for him) about his experience at Randolph:

Only about ten hours left to go here now, though we don't leave here for a little over two weeks. I get my final check on air work tomorrow morning. I've only had one other so far, and I shouldn't have any trouble with this one. Then I have an instrument check the last hour I'm here. So I'm nearly through. From what I hear I guess they don't "wash them out" at Kelly or Brooks [advanced training bases]. They figure anyone who can get there can fly too well to be let go.

We have been having swell weather here all week, and last night was especially nice. I flew from 8:00pm to 9:15pm. They have four zones, and last night they put two of us in each zone, one at 1,500ft and the other at 2,500ft. Then they call in the lower one (the man in Zone One at 1,500ft) and then upper one, then lower two etc. I was in lower four. We made four landings each – one with floodlights, one with floodlights and wingtip lights and finally two with nothing but wingtip lights. It's really swell flying at night. We have one more hour or so, and this last time we release a flare and land by the light of the flare. They are big flares and cost about $75 apiece. They float down on 15ft parachutes.

Guess all I'm talking about is flying, but that's about all we do down here. Some of the boys flew last night until 11:30pm. I was home by 10:30pm last night and started flying again at 7:45am this morning. Had aerobatics this morning and can do them as well as my instructor.

With completion of basic training in late July, it was just a 20-mile drive through San Antonio for Bill and his 236 40-F classmates to reach Kelly Field, where their advanced training would take place. Known as "the Cradle of Early American Military Aviation," Kelly Field had been turning out pilots for the US Army since 1917. It had just been designated the home of the Advanced Training Facility for the Gulf Coast Training Command, and a major upgrade and expansion project was well under way. A new operations hangar had opened a few months prior, and new barracks, classroom buildings and warehouses were under construction.

The accommodations proved a shock for the men of Class 40-F when they arrived at Kelly. After enjoying the relatively comfortable barracks at Randolph Field, they were now directed to a large tent city that would be their temporary home until Kelly's new barracks were completed in late September. But the discomforts of tent living were secondary concerns for Bill and his classmates. They were at Kelly to fly, and fly they would.

When student pilots reached the advanced training phase, they were assigned to one of two groups. For most of them, this assignment would determine the course of their military flying career for the foreseeable future. Single-engined pilots could expect to fly pursuits (soon to be renamed "fighters" by the USAAC), reconnaissance aircraft, attack aircraft (light bombers) or utility aircraft. Multi-engined pilots likely were headed for medium bombers, heavy bombers or transports. Perhaps because Bill had shown such talent in aerobatics during basic training (or perhaps by simple luck of the draw), the USAAC designated him for single-engined training. From the looks of things, pursuits were in his future.

Having mastered the techniques for controlling an aircraft in basic training, Bill would now learn how to apply that knowledge for military purposes during the advanced training course. Instrument training would continue, but now much of it took place on the ground in a stationary Link trainer – an ingenious device that was basically a cockpit in a box with instruments and controls. The Link provided a way for new pilots to become comfortable with blind flying without subjecting them to the dangers of flying in clouds or darkness before they became capable of doing so safely. The Link moved on its stand when the pilot inside moved the controls, giving a reasonable sensation of flight. An instructor would communicate directions to the pilot, who would then rely on the Link's instruments to perform the maneuver. A recorder kept track of how closely the pilot managed to follow his instructions, and the instructor would issue a critique at the end of the session.

Mostly, however, advanced training was about logging flight hours. Single-engined trainees at Kelly flew North American BC-1 and AT-6 Texan aircraft, which were virtually identical and closely resembled the BT-9 in appearance. The advanced trainers had several important upgrades from the BT-9 – a 600hp engine and retractable landing gear, both of which helped to boost the aircraft's top speed to just over 200mph. In addition, their wings had been redesigned to improve stall characteristics, and they mounted a single, forward-firing 0.30-caliber machine gun for gunnery training.[3]

The Texan was a fully aerobatic aircraft, and now pilots would test their aerobatics skills against one another as part of their training. The two contests used to simulate aerial combat were "rat racing," in which one pilot would lead and put his Texan through all manner of maneuvers while a second pilot attempted to follow the same maneuvers, and the classic "dogfight," when two pilots would meet in the sky and try to maneuver onto each other's tail. Bill was considered one of the "hot rocks" of Class 40-F, and the skills and confidence he developed in these contests would serve him well in the future when he went to war.

Two other key elements of advanced training were cross-country navigation and formation flying. Using the map-reading skills learned in basic training, the pilots would plot a cross-country route to an assigned destination. Taking off in five-minute intervals, the pilots would make their way to a distant airfield – Dallas, for instance – and check in there, then fly back. Sometimes the flights were timed so the return flight would take place in the dark.

Formation flying began in groups of three. Pilots would take off together and perform a series of maneuvers while holding position relative to each other. This required extreme concentration, especially in rough weather, as the wingmen adjusted their throttles and controls to stay with their leader. The leader, in turn, had to fly as smoothly as possible and make turns gently enough to avoid colliding with a wingman. The flight would then land in formation. As pilots gained proficiency at formation flying, the flights were increased in size to six and up, and the leaders could maneuver more aggressively.

Of the 232 flying cadets who completed training in Class 40-F, only two suffered accidents during advanced training. Bill's flying record remained unblemished throughout his flight training, and he graduated with the class on October 4, 1940.

Graduation for pilots completing USAAC flight training was normally quite a formal affair, but this was not the case for Class 40-F. The commandant of the Kelly Field Advanced Flying School, Col Hubert R. Harmon, was scheduled to make a graduation speech to the cadets. Harmon, however, was called away for the funeral of a family member and could not attend the ceremonies. Rather than reschedule the graduation, it was decided to dispense with Harmon's speech and allow several of the cadets (Bill was not among them) to deliver extemporaneous speeches. Then Capt C. A. Clark, Jr., adjutant of the airfield, administered a mass oath of office to the new officers to complete the event. With a shining set of pilot's wings attached to the breast of his new dress blouse, Bill was now 2Lt William N. Reed, USAAC Reserve.

It was common for cadets to invite family members, sweethearts and friends to their flight school graduation, and Bill was no exception. His steady date from high school days, "Mick" Forbes, traveled with her mother to San Antonio to witness Bill's big day. It also was common for couples to announce their engagement or even marry at the end of flight training, but if "Mick" was expecting that, Bill disappointed her. He had two main focuses in life – flying and taking care of his mother. Despite Bill's affection for "Mick," she did not have a place in his short-term plans.

For all the excitement of graduation day, what interested the new officers most was the posting of their first duty assignments. Most single-engined pilots hoped to be sent to frontline pursuit outfits, but the USAAC was in a state of rapid expansion and needed instructor pilots to shepherd those behind them through training. Of the four members of Class 40-F who would later fly for China with Bill in the American Volunteer Group (AVG), only Charles W. Sawyer and Lacy F. Mangleburg went to frontline squadrons. Bill, along with Matthew "Kirk" Kuykendall and Albert "Red" Probst, got the next best thing. They would go back to Randolph Field briefly for further pursuit training, then report to Barksdale Field in Louisiana for service there as pursuit instructors in the new Specialized Flying School for single-engined pilots.[4]

When Bill arrived at Barksdale Field toward the end of October, he found the airbase much to his liking. Less than a decade old, Barksdale was a sprawling facility of some 20,000 acres in the northwest corner of Louisiana just outside Shreveport. It was big enough to contain bombing and gunnery ranges within the boundaries of the property. The flightline boasted two huge hangars built to house airships, although none was assigned to the base. New billets had been added in 1936–37 when the base was headquarters for the 3rd Attack Group, and Bill was assigned comfortable accommodation in the Bachelor Officers Quarters.[5]

Barksdale was in transition from an operational base to a training facility, the 27th Bombardment Group having just departed for the Philippines and the new Advanced Specialized Training School of the Southeast Air Corps Training Center still setting up shop. Three school squadrons – the 87th, 88th and 89th – would provide specialized training for single-engined and multi-engined pilots, navigators and bombardiers. Bill's pursuit students would be flying Texan trainers plus aging Seversky P-35 and Curtiss P-36 fighters as they developed their skills at formation flying, tactical flying and aerial gunnery.

Bill did not leave an account of his first flight in an actual fighter aircraft, but his letters from this period give glimpses into his activities in the air and on the ground. On November 27 he made what he termed a "performance flight" and learned a painful lesson. Climbing in one of the school's fighters to an altitude of 30,000ft, he pushed over into a power dive. Unfortunately, he had developed a head cold several days prior. "I came down too fast and the pressure didn't equalize in my right ear," he wrote to his mother. "Nothing serious, but it has to snap back to normal before I can fly again." But his mind was not focused exclusively on flying. In the same letter, he looked forward to going home on leave over the Christmas season. He also reported that he had been assigned additional duty as the squadron's supply officer – "a lot of added work but good experience" – and told Mayme about playing in a basketball game pitting his team of instructors against the cadets' team.

At Barksdale, Bill got his first taste of the life he would lead as an officer and a gentleman in the USAAC. His off-duty time was his own, and when he did not find much of interest in the nearby town of Shreveport, he turned to culture, starting a class in Spanish language. With ready access to USAAC aircraft, he also had a level of mobility that was unknown to the average young American in 1940. More than once, Bill used the pretext of honing his cross-country navigational skills to make weekend trips by air to visit old friends in San Antonio, Topeka and other distant cities.

His financial situation was looking up, too. After earning $75 per month while in training, his monthly pay jumped to $205 when he became a second lieutenant. He soon started sending money home to his mother. Since all his siblings were married with families of their own to nurture and support, Bill took it upon himself to take care of Mayme financially. This would continue throughout the rest of his life – and beyond. A recurring topic in his letters to her was his life insurance policies, which listed her as the beneficiary.

When Bill came home on leave to Marion for Christmas 1940, he felt confident enough of his finances to purchase his first automobile, a late-model Plymouth convertible. After a hard night of partying on New Year's Eve, he departed in the Plymouth toward evening on January 1, 1941, to return to duty. His route would take him west to Des Moines, then almost due south to Shreveport, about 850 miles away.

On his return, Bill saw that the flying school had received eight new airplanes during his absence. These were Republic AT-12 Guardsman trainers, a two-seat variant of the Seversky P-35 fighter intended for Sweden but impounded by the USAAC when the US government declared a short-lived embargo against exporting weapons to any nation other than Great Britain. With additional aircraft available, Bill looked forward to building up his flying hours in the months ahead. He was also eager to get a chance to fly the USAAC's frontline fighter of the day, the Curtiss P-40. A modification of the company's P-36, the P-40 (featuring an Allison V12 liquid-cooled engine producing 1,040hp) was capable of about 350mph in level flight. Bill apparently got his wish to fly the P-40 sometime in the spring of 1941, but he did not leave a description of the experience.

A break in the routine came in March when Bill delivered an aircraft (type unknown) to Los Angeles. He wrote this account to Mayme on his return:

> Got back to Barksdale Thursday morning, early. Spent two nights and two days on the train from Los Angeles, but had Pullman so it wasn't so bad. Didn't see much of Los Angeles, though. Got in there about 2:30pm last Monday and left at 8:15pm the same night. Flew over some awfully pretty scenery as far as mountains etc. go, but much of the trip, in fact most of it, was over desert and sage brush.

An even more exciting break came on April 9, when Bill's squadron departed for Eglin Field, Florida, for a week of aerial gunnery practice on the former Valparaiso Bombing and Gunnery Range. At Eglin, Bill and his students spent their flying time attacking fixed targets on the ground and practicing air-to-air gunnery over the Gulf of Mexico by firing at a sleeve towed behind another aircraft. The bullets in each pilot's plane were painted a different color, and when they hit the target they left a telltale mark so the pilots could be graded on their marksmanship. When they returned to Barksdale, word came through that the entire advanced single-engined flying school, including the 39 cadets of Class 41-D, would be moving to a brand-new base at Selma, Alabama, when it opened on May 2, 1941.

When Bill arrived at Selma Army Air Base, he found visual proof of the USAAC's rapid expansion taking place at the time. Hewn from cotton fields and cattle-grazing land, the base featured modern one-story billets constructed out of concrete blocks, with a screened porch running the length of each building. Two temporary runways were available, as the first permanent runway was still under construction. Parts of the parking apron had been completed and some work was being done in the main hangar, but aircraft maintenance work took place outside. Most of the groundcrew (sheet metal workers, mechanics, parachute riggers, etc.) were from Wright Field in Dayton, Ohio, and were a mixture of civilians and military personnel.[6]

Bill was only at Selma about a week before he returned to Eglin Field for another round of gunnery training. While there, he wrote to his mother that he had been flying six to seven hours a day, first while training a class of cadets and then while running a school for instructors. He also described a recent reunion with an old high school buddy:

I was in San Antonio two or three weeks ago and stopped at Randolph. I ran through a list of the new cadets, and sure enough Don Goodyear's name was on it, so I went over to his room. He was sitting at a desk writing, and his three room-mates were sitting or lying around the room. I knocked and walked in. You should have seen them snap into a good "brace." I didn't have the heart to keep them that way. Don was certainly glad to see me, as he was in the very first stage of being a "do-do," and that's plenty tough.

Bill also told his mother that he hoped to visit nephew Dick Reed soon. Dick had just followed Bill into the USAAC and was in primary flight training at Grider Field in Pine Bluff, Arkansas. The letter contained a seemingly innocuous postscript:

Had an offer of $600 a month and expenses from Curtiss Aircraft.

Bill's postscript was not quite accurate. The job offer actually came from the Central Aircraft Manufacturing Company, Federal Inc., which was the Curtiss-Wright sales representative in China. CAMCO, as the company was known, had been assembling Curtiss aircraft in its factories in China since 1933. Now, it was involved in a new and more complicated project to boost the capability of the Chinese Air Force (CAF).

From their remote capital city of Chungking deep in the interior of China, Chiang Kai-shek and his Nationalist government had been holding out against the Japanese invaders for three years. The Japanese had captured the key Chinese cities of Peiping, Nanking, Shanghai and Hankow with relative ease in 1937–38, but the Chinese had finally halted their advance at Tsaoyang in mountainous Hupeh (Hubei) Province and to the south at Changsha in mid-1939. With the ensuing stalemate, the Japanese turned to a strategy of attrition. They captured port cities on the Chinese coast to cut off imports of much-needed supplies and arms to the interior, while stripping the countryside of indigenous Chinese resources to supply their own troops. At the same time, Japanese aircraft continued to bomb the cities of free China, including the new capital. Millions of Chinese civilians died.

China's situation became even more precarious with the outbreak of war in Europe. When Germany, an ally of Japan, defeated

France in June 1940, the port city of Hanoi in French Indochina (Vietnam) was closed to shipments bound for China. That left Rangoon (Yangon), in the British colony of Burma (Myanmar), as the last port of entry for China-bound goods. From Rangoon, supplies could be shipped north by rail to the junction with the new "Burma Road" and trucked from there into China, a total distance of more than 800 miles. It was a slender thread, but it was the only link China had to the outside world. If Great Britain went to war with China, as looked increasingly likely in the spring of 1941, the Burma supply route would be threatened unless it could be defended from air attack.

After four years of battling the Japanese with obsolete aircraft and a dwindling number of qualified pilots, the CAF was in no condition to take on this task. Claire Lee Chennault, a retired USAAC pilot who had spent a turbulent 20-year military career promoting pursuit aviation, had been employed by the Chinese government since 1937 to upgrade the nation's air defense system. He had been working tirelessly to train more pilots, build new airfields and devise an air raid warning system, but even these efforts were insufficient to protect the Chinese people from enemy bombers. Understandably, their morale was crumbling under the constant threat of death raining down from the skies.

To meet the growing challenge of defending China and the Burma Road from air attack, Chiang and Chennault devised a new strategy. They would ask the United States to provide China with a task force of modern fighters and bombers, manned by well-trained American aircrew, to oppose the Japanese. Two combat groups of fighters – six squadrons – plus one group comprising three squadrons of twin-engined bombers should do the trick. Chennault doubted the US Government would buy in, given its current policy to avoid joining the wars in Europe and Asia, but he agreed to travel to Washington, D.C., to make the pitch. He arrived in late October 1940 in the company of CAF Gen Mow Pang Tsu, and they joined forces with financier Soong Tse-ven, Madame Chiang's brother and China's top representative in Washington, to prepare their campaign.[7]

It was slow going for Chennault at first. US military leaders, particularly USAAC chief of staff Gen H. H. "Hap" Arnold and the US Navy's chief of the Bureau of Aeronautics, Adm Jack Towers, were dead set against China's plan. They were both working at full speed to expand their own forces and had no interest in giving up 350 frontline combat aircraft and the men to fly them – especially to a retired low-level officer like Chennault. Eventually, however, Chennault and his Chinese compatriots found their way around the military's opposition.

In January 1941, the China team identified a circle of White House advisors who were sympathetic to the nation's plight and had influence in the administration of President Franklin D. Roosevelt. They convinced the latter to back Chennault's plan, and on April 15, 1941, the president agreed to allow reserve officers and enlisted men to resign from the US Army, US Navy and US Marine Corps and join the AVG in China. Chennault rounded up a crew of recruiters, headed by his old pal C. B. "Skip" Adair, and they immediately began scouring military airfields throughout the nation in search of volunteers. Their goal was to find enough men to staff the first of the two fighter groups envisioned in the plan.[8]

Chennault's volunteers would need airplanes to fly, and he was able to work around the arms embargo and obtain 100 Curtiss Hawk 81-A-2 fighters through a complicated arrangement involving the American and British governments. Known to the Royal Air Force (RAF) as the Tomahawk IIA, this aircraft was an export version of the USAAC's P-40B, and it was considered obsolete for combat over Europe. It would have to do for the AVG, however.[9]

RECRUITED

Adair had been on the road recruiting AVG pilots for about a month when he made a visit to Selma. There, he had been told, he could find the rarest of USAAC pilots – one with actual combat experience. Although 1Lt Albert "Ajax" Baumler was now a pursuit instructor at Selma, in 1936–37 he had flown fighters in Spain on the Republican side, shooting down several enemy aircraft. A pilot with experience like that could be an asset to Chennault in China. However, when Adair asked to speak to Baumler, he learned that the pilot was on temporary duty at Eglin Field. There was, however, another USAAC pilot keen to volunteer. Adair turned his attention to him.

Adair had only got a few minutes into his pitch to A. E. "Red" Probst before the latter was hanging on every word. He agreed to sign up that same afternoon. Not only that, but Probst introduced Adair to his 40-F classmates and buddies Bill Reed and "Kirk" Kuykendall. Bill and "Kirk" listened intently as Adair explained the offer. The two pilots would be allowed to resign their commissions with no repercussions to become employees of CAMCO. The company would pay their expenses to travel to the Far East. There, they would, in the words of the contract, "perform such duties as the employer may direct" for one year. Those duties, Adair told them, likely would involve flying combat for China in P-40s to protect the Burma Road and Chinese cities from Japanese air attacks. Both young men perked up when they heard that, having spent several wearisome months boring holes in the sky for Training Command. Now Adair was offering them the adventure of a lifetime.

Still in debt from college, Bill was particularly interested in the pay offer of $600 per month – almost triple what he was making in the USAAC. Adair also told them of the rumor, which turned out to be true, that the pilots would be paid a bonus of $500 for each enemy aircraft they destroyed. In addition, CAMCO would pay the premiums on a $10,000 US Government life insurance policy and cover travel expenses up to $500 for their return trip when the contract expired. Another factor, shared by most USAAC instructors, was that in the event of war they feared being stuck in Training Command and missing the opportunity to get into combat. When Adair finished talking, Bill and "Kirk" joined "Red" in agreeing to sign up. Adair told them they would leave for Asia by ship from San Francisco in the third week of July.

Just like that, Bill and his two buddies were civilians, on their way to an exciting future. Bill wrote a letter to Mayme telling her what he had done (see Introduction), then packed the Plymouth with his belongings and headed north toward Iowa. He arrived in Marion in the first week in July. Bill had about ten days at home to say his goodbyes to family and friends. Fortunately, Dick arranged to get a few days of leave from USAAC flight training at the same time, and they made plans for Bill to drive him back to Randolph Field on the first leg of Bill's road trip to the West Coast. It was not an easy parting for Bill and his mother. On arriving in San Francisco, Bill wrote this in a letter to Mayme:

> There is no way, Mom, that I could possibly tell you how hard it was to leave last Monday, and how badly I felt because you took it so hard. I knew it was impossible to ever reconcile you to the fact of my going, but I think I'm doing right; and if I only had the assurance that you would believe in my judgment and not worry too much, it would make it much easier for me. I promise you that I will write as often as possible.

Bill and Dick rolled out of Marion on Monday morning, July 14, 1941. They drove west to Des Moines, then turned south. Their first objective was to pick up "Kirk" Kuykendall in his Central Texas hometown of San Saba, deep in pecan country. The three of them then continued south to San Antonio. They drove fast through the night and arrived at Randolph Field at about 0900hrs. After an 18-hour layover, during which they said goodbye to Dick and wished him well in his next phase of flight training, Bill and "Kirk" "highballed it" west toward California. Reaching Los Angeles, they took the Pacific Coast Highway north to San Francisco, arriving in the fog-bound city at about 1600hrs on Thursday, July 17, to check in at the Hotel Bellevue (now The Marker San Francisco) on the corner of Geary and Taylor Streets. Bill had not slept in a bed since Sunday night and was glad to have the 3,000-mile road trip behind him.[10]

CAMCO used the Hotel Bellevue as its local headquarters, and had arranged for all the volunteers to stay there until their ship departed for Asia. One of the AVG contingent later described the hotel as "small and filled with well-worn furnishings" but clean and comfortable.[11] It was a low-profile facility, just right for CAMCO's somewhat clandestine purposes.

When Bill and "Kirk" checked in, the desk clerk handed them each an envelope containing $100 in expense money, along with keys to the room they would be sharing. They were also instructed to check in at the CAMCO office, which was located in room 314. There, they met Mrs. Ruth Hamilton, a CAMCO secretary, and handed over their passports to her. She told them the ship would be leaving in several days, and they were free to enjoy the city until then. They were also required to check in at the office daily between 1300–1500hrs in case there were sailing instructions or other news for them.

Bill's first order of business was to sell the Plymouth. He had decided to drive the car across the country because he figured it might be worth more money on the West Coast than in Iowa. It did not quite work out that way. Although he got a good price for the car – $800 – the dealer that bought it would only give him $650 in cash plus a credit for $150 on the purchase of a new car at a later date. Bill knew it was a long shot that he would ever use the credit voucher, but he had little choice but to accept the deal. "Naturally, I took an awful kicking selling it on such short notice, but at least it's off my mind now," he wrote to Mayme a few days later.

Bill and "Kirk" had several days to see the sights in San Francisco while the rest of the AVG contingent trickled in to the Hotel Bellevue. One day they ventured down to the docks to watch their ship, the Motor Ship (MS) *Bloemfontein* of the Java–Pacific Line, being loaded. By Sunday afternoon, all the men had arrived (15 pilots and ten groundcrew), and they gathered in the AVG office for a short organizational meeting with recruiter "Skip" Adair. Then many of them adjourned to the Hotel Bellevue's cocktail lounge to get better acquainted. After a few rounds of drinks, Bill joined three of his new comrades – fellow former USAAC pilots George McMillan, Robert T. Smith and Paul Greene – for dinner at a nearby steak house. They had been instructed not to speak in public about their mission, so it is likely their conversation centered more generally on their flying experiences.[12]

Finally, on the morning of Tuesday, July 22, a small fleet of taxicabs carried the travelers and their baggage to the dock area and dropped them off next to MS *Bloemfontein*. The men scrambled up the gangplank and were met by a Dutch ship's officer who directed them to their cabins. At about noon the ship cast off, and MS *Bloemfontein* began to move away from the dock.

Bill Reed had no idea what the coming year would hold, but he knew his next big adventure was under way.

PART TWO

A Grand Experiment – the AVG

4

"Day after day passed by uneventfully"

A group of sturdy young men lined the stern of MS *Bloemfontein* as it slowly navigated away from its dock in San Francisco on the afternoon of July 22, 1941[1] and headed west toward the Pacific Ocean. They watched Fisherman's Wharf and Coit Tower on Telegraph Hill pass on the port side, then shifted their gazes to Alcatraz Island on the starboard. How many of the 300 or so inmates of the island prison would have traded their incarcerations for the unknown fates of the AVG condottieri aboard the ship? The volunteers looked up as the vessel passed under the orange span of the Golden Gate Bridge, then watched as the huge structure slowly disappeared from view.

The group began to disperse when the Marin Headlands on the California coast slipped below the horizon, but a few lingered to ponder further what lay ahead for them in the coming year. One of those at the rail was 24-year-old Bill Reed, who, until a few weeks prior, had been serving as a flight instructor in the USAAC. Now he was traveling on a civilian passport, destination Rangoon, Burma. His passport listed his occupation as shipping clerk, a feeble effort by the US Government to disguise the true purpose of his journey. In a few weeks he would be flying fighters for China.

"I know I was not alone in my thoughts of home and how long it would be until I returned to those fading shores," Reed wrote later. "The rails of the afterdeck were lined with passengers whose pensive faces reflected thoughts similar to my own."

MS *Bloemfontein* (soon nicknamed "The Bloom" by the AVG passengers) was a relatively modern 12,000-ton cargo ship of the Dutch-owned Java–Pacific Line. In its hold were goods bound for various ports in Asia, including automobiles and large containers of Quaker Oats like the ones Bill had loaded in Cedar Rapids during his college years. The ship also had accommodation for about 100 passengers. The cabins were clean, the food was hearty and the Javanese cabin boys were attentive to the travelers' needs. There were limited facilities for entertainment and exercise, including badminton, shuffleboard and even a swimming pool.

Among the 86 passengers for this voyage with Bill Reed were 24 other men who had recently signed contracts with CAMCO to serve for one year in the AVG. They were the second group of recruits to leave for training in Burma, and others would follow them to the British colony on the Bay of Bengal between India and China. About half of the AVG passengers were pilots, some of whom had experienced sea duty while serving in the US Navy. They were the lucky ones, because MS *Bloemfontein* was only a few hours out of San Francisco when the Pacific Ocean asserted its power to the discomfort of all but a handful of passengers aboard the ship. Heavy seas, with waves estimated at 15ft or more, began to roll the vessel fore to aft and side to side.

Bill had not been worried about seasickness when he boarded the ship, figuring his flying experience had prepared him for the ocean voyage. This, despite the fact, as he noted in his diary, that the largest vessel he had ever ridden prior to boarding MS *Bloemfontein* was a ferry on the Mississippi River. He figured wrong. When he began to feel woozy, he retreated to his cabin to lie down on its built-in bed. It was a good plan, but poorly executed:

> Unthinkingly, I left the porthole open, and it wasn't long before a good portion of the Pacific was in the cabin with me. I had one of the Javanese cabin boys change the linen. By this time I began to notice an unpleasant feeling in my stomach, so I just got back

in bed and stayed there through the evening meal and the first night at sea. By morning I was feeling fine and had my appetite back. From reports at breakfast and on deck, I gathered that I wasn't the only one in my misery that first day out.

The initial leg of MS *Bloemfontein*'s voyage to the Far East would take the ship to Pearl Harbor, Hawaii, in a sailing time of five to six days. Now with a calm sea and sunny skies, the passengers began to relax and enjoy the trip. Most of the AVG volunteers were not acquainted prior to sailing, so they spent their time getting to know one another. Bill Reed and "Kirk" Kuykendall were buddies, having trained together and instructed in the same fighter training outfit in Alabama. They soon made friends with Robert "R. T." Smith and Paul "P. J." Greene, two more refugees from Training Command. Other USAAC pilots were Robert "Duke" Hedman, George McMillan, Ed Liebolt, Max Hammer, Frank Schiel and Bill "Black Mac" McGarry. Former US Navy pilots were Bert Christman, Ben Foshee, David "Tex" Hill, Tom Jones and Ed Rector. None of the latter, naturally, had flown a USAAC P-40, nor had Smith or Greene. Rounding out the AVG contingent were ten former USAAC enlisted men who would serve in various technical capacities on the ground. Four years later at the end of World War II, five of these 25 "Bloom Boys" would be dead.

The AVG recruits also socialized with their fellow passengers, who included missionaries, teachers, students and others. Of special interest to Iowa native Bill Reed was a Chinese couple, both Ph.Ds., who had been teaching at Iowa State College in Ames and were now returning to their native China to try to help in the nation's war against Japan. He also got to know American physician Dr. Adele B. Cohn, who was on her way to China to work with the Red Cross teaching Chinese doctors how to treat tuberculosis.

Then there was Baron Gustav Adolf Steengracht von Moyland (spelled "van Mooiland" on the ship's roster of passengers), who claimed he was a Dutchman headed to Java to join the Netherlands East Indies Air Force but was actually a German diplomat on a secret mission to Asia. Shortly after his birth in 1902, Moyland became a naturalized citizen of Prussia and the German Empire. He studied law and economics and was a practicing lawyer prior to joining the Nazi Party and its Storm Detachment, the original paramilitary wing of the Party, in 1933. In 1935 Moyland went to work for the Office for Foreign Matters and in 1938 he became an assistant to Joachim von Ribbentrop, Nazi Germany's foreign minister.[2]

So much for all the secrecy surrounding the AVG. If Moyland did not already know about the volunteers when he boarded MS *Bloemfontein*, he certainly had plenty to report about them to his superiors – and their Japanese allies – by the time he left the ship.

Several months after arriving in Burma, Bill Reed wrote a detailed account of his sea voyage. We pick up his travelogue on July 27, 1941, as MS *Bloemfontein* neared Hawaii:

> The day before we were to dock in Honolulu we were met by eight US destroyers headed east. One of them pulled over beside us to determine who we were and where we were bound etc. The next morning most of us were up bright and early. Sure enough, land was in sight. It wasn't long before the pilot was aboard and we were making our way past Diamond Head and Waikiki Beach into the harbor of Honolulu. We were to take on water and fuel oil here, so there was only about half a day to shop and see what could be seen of the island in that short time. My friend "Kirk" and I went first to the Soldiers & Sailors Club, where we got off some mail, and then to Hickam Field, the Army air base on the island. I bought about $75 worth of clothes, camera etc. here in the morning, and then we went back to town and visited a few of the better-looking cafes and hotel bars. We got back to the boat just at the deadline – 4 pm – and before long we were once more under way. This time the destination was unknown, except to members of the crew, who proved to be very close-mouthed.
>
> Day after day passed by uneventfully, with nothing to do but read, play bridge or watch the waves go by. Once in a while a whale would be seen – or rather the vapor and water

which spouted into the air when the whale emptied its lungs and took on a fresh cargo of oxygen. Only once did I actually spot the body of a whale itself. There were lots of flying fish and occasional schools of porpoise. I kept checking our general course by noting the position of stars at night. We gradually lost sight of the Big Dipper and the North Star. Our course was south and west, and soon the Southern Cross and Scorpio and Centaur were visible. Finally, we were so far south that the cross appeared almost overhead early in the evening. About this time the course changed to directly west, and we decided that more than likely some Australian port would be our next stop.

By this time, some 16–17 days had passed, and the passengers were pretty bored with shuffleboard, bridge etc. I was plenty tired of the seas myself, though the time passed more quickly because of a bridge session that I was involved in. A mechanic from my group named [Jasper] Harrington teamed with me against the female M.D. [Dr. Cohn] and Mr. [W. F.] Giddings, a rubber planter from Sumatra. There was no money involved in the game, but we were keeping a running score, and according to the agreement, the team with the highest score when Manila was reached was to be treated to a round of drinks at the city's nicest night club by the losers. Our opponents really should have beaten us soundly, as they were well-versed in bridge rules etc., whereas Harrington and I played a wild game, relying more on plain card sense than anything else. We ran into a phenomenal bit of luck, though, and night after night we would send them away talking to themselves. But now, before I get completely sidetracked, let's get to our second stop – Brisbane, Australia.

We had a day's notice that we were to dock, so early on the morning of August 10 I was on deck. Once more the pilot came aboard, and we began to wend our way through the channels that led to a wide river. The town of Brisbane was about ten miles up the river. We arrived on a Sunday, and because of their Sunday laws almost everything was closed. We were allowed to go ashore at 10 am, with instructions to be back aboard by 10 pm. I spent the day wandering around the town seeing the sights. The streets seemed filled with people in uniforms. I was not much impressed with anything that I saw. It was rather frightening to get into a taxi, though, and go whizzing down the left side of the road. Early in the evening, while I was on the main street of the city looking at an American display in a show window of a large department store, two Australian soldiers escorting a rather nice-looking girl came along and struck up a conversation. Seems that they knew I was American by the clothes I was wearing. One of the soldiers bought me RAF "wings" and pinned them on my gabardine topcoat. The weather was rather cold, for the winter season in Australia begins when summer comes in the States. They were a nice escort, though, and when I left I promised the girl I would write her. Still have her card but haven't written.

Got back to the boat in good time and found that a lot of the boys had celebrated plenty during their stay. I didn't stay up to watch the ship leave Brisbane, because it was nearly midnight before they lifted anchor.

We now knew we were headed for Manila, and that it was a trip of some six–seven days. A pilot stayed on our ship, for we were hugging the northeast coast of Australia, and there were countless coral islands, some with a little lighthouse and keeper's house, but mostly uninhabited. After several days we were passing the rather narrow Torres Strait, and on the third or fourth day we came to Thursday Island, where we let the pilot off. From here we headed north and west, and on about the sixth day out of Brisbane we began to encounter the southernmost islands of the Philippine chain. Also, we encountered a few more of Uncle Sam's destroyers and cruisers, and carried on a code conversation by means of a signal light with one of them.

It was on this trip from Brisbane to Manila that we encountered the most unusual sight of the whole voyage. It was a phosphorescent phenomenon of some sort, and we noticed it from about 9 pm to 1 am on the fourth night out. The sky was clear, with only a few nebulous-appearing clouds to be seen, but the sea was a rather opaque, milky color, and as far as the eye could see a sort of cold light seemed to emanate from the surface of the water.

At last, though, we were in Manila, and after a few hours of dealing with the harbor inspectors, passport officials etc., we were ready to go ashore. From the approach into the harbor, the part of Manila facing the sea looked fairly modern and attractive. I was rather disappointed, though, in the first tour through the downtown district. True, there were some very nice buildings, mostly modern official houses (customs, city hall, legations etc.), but the greater part of the true downtown was made up of native shops facing each other across narrow, dirty streets. It was not as Americanized as I had imagined. Away from the city were some rather nice apartments and suburban dwellings and a great profusion of flowers and flowering vines, which added much to the appearance.

We stayed in Manila for two or three days, and most of these were spent visiting Nichols Field and the surrounding territory. At that time there didn't seem to be a great deal of activity there, and very few planes. "Kirk" had just recovered from a severe cold, and the ship's doctor told him he would like to see an X-ray of his chest; we took care of this matter through the cooperation of the medical corps at Nichols and found out that nothing was wrong with him. That night we hit a few of the clubs, but for the most part they weren't so hot. The nicest place was the Jai Alai Club, but we weren't dressed for the occasion. Among other places we visited were the Santa Anna (reputedly the world's largest cabaret), Legaspi Gardens (seemingly a great hangout for sailors) and the Metro Gardens (where they had two good orchestras).

We left Manila early one Friday morning, and once more we knew our destination – Batavia, Java. Many of our passengers had been left at Manila, and a few new ones had joined us. About the only interesting ones were five Free French people – four men and one girl – and she was really all right! Unfortunately, though, my college French (two years) wasn't enough of a basis to strike up a conversation – especially in the face of the fact that those four Frenchmen more or less formed a bodyguard for her.

It was only a trip of two–three days, though, when we crossed the Equator again. We crossed it first on the Honolulu–Brisbane trip and had quite a ceremony. Then going to Manila we crossed it again going north. We reached Batavia early one afternoon in the latter part of August. It was a nice, busy-looking place, though the city itself was four–six miles from the harbor. I like the Javanese people, and I think they are the cleanest of all the peoples in the eastern countries I have visited. Batavia is pretty well settled and managed by the Dutch. All of the hotels and large stores were operated by them. One thing the Dutch love to do is eat, and I give them due credit for their excellent cooking. I gained weight during the trip.

I visited the governor's residence – or rather the grounds around his palace – in a small town about 40 miles inland from Batavia. The shops in Batavia are places to find good buys in wood carving and silver work. Also, they are full of "batiks" [dyed textiles] and crocodile skins. We stayed in Batavia three–four days and finally boarded another ship, the sister ship of the *Bloemfontein* – the *Jagersfontein* – and set out for Singapore. The trip took only two nights and a day, and it was uneventful except for a nice dinner and patriotic ceremony that took place the first night out on the occasion of the Dutch queen's birthday.

About September 3 we entered the harbor of Singapore. It seemed an awfully busy place, full of commercial craft, native sampans and a few smaller British naval vessels. It didn't take us long to clear ship, and we were met by some British soldiers with trucks and, together with our baggage, we were whisked right through downtown Singapore to a British camp north of town. It was a rough-looking place, and we were told that arrangements had been made for us to stay there while in Singapore. None of us liked it very well, but we got tents set up in a little section bordering the jungle (we called it "Cobraville") and spent the night there. Then the next day we found that the British couldn't have us staying there (as we were nothing more than American civilians, officially), so we were assigned to various hotels in Singapore. "Kirk" and I drew the Seaview, and it proved very nice.

We stayed in Singapore until September 12, and I really got a chance to wander around the place. There are some good department stores there (British) and thousands of native shops. I had more fun arguing the price down with these native shopkeepers than I had doing most anything else. I know I always paid them double, but I thought I had them down plenty when I bought. The streets of Singapore were always filled with taxis and rickshaws, hurrying masses of natives (Chinese, Indians, Malayans etc.) and quite a few Europeans. It was a show itself to sit along the way and watch them. There were a few pestering snake charmers and magicians, but one show by them was enough.

I stayed out at the Seaview quite a bit of the time, for it was a very nice spot, with a shade lawn bordering the harbor and plenty of reading material etc. The food was excellent.

Speaking of food reminds me of the Chinese banquet which the Chinese Consul at Singapore gave in our honor. It was held at the Happy World Cabaret and was complete even to the chopsticks. I couldn't count the various courses, but I ate some things that I knew positively I would never eat again. Among them were shark fin and soybean cakes. I was no expert with the chopsticks, but I still wouldn't starve if I had to use them. I remember one of the courses consisted of chicken served with the head still attached. Another was a small pig, roasted whole until the skin was crackling. The first time it was placed on the table we ate just this crackling skin; then it was taken away and, after an intervening course, brought back and we ate the pork. Between courses we talked to the host and cracked watermelon seeds and ate the kernel, which I found a very common custom. After the dinner I visited the cabaret but didn't dance. I think there was every nationality represented among the girls except whites – all the dark races.

One day, two or three of us visited the airport and found some American navy men there helping the English maintain and assemble some American Brewsters [Buffalo fighters].

Finally, on September 11 or 12, we were able to secure passage to Rangoon on a Norwegian steamer called the *Hai Hing*[3]. It was a ship which normally engaged in carrying Chinese from Hong Kong to various points, and it only had good accommodations for nine or ten. But we put 23 aboard[4] some way or another, and we managed all right, though we had to eat in shifts. The captain was a nice guy and talked much of his travels in America. It was a three-day trip to Rangoon, which went by rapidly. The water along the route was full of flying fish. We were blacked out, as we had been most of the trip, but we could hear news broadcasts from the States. I saw quite a few small water snakes, and the captain told me they were quite poisonous.

Early on the morning of September 15 we started up the Rangoon River, and about 8 am we were offshore from Rangoon. Soon we were alongside the docks and were met by Adair and Hastey [AVG representatives]. We got our baggage through customs and all went to the Strand Hotel, where the company had a nice dinner arranged for us. During dinner I learned we were to entrain that same afternoon for "Point A," [Toungoo] Burma. I did get time enough, though, after eating to take a look around Rangoon. I went out to the zoo and then just rode around in a taxi. I was most impressed by two very large pagodas, both covered in gold leaf.

We all boarded the narrow-gauge passenger train and soon were skimming (and bouncing) through the rice paddies of Burma. Stopped in Pegu, Burma, for dinner and found that we would arrive at our destination shortly after 9 pm. Sure enough, the train jolted to a stop shortly after 9, and I knew we were there, for outside the coaches I could hear the din of welcoming American voices, which meant that those who had been on the boats before us had turned out en masse to welcome us. Probst, an ex-roommate of mine in flying school, was among them, and he took a bunch of us in a station wagon and started for the airfield, which lay some six–eight miles along the Burma Road from the village. We were soon there, and everyone congregated in the bar. There was much beer and more loud visiting and renewing of acquaintances. I found that I was assigned to the Third Pursuit Squadron and met my squadron leader, A. E. Olson, who seemed to be a very nice fellow.

The thing I was most interested in, though, was some mail that Probst had picked up for me, and as soon as possible I went over to his barracks and got it. Letters from Mom, Emma and Father Stemm[5]. I read them by flashlight, and the bugs almost ate me up. Finally, I crawled under the mosquito net in my barracks, and after a bit of thinking the situation over, was asleep.

"Don't be too much concerned, will you?"

Bill Reed awoke to the sound of a gong rung by the Burmese houseboy at 0530hrs on September 16, 1941, his first full day in Burma. He was lying on a narrow, slatted cot with a decidedly thin straw mattress and was cocooned by mosquito netting. The cot sat toward the center of a half-walled, clear-span barracks building. A ceiling fan turned slowly, and above that Reed could see the underside of a bamboo thatched roof. From outside came a chorus of chirps and twitters sung by the birds and other creatures of the surrounding jungle.

Soon Reed and the 17 other pilots of the 3rd Pursuit Squadron (PS) began to stir. They dressed and made their way to the four-hole latrine out back, then proceeded to the nearby mess hall for breakfast, joined by the men of the 1st and 2nd PSs. The food was prepared by a native contractor, and after the fine fare of the MS *Bloemfontein* and the Seaview Hotel, it was a tough swallow. Sure, there was some bitching, but these men had not come to Burma for the food. Bill's overall first impression of the Toungoo setup was favorable:

> We have a pretty nice place here. It is what you might call roughing it in a mild sense of the word, for we live in sort of a barracks built of bamboo; and the place is more or less hewn from the surrounding jungle, but I like it so far. I'm going to buy

a bicycle tomorrow. All of the buildings are scattered out and it's too much walking going from one to the other. Besides, it's too hot to move around much. They say this is the cool season, but the temperature during the day runs from 100 to 105. So far it has rained a little every day, but I think the real rainy season is almost over. We played softball last night and our outfit won. We have a movie every other night, and while they aren't the latest films, they aren't too old either.[1]

Right away, the men became aware of another condition at Toungoo, which Bill later described in a letter:

My main objection to the place, however, is the bug situation. There are millions and millions of them – all kinds, shapes and colors. They get in everything and make life miserable in many ways. They even get through the mosquito netting over the bed. We have killed half a dozen or so scorpions in the barracks, and one centipede that measured about six inches. The worst nuisances are the mosquitos and gnats, etc.[2]

About a mile from the barracks complex was Kyedaw airfield, which would be the home base of the AVG for the next three months. Located in the Sittang River Valley about 175 miles north of Rangoon, Kyedaw had a single, 4,000ft macadam runway running north–south, a low control tower, a few hangars and several administration buildings.

Like just about every detail concerning the AVG, Kyedaw was a product of compromise. The original plan had been for the AVG to train in China, but the vulnerability of Chinese airfields to Japanese air attack and the difficulty of ferrying new P-40s from their assembly plant in Rangoon to China argued against that plan. Instead, the RAF agreed to provide its airfield at Kyedaw – unloved and little-used because of its remote jungle setting – to the AVG for training. Here, newly assembled P-40s could be flown up from Rangoon in less than an hour, and training could take place unmolested because Great Britain and Japan were still at peace.

Two shipments of personnel had preceded the MS *Bloemfontein* crew to Rangoon. Over breakfast, these "old hands" of the AVG, who had been in Burma all of about a month, brought the new recruits up to speed on what had been happening at Kyedaw. It was not a pretty story.

The AVG had been officially "constituted" on August 1, 1941, four days after the advance party of men arrived. Most of the latter were technicians, and they went right to work at Rangoon's Mingaladon airdrome assembling the AVG's 100 P-40 fighters. The aircraft had been delivered to Burma by ship in large crates, with the wings separate from the fuselages. Lacking sufficient facilities and tools to rebuild the Curtiss fighters, the assembly crew made slow progress. By mid-August only three aircraft had been assembled, tested and flown to Kyedaw. New planes had been dribbling in a few at a time since then, and a total of 40[3] had been delivered to Kyedaw by the time Bill arrived.

With the arrival on August 16 of the second shipment of personnel, which included about 40 pilots, the AVG was organized into four squadrons – the headquarters squadron and three pursuit squadrons. Arvid E. Olson, Jr., a former USAAC pilot who had flown P-40s in the 8th Pursuit Group (PG), was appointed commanding officer of the 3rd PS, and most of the pilots he chose for the squadron also were ex-USAAC. Bill heard a lot of complaining over breakfast, and of the 12 squadron pilots he met that day, fully half would quit the AVG without ever flying a combat mission. On a brighter note, Bill took an immediate shine to pilot Neil G. Martin, who had flown with Olson in the 8th PG and, before that, had been a football star at the University of Arkansas. In the weeks ahead, the two young men would form a close friendship.

As might be expected, the new pilots were eager to learn more about the man in charge of the AVG, Claire Lee Chennault. "The Colonel," as he was called by the AVG in reference to his rank in the CAF, was up in Kunming, China, on business and would not meet the latest arrivals for a few more days. Later, he would earn another appellation from his admiring pilots – "The Old Man."

Chennault eventually became world famous, but at this point in time he was an unknown quantity. The talk by the old hands at breakfast was of a wiry man about 50 years old, with a leathery face and a pronounced Louisiana accent. His deep voice sometimes sounded more like a growl. They knew he had been in China since 1937 trying to build a functioning CAF, and had spent 20 years before then as a pursuit pilot in the USAAC, retiring with the rank of captain. Although he had not experienced combat in World War I, he seemed to know a lot about fighter tactics and have strong opinions about how best to fight the Japanese in the air. Chennault made a distinct impression, no doubt about that. Time would tell if he knew what he was talking about.

After breakfast, the pilots made their way over to the Kyedaw flightline, where about three-dozen P-40s awaited them. As previously noted, technically, these planes were not P-40s at all but British-spec Hawk 81-A-2s. That meant they had various internal differences from USAAC P-40Bs, ranging from larger-caliber machine guns in the wings to simplified seat belts for the pilot and weak civilian radios. Outwardly, the planes looked identical to the P-40s Reed had flown in the USAAC except for their green-and-brown camouflage scheme and CAF insignia, which consisted of a 12-point white sun on a light-blue disc applied to the tops and bottoms of both wings. Despite the differences, the Hawk 81-A-2s remained "P-40s" in AVG parlance.

The fighters were in various states of repair. Those on flight status were parked side-by-side along the taxiways leading to the runway, arranged by squadrons. Three fresh examples had just arrived from Rangoon the previous day. These planes lacked guns, radios and oxygen tanks, all of which would be installed by groundcrew at Kyedaw as time allowed.

Perhaps a half-dozen fighters were in the airfield's large hangar, where technicians were busy making minor repairs to crumpled wingtips, battered propellers and bent undercarriage legs that had been damaged in landing accidents as pilots were trying to master their new mounts. Still others, more seriously damaged, were sitting in a field next to the hangar. There, they could be stripped for parts needed to keep the flyable P-40s in service. Two planes no longer existed, having been destroyed in a mid-air collision that claimed the life of 2nd PS pilot John Armstrong on September 8.

The new pilots were given time to look over the Hawks and acquaint – or reacquaint in Bill's case – themselves with the cockpit layout. But soon the sun was high and the clock approached 1230hrs, when work ceased for the day to avoid the extreme afternoon heat. Checkout flights would begin the following morning.

Bill made his first flight in an AVG P-40s just two days after arriving at Kyedaw. His new pal Neil Martin checked out Bill on cockpit procedures, reminded him of the fighter's strong torque pull to the left on the takeoff run and wished him well. Despite his long layoff from flying, Bill cleared the runway with no problem. He spent the next hour wearing the rust off his flying skills by performing maneuvers, including on- and off-power stalls, slow rolls, snap rolls, split-esses, loops and spins. When he rolled the aircraft over on its back and pulled the control stick into his lap, the Hawk responded in an exhilarating power dive, just as Bill knew it would. At the end of the hour, he brought the fighter in for a smooth landing, to his great relief. Bill reported in a newspaper interview months later that he became completely comfortable in the P-40 after further flights over the next few days. He wrote this about his first flight in a letter to his mother dated September 17:

Flew today for the first time in two-and-a-half months. It seemed strange at first, but it doesn't take long to get back in the groove.

The new pilots got their first taste of "The Colonel" when Chennault flew in from Kunming later that week. He gave them a brief welcome speech over dinner and then spent time chatting with them after the meal. They found him pretty much as advertised – the heavily lined, leathery face; the Louisiana drawl that was hard to understand at first; the unmistakable air of a man in full command.[4] At the same time, he exhibited the charm that had made him a favorite of subordinates throughout his USAAC career. He was warm, easy to talk to and disinterested in the dogma of military rank and discipline.[5] As a result, the AVG operated on a first-name basis, there was no saluting and the dress code was come-as-you-are.

In a few days, Chennault began a series of lectures in which he explained to the AVG pilots how they would be able to defeat the Japanese in aerial combat. He had very strong opinions about the employment of fighter aircraft in defense against enemy bombers, which he had laid out in his 1933 treatise, *The Role of Defensive Pursuit*. He had further refined his thinking during the previous four years in China while closely observing the capabilities of the Japanese bombers and fighters attacking the country and the tactics they employed against the inferior CAF. The time for testing his theories in combat was approaching rapidly. With the AVG, Chennault had just the force he needed to find out if they worked.

For his system to succeed, he needed three equally important elements: an adequate force of heavily armed, well-flown fighters; sufficient warning of approaching enemy formations; and effective air-ground radio communication to direct his fighters to the enemy. He was already well along in building an air-raid warning net consisting of ground observers throughout China who reported into centralized stations that could correlate the information and pass along instructions to the interceptor force by radio. The next step in his plan was to move the AVG to China when training was complete to defend population centers and the northern stretch of the Burma Road. At the time, it was assumed that the British would be able to defend the route from Rangoon to the Chinese border, keeping open the last remaining route for sending vital supplies and munitions to China.

A new shipment of AVG pilots arrived at Kyedaw on October 11, and that evening Bill gathered with the others in the mess hall so Chennault could resume the lectures on tactics he had started when the first pilots arrived in August. The "Old Man," as the pilots now called him out of earshot, spoke off the cuff with no notes. He used a blackboard to illustrate his points and provided handouts showing the outlines of Japanese aircraft his pilots could expect to encounter.

Chennault referred to enemy fighters as "Zeros" as a general term, having seen the Imperial Japanese Naval Air Force's outstanding Mitsubishi A6M2 Type 0 in action over China the previous year. As it turned out, the AVG would actually engage Imperial Japanese Army Air Force (IJAAF) Nakajima Ki-27 (lightly armed with fixed landing gear) and Nakajima Ki-43 Hayabusa (similar in layout and performance to the Zero-sen) fighters. All three types were low-wing monoplanes with radial engines, so it was easy to misidentify them in the heat of a swirling aerial battle. The Japanese fighters adhered to the same design philosophy, their designers choosing lightweight construction to achieve speed, maneuverability, long range and a high rate-of-climb. Unlike their American counterparts, the Japanese eschewed armor plating and self-sealing fuel tanks in exchange for higher performance.

Chennault told his pilots that their Hawks, although considered obsolete in some circles, had strengths – high speed and heavy firepower – they could use to their advantage in combat with Japanese aircraft. And although the P-40 was inferior to the enemy fighters in several key measures, particularly maneuverability and rate-of-climb, the pilots could offset these factors by adhering to the "Old Man's" tactics.

Despite the popular contemporary Western cartoon image of the Japanese fighter pilot as a buck-toothed fool wearing thick glasses, Chennault knew his enemy was well trained, highly disciplined and fully capable of shooting down AVG P-40s if they were flown haphazardly. The favored tactic of Japanese fighters was to attack from above and then draw their opponents into a turning fight, bringing their superior maneuverability into play in one-on-one combats. This had been the pattern established on the Western Front during World War I, and it remained in place in most air forces of the world during the 1920s and 1930s.

At this point in history, Chennault envisioned using his fighters almost exclusively in an air-to-air role. Later, he would develop fighter-bomber tactics as well, but for now his focus was on defending friendly territory from Japanese air attack. Having studied the advancements in fighter tactics developed in the Spanish Civil War and the Battle of Britain, Chennault was able to roll out a new way for the AVG to fight in the sky. For starters, he told the pilots to forget the three-plane V formation they had been taught in the US, as it was unwieldy in an actual combat environment. Instead, the pilots would fly in two-plane elements, with the leader doing the shooting and the wingman supporting him by guarding the rear from approaching enemy fighters. Every effort should be made to hold the element together throughout an engagement. Multiple elements could be combined to form a flight, depending on the nature of the mission at hand.

When an enemy formation approaches, Chennault instructed, the AVG pilots should avoid combat until they had climbed above the attackers. When they had reached an advantageous position, they should dive on the enemy planes, make a firing pass and then continue down, using their superior diving speed to clear their tails of enemy fighters. Once clear, the fighters could zoom back up above the enemy and repeat their attacks. Under no circumstances should AVG pilots attempt to make a climbing attack or to get sucked into a turning fight. Some months later, Chennault wrote a memo expanding on this point, saying in part:

It should be obvious to anyone that an attempt to climb toward or within visual range of an enemy equipped with aircraft which have a superior rate-of-climb and who is invariably present in superior numbers ought to result in sudden death. While membership in the "DIE YOUNG CLUB" may be highly prized by some, (our) objective is to destroy hostile aircraft with minimum losses of our own.[6]

Subsequent lectures would cover topics such as night combat and China's early warning net. Chennault also took an active part in the AVG's flight training, spending most mornings on the flightline at Kyedaw holding a set of field glasses to his face as he observed the pilots practicing what he preached. Training missions included formation flying and one-on-one dogfight practice.

It was important for Chennault's pilots to master formation flying, because he wanted them to be capable of attacking enemy formation en masse, as opposed to the single attacks made in a string that they had been taught by the USAAC and US Navy. The formation positioned the planes in line-abreast, with the flight leader and his wingman in the middle and element leaders with their wingmen on either side. It was relatively easy for the pilots to hold position as long as the formation was traveling in a straight line, but they had to be on their toes when the formation leader decided to turn. The formation could not simply turn on a flat plane, because that would risk a collision. Instead, each aircraft needed to maintain its position relative to the leader's wingtip – the ones on the inside of the turn would need to dive as they turned, while the ones on the outside had to climb. And the leader had to ensure that the formation was high enough above the ground or the cloud deck to provide space for the lower planes to complete the turn without crashing or losing sight of their leader.

All pilots learned how to fly in formation during military flight training, but not all continued to practice it in service. For instance, flying boat and reconnaissance pilots, of which there were several in the AVG, had been flying single-plane missions most of the time before coming to Burma. So Chennault watched from the ground as his pilots honed their skills at formation flying. He made notes and critiqued them when they landed.

It might seem illogical that Chennault, who lectured his pilots to avoid dogfighting against enemy fighters, included two-plane mock combats in his training syllabus. But he knew that there was no better way for pilots to build confidence in their ability to fly the P-40 than to match their skills one-on-one with another pilot. Flight Leader Lacy Mangleburg was generally acknowledged to be the top dogfighter in the 3rd PS, although Bill was among the upper echelon of pilots and R. T. Smith was an up-and-coming talent. On October 22, Mangleburg and Smith squared off in the sky over Kyedaw, and Smith took the measure of his more experienced opponent in two of the three engagements. Twelve days later, Smith took on Bill, as the former reported in his diary entry for November 3:

> Last period had a combat with Reed. We broke about even, and if anything, he had the edge. But my ship was fully loaded with ammunition, weighing about 400lb, so he had quite an advantage.

While Chennault was encouraging his pilots to master their P-40s, he was nurturing a strong competitive spirit among them as well.

LIFE AT KYEDAW

As the monsoon season of 1941 gave way to improved fall weather, the flying activities at Kyedaw airfield picked up. In addition to building up flight hours in his log book, Bill tended to his duties as the squadron's supply and transportation officer. The job mostly consisted of signing off on work done by ground personnel, but it still required a commitment of his time and attention. Bill nevertheless managed to send a letter home every week to ten days. He was careful to keep the letters on the light side, mostly telling his family in Iowa of inconsequential matters such as the quality of the mess hall food and various recreation activities such as sightseeing trips and inter-squadron sports competitions. The closest he came to discussing flying was an occasional mention of the weather. In nearly every letter he urged his mother to take care of herself, and to not worry for his safety. He also regularly berated her for not spending more of the money – a hefty $500 per month – he was having sent home to their joint bank account. And he always included a plea for more mail from home. What follows is a sampling of quotes from his letters during this period.

> September 30
> By now, Mom, that bank statement should have taken a definite trend upward, and in the black ink, too. And so help me, if you

don't start using it to fit whatever purposes you see fit, I will have to write the bank and have them send the check to you each month. But I've told you all that before, so I won't go into it again. I have changed the allotment, and beginning next month, that is for the month of October, the deposit at the bank should be $500.

October 8
I spun in on my bicycle coming back from the mess hall the other day and broke some spokes out of my wheel, but it only cost me one rupee to get it fixed. These native merchants are pretty shrewd, and it's really an experience to argue with them. Some of them get angry if you take their first price and don't give them any argument over it. I'm still feeling swell, and so far the food, climate etc. are agreeing with me.

October 16
Everything is going along smoothly here, although it's impossible for me to tell you much about the work we are doing. The rainy season is over now, and the weather much improved. With good flying weather, the time seems to pass more rapidly. The meals have shown definite improvement since we fired the outfit that was in charge when we arrived, but there's much to be done along those lines still. At least we don't get beef (water buffalo) every noon and night now.

I lost 100 rupees last week. It amounts to about $33. Guess I left it in a shirt which I sent to the laundry. I asked the laundryman, who is a native, whether any of his workers reported it, but no such luck. He said two of them quit. I imagine they went into retirement on such a sum. I don't need it, but it irks me a little to be so careless.

October 17
Got interrupted last night and had to make a ferry trip to Rangoon, but got back late this afternoon. Spent a very uncomfortable night on a narrow-gauge train which averaged

about 20mph, stops included. Didn't have a chance to do much shopping in Rangoon but did manage to buy some Christmas cards, which I plan to mail tomorrow. Seems strange to be mailing cards two months in advance, but that's about the time it usually takes. Another thing that seems strange is to listen to the radio here at night and hear the announcer in the US say that it's early morning of the day you've just finished. In other words, when it's Friday night here, it's Friday morning there.

October 28
Last Friday night we had a big charity dance at the nearby town we call Point A [Toungoo]. It was quite an affair, and I dressed in my summer tux and everything. Seemed rather strange to put on such airs out here in the wilderness, but it was a lot of fun. Before the dance, seven of the pilots and the two nurses went in to have dinner with an English teakwood dealer. I was one of the seven, and it was a very fine dinner. The host, whom I had met before, proved to be a good fellow. He's been out here 21 years now, thus had a fine collection of curios. If you haven't done so already, Mom, please send the Bossier National Bank the $75 I owe them. I'm disappointed that you haven't drawn out more money than the $50 you mentioned in your last letter. Starting with September 31 [sic], there should have been $500 deposited the last day of each month. I want you to use as much as you need, but at least $100 a month. Use it any way you see fit – if Laurence needs some, let him have it. It's there for you to use, as I have told you many times before.

You probably wouldn't recognize me now, Mom, because I've got a nice black mustache – no foolin', I'm a regular Ronald Coleman! All except one or two of the boys in the barracks are growing one. I didn't have much trouble because my whiskers are so black.

November 19
The weather is much nicer now. The days are still quite warm – around 90 degrees from noon on – but the nights and early

mornings are cool enough to warrant at least a sheet over you. It hasn't rained for several weeks now, either. The skies are clear except of those billowy cumulus clouds which mushroom up over the nearby mountain ranges in the heat of the day. The bugs are the same as always – thick and blood thirsty.

I got my first raise in salary and in position this month. I'm now a flight leader, with $75 more a month. I have a plane of my own now, and I'm pretty proud of it.

Every day seems very much the same. We get up at 5:30 every morning, breakfast at 6 and start work at 6:30. The morning is broken up by tea and sandwiches, and we stop work at noon, that is, with the exception of paperwork and administrative jobs that have to be taken care of. Most of the boys take naps every afternoon, because it really is too hot to do much. I nap sometimes, but lately I've been roaming around the surrounding territory, and then later in the afternoon play either softball or volleyball. We [3rd PS] still are the class of the field in all athletic contests. A couple of my friends and I have taken up one of the native games called "Chin-Lon." It is a game played with a ball made of woven, dried cane shoots, and the players stand in a circle and keep the ball in the air by kicking it or hitting it with any part of the body except the hand and forearm. The native boys are still too good for us, but it won't be long now.

November 29
I just heard one of our ships come in from Rangoon, and I'm hoping it brought some mail from home. You all have been doing fine so far, but one thing that you can't possibly do is send too much mail. Aside from the mail I get from you folks, there isn't much other news from the States. Emma (in San Antonio) has written three times, a girl from Selma wrote one letter, Mick [Forbes] has written once or twice, Dick has written two or three times, a girl from Shreveport wrote to Kirk and me once, Ben Buckley wrote one letter, and I guess that is about the extent of it.

Today is a maintenance day, and the only thing to [do] is check up on the work the men are doing on the planes and take care of necessary paperwork that you haven't had time to take care of during the week. I always have a lot of that piled up, because I have a lot of equipment checked out to me that has to be signed for and occasionally accounted for.

I had hoped to get up to Mandalay before leaving here, but now it looks as if that is out. I think that we'll be gone from here very shortly – within a week or so. I hope that we do, for the time seems to go so much faster when you are starting over at some new location. It's just when the novelty wears off that the time begins to lag.

I hope you haven't been worried too much by the situation in this part of the world. Aside from glancing occasionally at the headlines of the Rangoon paper, I hardly know the score on the war at all. I haven't listened to a newscast from America for some time now, and I don't know exactly what they are saying, but don't be too much concerned, will you?

What Bill did not tell his family was that he could see the threat of war with Japan growing by the day, and that the AVG was racing against time to be combat-ready when the shooting started. He did not mention the deaths of two pilots in flying accidents since his arrival in Burma. Nor did Bill tell the family about the steady string of landing and takeoff crackups that were whittling down the AVG's supply of fighters – including one mishap of his own when he landed long, ran off the end of the runway and nosed up after hitting a stump.

On October 20, Chennault gave a lecture in which he informed his men that the Japanese were massing troops on Thailand's border with Burma – a clear threat to the British colony. He ordered that all of the AVG's P-40s would now be armed, and announced a new policy that would place a flight of fighters on intercept alert from dawn to dusk. The responsibility for providing the alert flight would rotate among the three squadrons. The alert system got its first test just six days later.

Bill was one of the six pilots on alert duty on October 26 when "a strange silver ship"[7] was spotted flying at 6,000ft near Kyedaw. Neither the RAF in Rangoon nor the AVG had any uncamouflaged aircraft, so Chennault ordered the alert flight to scramble and check it out. Bill taxied out with the others, but the engine in his P-40 cut out as he was in his takeoff roll, so he had to abort and taxi back to the 3rd PS's parking area while the others climbed toward the last reported location of the snooper. The remaining pilots searched in vain for the intruder until they heard the command "free beer" on their radios – the code phrase recalling them to base.[8] The same thing happened the following day. Later it was learned that the snooper had been a long-range Japanese reconnaissance plane based in Hanoi, French Indochina (Vietnam). Bill, of course, mentioned none of this in his October 28 letter to Mayme.

In a similar vein, Bill's next letter failed to mention that the 3rd PS had commenced practice firing on the gunnery range on November 11, or that the squadron adopted the nickname "Hell's Angels" at about the same time. He did report that he had been assigned a fighter of his own, which carried the number 75 in white on the fuselage. He did not tell her about painting a "sharksmouth" marking on the nose of the plane or the addition of a voluptuous nude female "angel" artwork that Bill's crew chief Stan Regis added in red just forward of the windshield.

With the arrival of December, rumors spread about the AVG's impending move to China. The "Old Man" lectured the men about conditions and customs in the country. A few days later he ordered an 18-ship formation flight, which everyone assumed was practice for the coming cross-country trip to Kunming. Next came a big mock dogfight on December 4, pitting 12 P-40s of the 3rd PS against a similar number from the 2nd PS. On December 6, a convoy of AVG trucks left for Kunming carrying tools, parts, personnel and the excess baggage of the pilots and maintenance men who were soon to follow. Bill and the other pilots were left with bare minimum wardrobes, which amounted to little more than a toothbrush and several changes of underwear. Again, none of this – except the rumors – made it into Bill's letters home.

The official 3rd PS diary of events for the following day reads as follows:

Sunday services in the morning, nothing new to do except go hunting, take pictures or ride up into the mountains on sightseeing buses that are gotten by members of the group for such purposes. No ball game today.

The date of that report is December 7, 1941, because the calendar in Asia is one day ahead of the United States and the rest of the western hemisphere. The boredom described in the entry would end 24 hours later.

6

"I dove and attacked them head-on"

Bill and the other "Hell's Angels" pilots had just finished breakfast and arrived at the ready room on the flightline at Kyedaw on December 8, 1941, when a fellow rushed in with news he had just heard over the radio – the Japanese had bombed the US naval base at Pearl Harbor, Hawaii, plus other American and British targets in the Philippine Islands, Wake Island, Singapore and Thailand. The room went quiet for a moment and then, as R. T. Smith recorded in his diary, "Everybody stood around laughing and kidding about it, although it was easy to see there was really plenty of tension."

Before long Chennault walked into the ready room and announced that he was placing the AVG on a war footing. He designated the 3rd PS, under Arvid E. "Oley" Olson, Jr., as the "assault echelon," with Olson as the group commander in the air. He also told the squadron that it would be moving to Rangoon to bolster the RAF's air defenses there. The other two squadrons would take support and reserve roles for the time being.

Several pilots trooped outside and began watching the skies to the east, fully expecting to see a formation of Japanese bombers appear over the horizon at any moment. The "Hell's Angels" spent the rest of the day standing by their fighters for immediate takeoff in the event of an attack, but none came. The next day passed much the same, except for a visit by a single enemy observation plane, which made a quick getaway when two flights of P-40s scrambled to give chase.

That night was a full moon with clear skies, so six fighters were placed on alert in anticipation of an attack. The air raid siren awakened Bill, who was not on the alert crew, at 0300hrs, and he joined the others racing for the trenches outside the barracks to take cover while the P-40s roared into the sky. An hour's search revealed no enemy aircraft (they had bombed Pegu, about 30 miles south of Toungoo), and soon the fighters were circling the field to prepare for landing in the dark. Groundcrew had positioned trucks at each end of the runway and switched on their lights, so the pilots could see to land. Five of them got down safely, but David L. "Tex" Hill of the 2nd PS, who had accompanied Bill to Asia aboard the MS *Bloemfontein*, landed long and ran off the end of the runway. He was not hurt, but his P-40 "No. 48" was damaged beyond repair. Bill volunteered for alert duty the following night, but no raiders came over.

It was not that the Japanese were holding back. However, their primary objectives in Asia during the opening days of the war were to take Hong Kong and Singapore. In preparation, the IJAAF had moved its 3rd Air Division from China to Saigon the previous month, and much of this force was transferred into Thailand on the first day of fighting. From there, IJAAF bombers and fighters ranged far down the Malay Peninsula to support troop landings at Khota Bharu and a ground advance across the Thai border into Malaya. The Japanese envisioned a relatively quick campaign, after which they could turn their attention to the invasion of Burma.

MOVE TO RANGOON

Chennault sent Erik Shilling, in an unarmed P-40 modified to carry an aerial camera, on a photo-reconnaissance mission over Bangkok, Thailand, on December 10. Shilling, with two fighter escorts, photographed Bangkok's dock area and Don Muang airdrome, then returned safely to Kyedaw. His pictures revealed more than 90 Japanese aircraft at Don Muang, and that was enough to convince Chennault to take action.

Orders sending the "Hell's Angels" to Rangoon arrived the next day, and 20 technicians moved out by train at 2135hrs. They reached the city at 0740hrs on December 12 and continued by road to Mingaladon airdrome, just outside Rangoon. Others traveled by truck, carrying spare parts, tools and other items needed to support the squadron's operations. Meanwhile, Bill took off from Kyedaw in his P-40 "No. 75" along with 17 other pilots at about 0930hrs for the 40-minute flight to Mingaladon. They arrived without incident and immediately dispersed their planes around the airfield, then set off for their new quarters in the nearby officers' barracks.

Bill and his buddy Neil Martin found accommodations in one of the two-man rooms, their friendship having grown during the time at Kyedaw. Like Bill, Neil had been a standout college football player, starring in the backfield for the University of Arkansas. As Bill later wrote in a letter, "From the very first Neil and I seemed to 'hit it off.' We did everything together – played baseball, volleyball, went on picture-taking hikes and bicycle rides, etc. Mainly due to Neil's ability, our squadron won all the inter-squadron athletic contests. Everyone in the group was his friend."

The gravel runways at Mingaladon were laid out in the shape of an "A," and the "Hell's Angels" were assigned to the east–west runway, which was the cross piece of the "A." The fighters were divided into two flights of nine aircraft apiece: Bill's flight, under Neil Martin's command, was at one end of the runway and the other flight, under George McMillan, at the far end. The "Hell's Angels" shared the airfield with the RAF's No. 67 Sqn, which was equipped with about 30 Buffalo I fighters. Originally developed in the late 1930s to be operated from aircraft carriers by the US Navy, the barrel-shaped Buffalo I was slightly inferior to the P-40 in most measures of combat capability.

Tensions were rising. A Japanese snooper was spotted high over Rangoon on December 12, suggesting to the AVG pilots that an air raid would not be long in coming. But nothing happened. After spending the 12th settling in at Mingaladon, the "Hell's Angels" went on alert the following morning, with 16 P-40s and their pilots ready to take off at a moment's notice. About 1230hrs, the Burma Observation Corps phoned in a report to RAF headquarters that 27 Japanese bombers had crossed the Thai border heading eastward. The Buffalos scrambled first, followed by the AVG fighters. It was a mad dash because the two active runways crossed, but fortunately there were no collisions.

The interceptors climbed to 16,000ft, pilots scanning the sky for signs of the enemy formation as their hearts pounded with excitement. An hour of searching turned up nothing, however, because the Japanese had bombed Mergui – about 150 miles away – instead of Rangoon. On landing, Bill and the other AVG pilots complained that they had no radio contact with the RAF on the ground or in the air during the flight. That was no way to fight a war, but the British displayed no urgency in addressing the problem over the coming days. It was as if some of them viewed the "Hell's Angels" as interlopers into their war – at least in these opening days of the conflict. That attitude would soon change when the shooting started.

The next week passed with little excitement. Olson maintained his force on alert duty throughout daylight hours, but the sky over Rangoon remained empty of enemy aircraft. Daily patrols took place, and Bill flew four of them that week. The RAF began issuing passes allowing AVG personnel to visit the city. Most of the men headed straight for watering holes such as the Green Hotel and the Silver Grille. They found Rangoon a city on edge, as most residents – Burmese and British alike – expected the Japanese invasion to begin soon.[1] Should they flee to India or stay and see what life would be like under Japanese occupation? Those who could were planning to leave.

Over the radio came news of the Japanese advances. Penang Island, off the west coast of Malaya, and nearby Butterworth airfield fell on December 16 as Japanese troops moved southward down the Malay Peninsula. On the China coast, the British had retreated from Kowloon to Hong Kong Island, where they would be able to hold out for only another two weeks. In the Philippines, Japanese troops had landed at Viggan and Appari, on Luzon Island, and were advancing steadily toward Manila. There was no good news for the Allies anywhere in the Pacific.

In the excitement of the deployment to Rangoon and subsequent events, Bill did not have a chance to write a letter to his mother until December 17. When he did, he insisted as always that he was in no danger, and that Mayme need not worry about him. Nevertheless, the seriousness of Bill's situation comes through in his words:

> No telling when this will reach you, with the Pacific air routes definitely closed, but chances are that it may go westbound through India, Cairo, etc. Anyway, you will have heard from me prior to the arrival of this letter, for I will get a Christmas wire off to you as soon as I can get part of a day off duty. Those "yellow imps" have certainly raised hob with things, haven't they? I'll bet everyone in the States was shocked at the suddenness of the attack. I expected some sort of a break, but hardly anything that daring, and that far away from here. It has certainly interrupted my schedule! I've been on duty dawn to dusk since the 7th of December, and on the move plenty, too.
>
> I hope you will try not to worry, Mom. If I could tell you straight-out how things stood, I might be able to ease your mind a bit, but I know the details can't be sent through the mail, and it's better that I don't try. Please don't pay too much heed to rumors and newspaper items which are not officially confirmed. I'm all right and will continue to be, believe me!
>
> Hardly seems possible that Christmas is only a week or so away. The weather continues to be hot – around 90-95 degrees yet, and there are no signs whatsoever that it intends to change. I'm still in Burma, however no longer at "Point A" [Toungoo].
>
> All of us here are pulling for old "Uncle Sam" of course, and every news broadcast finds me with my ear at the receiver to hear news that they've started erasing Japanese battleships etc. out in the Pacific. I certainly hope this won't alter "Nephie's" [Dick Reed's] status. Hope he stays an instructor, although the

Japs, to my notion, are no more dangerous than some students I used to have.

Had the letter telling of your Christmas box. It sounded pretty swell. If those guys sink that en route – boy! Watch out! I've bought a lot of odds and ends over here with the idea of making gifts of them, but to get them checked and through customs etc. is too much of a job. Besides, Mom, you had your instructions from me to do my Christmas shopping, and I'm relying on you to do it. One thing I want to take you to task for is not using your checking account enough. I was thinking about it the other day, and I came to the conclusion that if I didn't keep at you hammer and tongs you would let that money lie down there in San Antonio in disuse – How about it?

I'm going to miss you all at Christmas, and especially you, Mom, but I'll be right there when Aunt Em says the blessing. Hope you are all together with the girls and families from Sioux Falls and Chicago, the folks from Stone City, and "Nephie" and Laurence. Next year you can bet that there's going to be an added mouth to feed. Maybe by then he'll only be able to speak Chinese or Burmese, and ask for rice and tea instead of turkey and trimmings, but he's going to be there nonetheless. Again, Mom, don't worry too much, and give my best wishes and regards to all.

The AVG went into action three days after Bill wrote his letter, but the combat did not take place over Rangoon. Late in the afternoon of December 20 a telegram arrived from Kunming with news that the AVG had fought off a Japanese bombing raid earlier that day. Chennault's air raid warning system had worked in its first live trial. When an estimated ten IJAAF Kawasaki Ki-48 "Lily" twin-engined bombers approached the city from the south without fighter escort, the 1st PS, recently transferred from Kyedaw, was waiting for them. In the combat that followed, the AVG pilots shot down at least three bombers without loss, although one fighter was force-landed short of Kunming due to fuel exhaustion.

The news of the AVG's successful first encounter with the enemy was greeted with mixed emotions by the "Hell's Angels" at Rangoon. As pilot R. T. Smith wrote on his diary that day, "That was damn good work, but we're all mad because they got into action before we did." No doubt Bill Reed shared those sentiments, but soon they would be forgotten.

Tensions continued to build in Rangoon over the next few days. Everyone knew a Japanese attack was coming, but when? The "Hell's Angels" were saddened by the news that Lacey Mangleburg had been killed on December 22 when he crashed during a ferry flight to Kunming. "Mangle" had died without getting a chance to test his prodigious flying skills in aerial combat.

INTO ACTION

The Japanese made their first bombing raid on Rangoon two days before Christmas. When Bill arrived at the Mingaladon flightline on the morning of Tuesday, December 23, he was notified that he would be flying "No. 69" in Blue Flight that day, as his "No. 75" was down for maintenance. It looked like another quiet day ahead for the "Hell's Angels." At about 0945hrs he climbed into the cockpit to check the plane's radio and oxygen equipment. As he was sitting there he noticed the rest of the pilots in his flight running from the alert tent toward their fighters. Scramble!

Bill jumped down from the plane and closed the door to the baggage compartment, then got back into the cockpit, hooked up his belts and started the engine. As soon as the exhaust note calmed down to a steady roar, Bill taxied out to the runway and took his position behind Blue Flight leader, Parker Dupouy, and his other wingman, Ralph Gunvordahl. Ahead of them was Neil Martin's flight, with Ken Jernstedt and Robert Brouk as his wingmen. Two other flights at the north end of the runway would take off as soon as Bill and the others cleared the field.

Blue Flight settled into a string formation behind Dupouy and began climbing for all the P-40s were worth. Bill expected this to be another false alarm, but when he tried to contact Dupouy by radio for information, he could not raise him. Apparently, Dupouy's radio transmitter was on the blink. Bill could only hold formation and wait to see what developed. He slipped on his oxygen mask when he reached 12,000ft as the climb continued for another 5,000ft.

By now the fighters were about ten miles southeast of Rangoon, and Bill scanned the sky for enemy aircraft but saw nothing. Before long Bill noticed Dupouy violently rocking his wings in the universal signal for attack. Now Bill saw a large formation of twin-engined bombers (Mitsubishi Ki-21s of the IJAAF, escorted by Ki-27 fighters) directly in front and at the same level as the P-40s. This was it! Immediately, all of Chennault's teachings went right out the window. The pilots had no thought of two-plane elements or coordinated attacks. It was every man for himself as the fighters piled into the enemy in a front quarter attack. Bill described it this way in a newspaper interview months later:

I forgot all caution and most of what Chennault had told us. Pressing the trigger, I sprayed the formation with lead. It was my first aerial attack and they looked so big – I expected to see them fall like plums out of a tree. It surprised me when none of them dropped. They just kept roaring on their mission.

Bill's diary entry for December 23 described how the battle developed:

After the first pass at them we were split up, and from then on it was more or less individual attacks. I went in from every angle, raking the flanks with long bursts. Just as I pulled up from one dive to make another attack, I saw Jernstedt pour a burst from close range, and apparently he found a bomb with one of his bullets, for the bomber burst into bright red flame and crashed right into Rangoon.

I continued my attacks, pouring lead at them. At last I got one in the left engine, and he dropped out of the formation. I made one more pass, and a Brewster followed me through. When I looked again the bomber was in flames. I talked to the

Brewster pilot [RAF] afterward, and he said that on his pass the rear gunner was dead. But the bombers maintained good formation and passed over Rangoon. They showered plenty of bombs down, but most of them missed the docks. Then I glanced over toward our field, Mingaladon, ten miles north of Rangoon. There, I saw two more clouds of bombers. I was too busy with the one I was with, though, so didn't go over the field.

Finally, after chasing them out over the gulf [of Martaban] I started back to the field. I looked at Rangoon, and it was a mess. Several large fires had broken out in the city, and dust and smoke columns hung thousands of feet over the city. Mingaladon airdrome was badly beat up, too, with one petrol dump burning and holes and craters in every runway. I found one I could land on, and brought it in. As I rolled to a stop I saw one lad lying in a grassy space, flat on his back, but waving a handkerchief. I taxied back to the line, then got a car and looked after him. He was hit in the back by shrapnel. Then I went back and checked up to see who was in.

The news was not good. Three pilots were unaccounted for, and one of them was Neil Martin. There was nothing to be done except wait and hope to hear the engine note of a P-40 returning to base, but none came. As soon as Bill's plane was refueled and rearmed, he was sent back up on patrol to be ready in case the Japanese tried another raid. The air raid alarm went off at 1300hrs when three Japanese reconnaissance planes were reported in the area, but the AVG pilots never found them. Bill wrote in his diary:

At last the sun began to get low, and we headed back over Rangoon, which was still burning, and home to Mingaladon. That night when I walked into my room to go to bed I was dead tired, but I couldn't sleep for quite a while thinking of Neil and the possibilities he might still be alive.

Two of the missing pilots had been found by the time Bill rolled into bed. P. J. Greene, who had traveled to Asia with Bill on MS

Bloemfontein, bailed out of his plane when it was hit by return fire from a bomber and he landed safely not far from the base. He walked in that afternoon. The other pilot, Henry Gilbert, was found dead in the wreckage of his fighter.

Neil Martin's fate was eventually determined several days later when his body was recovered from the burned-out remains of his P-40. According to eyewitness reports from other "Hell's Angels" pilots and Japanese aircrew involved in the action, Neil had led his flight into the side of the formation of Ki-21s and began taking fire from the gunners in several of the aircraft closest to him. He pulled up suddenly, exposing the vulnerable belly of his fighter, and the enemy gunners took full advantage of this by repeatedly hitting the aircraft. It immediately caught fire and went down trailing flames and smoke. Neil Martin's first combat was also his last. He was the first AVG pilot to be killed in action.[2]

Bill received credit for one bomber destroyed on December 23. When all of the pilots' reports were in, the AVG determined that the "Hell's Angels" had shot down 11 Japanese aircraft, probably destroyed five more and damaged ten[3] for the cost of three P-40s lost and several more damaged.[4] Although costly (the Japanese had lost seven Ki-21s), the raid was not altogether unsuccessful for the IJAAF. The bombers attacking Rangoon caused random damage to buildings and the population but missed the mountains of lend-lease supplies sitting on the docks awaiting shipment to China. The attack on Mingaladon was more effective. Bombs hit the runways, the main hangar and a fuel storage tank. Other buildings, including the mess hall and operations building, were damaged by bomb blasts. Ten British and 30 Burmese servicemen were killed[5], although there were no fatalities among the "Hell's Angels'" ground personnel.

For Bill and the rest of the 3rd PS, the war had changed in one day from a friendly rivalry with the other AVG squadrons to a deadly serious fight for survival. Bill had lost a good friend, but he had also taken at least one life – probably several (the Ki-21 typically had a crew of between five and seven). He would refer to the deaths of Neil and others often in his letters and diary over the next few months, but he never revealed his thoughts about the other side of the equation.

Everyone in Rangoon was on edge as Christmas Eve dawned, fully expecting a return visit from the Japanese. The evacuation of the city was well under way, leading AVG crew chief Frank Losonsky to observe, "Rangoon is like a ghost town, and it smells like a funeral."[6]

Bill got up before daylight at Mingaladon and took off at 0600hrs for an uneventful two-hour patrol before breakfast. There was time for him to take a brief walk around the airdrome to survey the damage from the previous day's air raid before he took off on a second patrol. An air raid alarm during lunchtime sent everyone scrambling for cover, but no enemy aircraft approached the field. By the end of the day Bill had flown six hours and fifteen minutes. He was dead tired when he went to bed. Still, he had enough energy to record some thoughts in his diary:

> Still no word of Neil, and the room seems empty. Would give a lot to be home just for tonight and tomorrow. Hope Mom isn't too lonesome and worried, and that the newspapers don't write up the raid too luridly. No lights or telephone since the raid, and most of the bearers and cooks have left. Meals are pretty scratchy. Another busy day, though, tomorrow.

Christmas Day 1941 was sunny and hot in Rangoon. The "Hell's Angels'" pilots spent a quiet morning in the alert tents at the north and south ends of their Mingaladon runway, six P-40s parked in the dispersal area nearby each tent. The air raid warning system was back up and running after a day off the air, so Bill and the other pilots were freed from the task of flying standing patrols.

Meanwhile, the IJAAF had responded to the drubbing handed out by the AVG and RAF on December 23 by flying in 25 new Type 1 (Ki-43) Hayabusa fighters to Thailand from Malaya to counter the Allied interceptors.[7] The Hayabusa (given the Allied reporting name "Oscar") was a low-wing monoplane with a radial engine, enclosed cockpit canopy and retractable landing gear. Lightweight construction and a big wing gave the plane outstanding maneuverability and a high rate-of-climb, but its armament consisted of just two light machine guns. In the air, the Hayabusa resembled the IJNAF's well-known Type 0 fighter closely enough that the AVG and RAF pilots did not realize they were two entirely different aircraft. To them, any Japanese fighter with retractable landing gear was a "Zero."

Bill was assigned to lead the second element of Parker Dupouy's flight on December 25, with Ken Jernstedt as his wingman. The third element was Lew Bishop and Bob Brouk. At about 1100hrs they got the call to stand by for takeoff. Bill walked out to his P-40 "No. 75" to check it over, and while doing so the order came to start engines. Bill jumped into the cockpit and fired up the big Allison engine, but then came word over the radio from the alert tent to shut down again. Bill takes up the story in his diary:

I relaxed, thinking that someone had just gotten jumpy and given a false alarm. My engine had hardly stopped sputtering when, very excitedly, they told us to get going. In a matter of a minute or two we were in the air and climbing as rapidly as a P-40 will climb. Two of our men, Bishop and Brouk, got in too big a hurry and took off out of turn. They didn't join us in the air, so that left us with a four-ship flight – Dupouy and Hodges, Jernstedt and me. I heard our patrol orders, "Orbit Hometown Angels 15" – circle Rangoon at 15,000ft – and this is what we proceeded to do. Fifteen minutes passed, then 30, and I began to think people were just nervous and we had another patrol for nothing. We swung to the north in our circle around the city of Rangoon, and just as Dupouy rocked his wings I saw the formation! As near as I could judge, there were either 27 or 30 bombers, and glinting wickedly in the sunlight about one-half mile behind were from nine to 15 pursuit planes. They were all from 5,000–6,000ft above us, and as we climbed toward them they passed over Mingaladon and dropped their bomb load.

I was cursing the operator who held us at 15,000ft as I climbed after them. I didn't quite reach the main formation of bombers, though, before I ran into a dogfight involving about two other P-40s and about nine "Model 0" Japanese pursuit planes. As I entered the fight I was fortunate in getting the drop on one Jap, and in a front quarter "head-on" attack I raked him with a long burst and saw tracers rake him through the length of the fuselage. He spun down and out of the fight, but I didn't get a chance to follow him, as two of his mates were about 500 yards off. I pulled around so I could meet them head-on should they attack, but strangely enough they started a gentle turn away from me in formation. I headed over that way, and one of them sort of dived gently away from the other. He looked like a cinch, so I started for him, but not for long. The other Jap, who had just flown along in a straight path, suddenly pulled up and turned down toward me. Had I followed through on my attack on the other one, he would have had me dead to rights. I turned into and under him and dove away.

Then I estimated where the bombers should be and headed that way, climbing and watching for pursuit. I reached 20,000ft and leveled out. I knew I was on the right track, for on my ascent I saw one bomber hit about two miles out in the gulf [of Martaban] in flames. I saw them off to my left then. Still they were in good formation. I couldn't see any pursuit planes – either ours or theirs. I dove and attacked them head-on, all guns blazing, and continued on past them. I pulled up out of range and gave chase again. Apparently I hadn't knocked any down. One had gotten out of formation, but he got back in. They were quite far off now, since I met them doing over 300[mph], and they were doing almost 200. But I decided to make a couple more passes. Then I saw a dogfight in progress just behind them a mile or so.

I was there in a moment, and as I entered the fracas I saw one P-40 going round and round with three Model 0s. I don't think the pilot of the P-40 saw me come into the fight. We went round and round, with no one getting in any very good bursts. The best shot I had was an overhead deflection shot, but as I squeezed the trigger only one 0.30-caliber fired. I dove away to clear my guns, and as I did so I saw the other P-40, who was also leaving the scrap. By now we were 140–150 miles across the gulf from Rangoon. I joined the other ship and found it was Dupouy.

We started back across the gulf at 17,000ft and had only gone about 30 miles out offshore of Moulmein when we spotted three Model 0s in a V formation below us, apparently headed home. We dropped down on their tails and surprised them. Dupouy was following me as I picked out the right-hand wingman. I fired from about 50 yards, and Dupouy fired behind me to the right. The Jap exploded right in my face. I pulled up sharply to the right to avoid hitting him, and Dupouy pulled up to the left. In doing so, his right wing clipped the other Jap wingman's ship right at the wing root, and that Jap spun into the gulf, too. The other Jap got the drop on me as I went by him, and after managing to meet him almost head-on in one turn, and losing ground in the next, I dove away. I climbed back up to get at him, but no one was to be seen.

I was damn low on gas, so I decided to head straight over the gulf in the general direction of Rangoon. I'd gone about five minutes when I met three more Model 0s at my level. I didn't even bother with them, but stuck my nose down and kept going for home. About that time the engine started spitting, and I had to switch [to the reserve fuel tank]. Thought the coast would never show up, but finally it did and soon I was back on Mingaladon, which had taken another beating, as had Rangoon.

Mingaladon indeed had taken another beating. Most of the Japanese bombs hit on the southeast corner of the airdrome, doing quite a bit of damage to the barracks buildings located there. Two AVG technicians were wounded by flying shrapnel, but not seriously. In the air, the "Hell's Angels" lost two of the 13 P-40s that had engaged the enemy. Both pilots survived being shot down and returned to the field the next day. Dupouy was not one of them – somehow he managed to nurse his P-40 back to a safe landing at Mingaladon with about three feet of its right wing and part of its aileron torn off from his collision.

Despite the damage to their field, the "Hell's Angels" felt good about their performance on Christmas Day. The squadron was credited with no fewer than 24 enemy bombers (both Ki-21s and Mitsubishi Ki-30s) and fighters (Ki-27s and Ki-43s) shot down, two aircraft probably destroyed and six more damaged, with all 13 of the participating pilots receiving at least one credit.[8]

Bill's share was two Japanese Hayabusa fighters destroyed. What he did not realize, and no doubt never learned, was that he was the first Allied pilot of the war to shoot down this type of aircraft. Many hundreds of Hayabusa would fall over the next three-and-a-half years, but Bill's victory over Mingaladon had a significance all of its own. The Hayabusa was not a bad aircraft, but Allied pilots would soon learn – as Bill already knew – how to counter its strengths and exploit its weaknesses.

The morale of the "Hell's Angels" was sky-high following the combats of December 23 and 25 despite the loss of Bill's friend Neil, who was highly regarded in the squadron. R. T. Smith, who had scored four victories plus a half share of another in the two combats, later noted:

> It was evident that suddenly the Hell's Angels squadron had come of age; in a matter of 48 hours we had progressed from an unknown quantity to a battle-tested unit, a dozen or so (men) who could now lay legitimate claim to being fighter pilots. The necessary ingredients were all there: flying ability, courage, determination, desire, opportunity and luck, all of them necessary for success and survival.[9]

Unbeknownst to the "Hell's Angels," the squadron would have no further combats over Rangoon, as the IJAAF turned its attention back to Malaya for the remainder of December. But that did not mean the AVG pilots could relax. Bill was not on the flying schedule for December 26, and when the air raid alarm sounded at about 1030hrs, he found himself face-to-face with Gen Sir Archibald Wavell, the British commander-in-chief for India. The two men shook hands while seven P-40s – all the "Hell's Angels" could muster – roared off the runway to hunt for incoming Japanese bombers. The intruders turned out to be two high-flying reconnaissance aircraft that turned tail for Thailand before the P-40s could reach them, however. The day's only other air activity came at about 1500hrs when a Japanese plane appeared over Rangoon and dropped leaflets warning of an imminent invasion of the city by parachute troops. Everyone expected the invasion to come that night, when a bright, full moon would illuminate the clear sky, but the paratroopers did not come.

Tensions remained high at Mingaladon, but Bill's main complaint was about the British-supplied meals. He noted, "The food situation is not so hot. Sardines for breakfast, and canned 'corn-willy' the rest of the day." The next three days passed quietly, without even a false air raid alarm on December 28. Twenty-four hours later, the "Hell's Angels" were ordered to move to Kunming, but it would take a few days for the 2nd PS to arrive from China to take their place.

Two Consolidated B-24 Liberator four-engined bombers of the USAAC flew into Mingaladon on December 29 carrying several high-ranking officials on an inspection tour of the war zone. "It was my job to see that they got refueled," Bill recorded in his diary. "We have three trucks left, but they have to be filled by hand from 40-gallon drums – four of us worked into the night on them. The B-24 has a 3,200-gallon capacity."

Most of the "Hell's Angels" pulled out of Rangoon on December 30. Ten pilots flew the remaining serviceable P-40s to Kyedaw airdrome at Toungoo, spent the night there and continued on to Kunming the next day. Groundcrews and the excess pilots rode the train to Toungoo, where transport planes of the China National Airline Corporation (known throughout Asia as CNAC) picked them up for the flight to China. Bill was not in either of these groups. He and Paul "P. J." Greene were to wait in Rangoon while repairs were completed to the squadron's remaining two P-40s and then fly them to China. Bill left for Kunming on New Year's Day 1942, as he described in his diary:

January 1 – Paul's plane wasn't ready to go, so he and I opened a can of soup and a can of beans for the most delicious meal in a week or so, and talked the situation over. I took off about noon for Point A [code for Toungoo], Burma, where I was to wait for Paul. Arrived okay and found Adkins and McMillan [two 3rd PS pilots] waiting for the weather to clear so they could go to Kunming, too. We all decided to go together the next day, so I borrowed a car and visited Miss Fields [a British nurse he had befriended] at the hospital. Walked right into a big tea party and sat by two IMS [Indian Medical Corps Service] colonels who talked my arm off about the raids on Rangoon. Drove Miss Fields and Miss Burns up to the top of the mountain near Thandosong and then back to the field, after dropping them off.

January 2 – Slept until I heard Greene coming in from Rangoon. Had breakfast and went over with Mac and Adkins to pick Paul up and get the weather report from Kunming. It was pretty "stinko," so we decided to go into town and buy a few knickknacks we might not be able to get in China. Back to the field, and we found that Lashio, Burma, had cleared, so we decided to eat lunch and take off for there. We finally got off about 2 p.m. and headed north to Mandalay, which we passed over about 3 p.m. and then to the east over some rugged mountains to Lashio, which was about 45 minutes from Mandalay. We were met at Lashio by Captain Wong. He took us to town, where we met Ed Hesser and "Dutch" Myers, two of Paul's friends. Had a marvelous dinner at Hesser's, followed by a mild poker game. I lost 50 rupees, and during the game I finally was persuaded to become a member of the "short snorter"[10] club. Greene and I both joined. The four of us stayed at the RAF headquarters overnight.

January 3 – Up fairly early, and a wonderfully cool morning – a welcome relief after the heat of Rangoon. Dutch and Ed came out, and we all visited the town. Lashio is a very pretty spot, nestling among the mountains. We finally took off for Kunming right after noon, also after CNAC, which pulled out about five minutes ahead of us. Thick, scattered, clouds all trip, and the most wild and rugged terrain I ever hope to fly over. We were around 12,000ft most of the trip, and the ground wasn't far beneath us, except when we went over a crevasse or gorge. I was glad to see the lake, on the [north] tip of which lies Kunming.

Kunming lies in a valley surrounded by mountains and is at the tip of a 20- to 25-mile-long lake [Dianchi]. Its elevation is about 6,500ft. It was great to see the fellows again, both those of our own squadron [who had only been here a day or two], and those of the First [who had been here almost a month]. Had the first hot shower since September 12, and then had a swell dinner. Kirk came over, and we had a long visit. Only thing wrong was Neil's not being here.

7

"This is no time to take a runout"

Bill had several deployments to Burma and western China ahead of him during the coming six months, but in the opening days of 1942 he stayed busy acclimatizing himself to Kunming – the city as well as the air base. He was favorably impressed by his new situation. The most noticeable change was in the climate. After the heat and humidity of Burma, Kunming – 700 miles north and some 6,000ft higher than Rangoon – was as cool as Iowa in the fall. He also appreciated Kunming's setting in a valley with mountains on three sides and the lake to the south.

Living conditions were also much improved over Burma. Unlike the communal quarters at Kyedaw and the battered barracks at Mingaladon, the "Hell's Angels" were now assigned to AVG Hostel No. 1, which had most of the comforts of a country club but without the golf course. Pilots lived in single rooms, and the complex also included a dining room with good food, a recreation room with a bar, indoor toilets and even a barber shop. A Chinese servant was assigned to each room to take care of housekeeping and laundry. Outside in the courtyard was a softball diamond, a volleyball court and a basketball hoop – Bill would make great use of all these amenities. Bill even signed up to take Chinese language lessons three evenings a week.

If there was a drawback to Hostel No. 1, it was the location on the far side of downtown Kunming from the airfield. That meant the men had to make a slow drive through the crowded streets of the city whenever they went on and off duty.[1] Evidence of earlier Japanese bombings was everywhere, with shattered and burned out buildings lining the streets and masses of refugees picking through the rubble seeking anything of value that they might trade for food and shelter.

Kunming's airfield was located on flat pastureland about two miles south of the city. The runways used by the P-40s were sod-covered, but a crew of several hundred Chinese workers was busy building a 7,000ft runway of crushed rock in the middle of the field. Bill and the others marveled at the ability of the Chinese to construct such a runway by hand, without the use of any modern machinery. Day after day the workers hammered rocks into gravel and carried the gravel in baskets to the runway. Once they placed the gravel, the Chinese would pull heavy concrete rollers over it by hand to compact the surface.

Bill started his first day at Kunming with another hot shower followed by a tasty breakfast. He spent the morning in his room, reacquainting himself with his belongings that had been transported by truck up the Burma Road from the "Hell's Angels'" former home in Toungoo. He was glad to find his warm clothing in the trunk.

Later, "Oley" Olson gathered the pilots for a squadron meeting, and Bill learned that he would be one of six assigned to night alert duty for the first week, starting that night. The night alert crew then made their way to the airfield, where they checked their planes and took a short flight to familiarize themselves with the territory around Kunming. They had dinner at the 1st PS's Hostel No. 2, which was close to the airfield, and then reported for duty at 1740hrs. Bill's diary entry for the day reads as follows:

Warmed our ships up and then retired to the alert shack. Played bridge for a while and then talked to a Chinese soldier named William King. We all went to sleep about midnight, for we had a man on duty at the telephone to call us in case of an alarm. There wasn't one, so we were awakened by the day alert crew at 5:30 and went back to our own hostel across town.

The "Hell's Angels" soon settled into a quiet routine, with pilots alternating from night alert to day alert to time off. After the hectic three weeks spent at Rangoon, the abundant down time was a luxury at first. The pilots enjoyed getting exercise in the afternoons, although Bill noted that he tired more quickly than normal due to the high altitude at Kunming. Free evenings passed with frequent card games, Bill often partnering with one of the two AVG nurses, Emma Jane "Red" Foster, at bridge.

Bill's private room at the hostel was a much-appreciated refuge. There, he could be alone to read, write letters and listen to classical music on his record player. It may seem out of character for a hell-for-leather, young fighter pilot to spend time lying on his bed, eyes closed, as he enjoyed works including Grieg's "Peer Gynt Suite" or Tchaikovsky's "Sixth Symphony," but that's what Bill often did while living at the Kunming hostel. The only drawback to Bill's room was the heating system – a charcoal pot that sat in the middle of the floor and barely took off the chill on winter evenings.

Bill and three other pilots joined the AVG chaplain, Paul Frillman, for their first visit to downtown Kunming on the afternoon of January 6. This gave Bill the opportunity to send cables home to his mother and to "Mick" Forbes. He also left some film for processing at a camera shop and bought a leopard skin from a Chinese merchant. Frillman, who spoke excellent Chinese, haggled with the merchant for Bill and succeeded in getting the price down significantly. The city of Kunming, packed with refugees from Japanese-occupied areas of China, offered a stark contrast to the pleasant AVG hostel. Bill described it in a letter shortly after arriving in China:

> It's really unbelievable how these people live. I had expected something pretty bad, but I had no idea that anyone could survive in the conditions that one sees in the city. The filth and disease defies description, and the people are crowded much worse than they are in any [American] big city tenement district. This is the old China, too, and it isn't all that uncommon to see

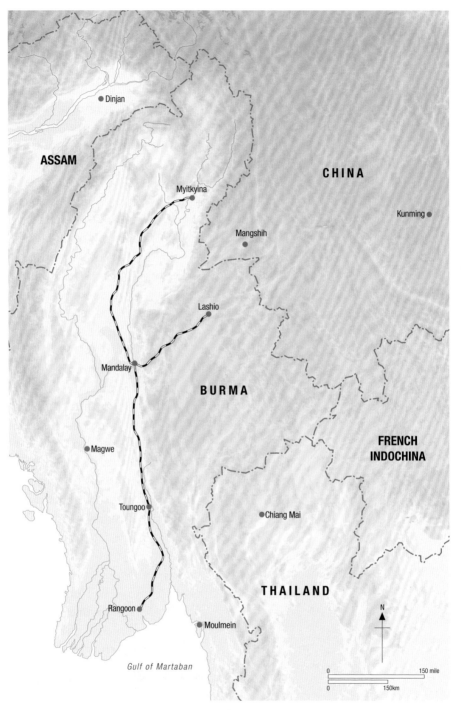

ASSAM

Dinjan

CHINA

Myitkyina

Mangshih

Kunming

Lashio

Mandalay

BURMA

Magwe

FRENCH
INDOCHINA

Toungoo

Chiang Mai

THAILAND

N

Rangoon

Moulmein

Gulf of Martaban

0   150 mile
0   150km

1

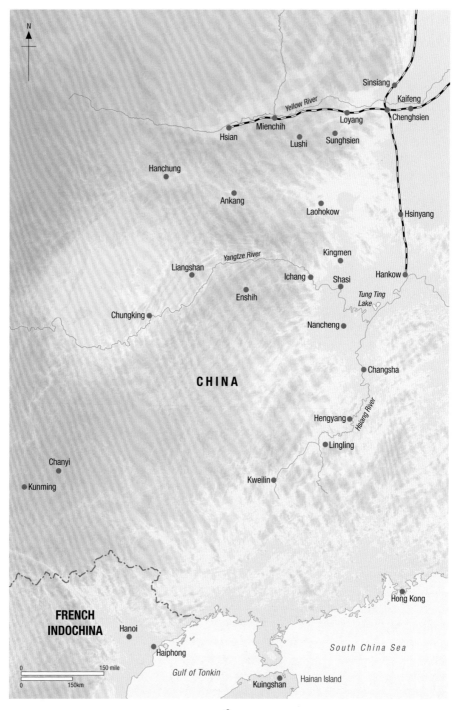

2

3

4

5

6

7

8

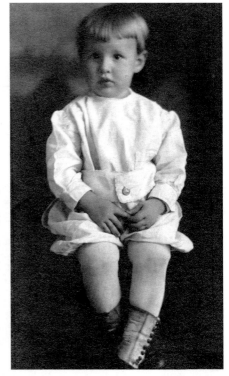

9

11

12

13

15

16

17

18

19

20

21   22

23

24

25

26

27

28

29

women whose feet have been bound in infancy until now they are just a continuation of the ankle. I understand that it is now against the law. But there are many other things that are much as one would find in reading about old China.

Of course, the rich Chinese drive new Buicks and Oldsmobiles etc., but for the very great majority, the rickshaw is the only means of conveyance. All the surrounding countryside, mountains and all, is laid out in tiny plots, each separated from its neighbor by a little dike, and full of vegetables or rice. They have utilized all of the available land, and every mountainside is terraced. Kunming, even though it is at such a high altitude, is at the tip of a 20-mile-long lake, and nestled in the surrounding mountains are several more smaller lakes.[2]

Amid the crowding and filth, Kunming was also a city on edge, as its citizens never knew when the next air attack might take place. Bill described a tense scene in another January letter:

Today, late in the afternoon, I was coming through town as usual when suddenly the mass of people on the sidewalks began running pell-mell, the shopkeepers commenced slamming the fronts of their little shops closed and things were in a very agitated state. I finally heard the words "Ching Bow," which mean air raid, and knew the reason for the commotion. It proved to be a false alarm, but it was quite an example of mob psychology at work. One can't blame them for becoming so panicky, for there are plenty of large bomb craters in the downtown district, and I know that with the crowded conditions that exist, many people must have been killed.

Novelty turned to familiarity and proceeded toward boredom for the "Hell's Angels" during their first two weeks in China. When Bill spent a sleepless night on January 9–10 "refighting the Rangoon battles about ten times," he spent the following day in the alert shack reading, writing letters and playing catch with some of the other pilots. Many of the "Hell's Angels," including Bill and his crew chief, Stan Regis, took advantage of the lull to repaint the "sharksmouth" markings on their P-40s. Soon rumors began to swirl that the AVG personnel would be allowed to resign and return to the US if they wished. Bill found the possibility "awfully tempting, but this is no time to take a runout. Caused plenty of thinking, though."

One evening, Chennault showed up at the "Hell's Angels" hostel with a visitor in tow. It was Gen Mao P'ang-chu (who anglicized his name to Peter T. Mow), chief of the CAF and an enthusiastic bridge player. Pretty soon a deck of cards appeared and the game was on. Bill partnered with "Oley" Olson against AVG adjutant Curtis E. Smith and the general. The game lasted until 2330hrs, with Bill reporting that his team lost by "a small margin." The general must have enjoyed the game, because he came back two more nights in the following week for rematches.

Chennault's warning net remained quiet until January 17, when unknown aircraft were reported near Mengtsze, about 140 miles south of Kunming. Bill was at the hostel having some teeth filled by the AVG dentist, Dr. E. W. Bruce, when the alarm sounded, so he missed the scramble. The alert flight, consisting of George McMillan, Chuck Older, Erik Shilling and Tommy Haywood, proceeded to track down three Japanese bombers (which they identified as "Type 97s") heading north from Hanoi and shoot them all down. Most of the "Hell's Angels" were waiting outside at Kunming when the P-40s returned, and the excitable Shilling gave them a show, performing three victory rolls during a low pass over the airfield before he landed.[3]

Meanwhile, 700 miles south in Rangoon, the 2nd PS had repeatedly engaged IJAAF aircraft as the enemy prepared for an all-out assault on the port city. The Imperial Japanese Army invaded south Burma on January 18, and two days later the IJAAF began a series of heavy raids against Rangoon and nearby Mingaladon airdrome. By the end of the month, AVG pilots had been credited with shooting down no fewer than 51 enemy bombers and fighters. RAF Buffalo pilots of No. 67 Sqn added a number of victories to this impressive total.

Word was beginning to filter back to the US of this rag-tag band of American volunteers who were giving the Japanese a bad time. The AVG's successes over Rangoon, starting in December, were important beyond their obvious military value. The Pacific War was now in its second month, and there had been precious little good news to report to the folks back home in the United States. From the first week in December 1941, when the Japanese bombed Pearl Harbor and invaded Bataan Island in the Philippines, one defeat after another had befallen US forces and their allies. Hong Kong and Wake Island had fallen by Christmas, and the Japanese invasion of Malaya was well under way by then. Soon Manila was declared an open city as American and Philippine troops were bottled up on the Bataan Peninsula. Japanese aircraft rained down bombs on far-flung targets including Singapore, Port Moresby and Rabaul. The siege of Singapore began at the end of January.

War news from the other side of the world offered no relief. In the USSR, German forces threatened Moscow, and in North Africa a British advance into Libya had been halted by the Germans and Italians near El Agheila on January 18.

War correspondents, eager to find anything positive to tell their readers back home, began to focus more attention on the unruly band of mercenary American fighter pilots that was taking such a heavy toll on the Japanese in the skies over Rangoon. The first reports of the "Hell's Angels'" December heroics had rated only a few paragraphs by the Associated Press, which for lack of a better term referred to the AVG in its story as the "International Air Force." That clearly would not do for such a colorful outfit, so the AVG representatives in Washington, D.C., asked Disney Studios to come up with an identity for the group. Thus was born the term "Flying Tigers," a name that took hold instantly and played a big part in making the AVG famous the world over. Disney artists came up with a design for a logo showing a cartoon tiger jumping through a V-for-Victory. Large decals of the design were shipped to China for application on the fuselages of the AVG P-40s.

On March 30, 1942, a multi-page spread on the AVG in *LIFE* magazine began with these sentences:

> One shining hope has emerged from three catastrophic months of war. That is the American Volunteer Group of fighter pilots, the so-called "Flying Tigers" of Burma and southeast China who paint the jaws of a shark on their Curtiss P-40s.

Ironically, Bill Reed and the rest of the AVG rarely if ever referred to themselves as "Flying Tigers."

DISAPPOINTING RIDE

Bill was feeling sick in the stomach when he awoke at the hostel on January 22. That was not good, since he was scheduled for alert duty. He vomited three times while he was getting dressed and skipped breakfast to head straight for the airfield. He did not want to miss his day on alert, because word was out that there might be some action brewing. After three weeks of relative inactivity, Bill was eager to take part.

Once in the alert shack Bill went straight to a cot and took a nap. He awoke several hours later feeling better, but he passed on lunch just to be safe. Sure enough, the alert crew got orders after lunch to prepare for a mission down toward the border. Ten twin-engined Russian-built Tupolev SB-2 bombers with Chinese aircrew were assigned to bomb Hanoi, with P-40s of the 1st PS providing escort. Six "Hell's Angels," including Bill, would form the assault echelon. Their job was to circle over Mengtsze to be in position to intercept any enemy aircraft pursuing the bombers on their return flight. The weather was overcast, and the bombers missed Hanoi but bombed Haiphong instead, losing one plane to antiaircraft fire. Bill's part in the mission was uneventful:

> Six of us, with Oley leading, left at 2:15, and we went to our location and circled for an hour or so without glimpsing any other planes. Landed at 4:15 [at Mengtze], and in another

hour-and-a-half were ready to go back home. Cleaned up and went to dinner, and ate the first solid food of the day. If the weather is right tomorrow, there is promise of more action. Hope my stomach is settled down in the morning, because I want to be ready to "put out" at maximum hp.

Although Bill felt better the next morning, the weather remained bad and the mission was postponed for a day. It was bright and clear at Kunming on January 24, and the mission was on. This time eight "Hell's Angels" would escort the bombers and the 1st PS would provide the assault echelon. "Oley" Olson led his P-40s to Mengtsze shortly after 0800hrs to refuel for their flight into French Indochina and back to Kunming. Bill reported in his diary:

Held our rendezvous with the bombers we were escorting about 11:15. Flew to our objective over two layers of overcast at about 23,000 feet average altitude. The bombers were so slow that we had to stall and twist along to keep from leaving them far back in our slipstream. Took one hour and 45 minutes to get there, and Oley decided that we couldn't hang around and escort them back. We left them near H [Hanoi] and came back. None of us had over 10 or 15 gallons left when we landed. Very disappointing ride, and very tiresome. We were up three hours and 15 minutes, which is stretching the range of our ships plenty. They carry 132 gallons. We were on oxygen three hours out of the 3:15 we were up. That tires me out, and I took a nap when we got back to our alert shack.

The dull routine resumed, as Bill had the next day off and then went on night alert duty for a week. During that week the 1st PS departed for Rangoon to reinforce the 2nd PS, leaving the "Hell's Angels" with sole responsibility for defending Kunming. It was not a daunting task, as the IJAAF was heavily engaged farther south and not particularly concerned with Kunming for the time being. In fact, it would be more than a year – long after the AVG disbanded – before Japanese bombers attempted another raid on

Kunming. A minor break in the routine came on February 3, as Bill reported in his diary:

> On alert again today. No sign of raids here since I came, except the day the boys intercepted three of them down south a ways. Took [Wingman Robert] Raines over to the gunnery range – or rather flew over to check my guns, and he accompanied me. It was his first gunnery mission. Two of my .30s and my two .50s fired all out, but the other two .30s didn't fire so well. Raines was spraying lead around the target like a Chinaman sowing rice. He'll get on to it. He'd better![4] At the end of the mission we came over the field and rolled, and from what they told me on the ground, Raines almost spun in.
>
> At 3:30 this afternoon we had a big meeting in the Chinese hangar, and Col Chennault and some high-ranking Chinese political figure spoke to us. Ten of us got beautifully embroidered silk hangings from the chief of the Chinese Air Force [Bill's bridge opponent, Gen Mow] and a nice card expressing appreciation for our work at Rangoon. Last Sunday I forgot to report that I received my Chinese Wings. I guess it's quite an honor, but I like my U.S.A. wings better.

Two days later Bill was back on alert when he received a call from operations scrambling him to intercept an observation aircraft seen at 30,000ft over the airfield. Bill had already earned bonuses of $500 for each of the three planes he shot down over Rangoon, and this looked like a good chance to add to his total. Not so, as it turned out:

> Raines, who was flying wing on me for the day, and I took off and climbed to 26,000–27,000 feet as fast as possible, but didn't see a thing. I almost froze though. Cruised around about an hour, and when we came in we found that the "enemy plane" had been Dupouy checking his ship. I was disappointed, for I had already counted that lone enemy as another increase in my banking account.

It had now been more than two months since Bill had received any mail from home, which had come to an abrupt halt when the war started. He had kept the letters received during his months at Toungoo, and on especially lonely nights would pull out the pack and re-read them. Realizing that mail was an impractical means of communication now, Bill had begun sending telegrams (which he called "wires") home every so often to ensure his family that he was okay. He could send and receive these from an office in downtown Kunming. After sending the first few wires to Mayme and receiving no replies, he realized that his mother was too thrifty to spend the money for a return message, so he started pre-paying for the reply when he sent her a message. The strategy worked – Mayme's messages were short and to the point, but at least Bill knew that no further tragedies had befallen his family. Bill also began trading wires with his old high-school flame, "Mick" Forbes, who was still living in the Marion area and presumably still waiting for Bill to take their relationship to the next step when he got home from the war.

By mid-February members of the 1st and 2nd PSs were returning to Kunming in twos and threes, as attrition steadily reduced the number of P-40s available at Mingaladon. The remaining AVG pilots continued to have great success at opposing enemy air raids on the city, but the Japanese were advancing steadily on the ground. Singapore fell on February 15, and British forces in lower Burma withdrew behind the Sittang River a few days later. The quiet routine continued at Kunming, but Bill did report a bit of personal excitement on February 18:

Today shouldn't have happened. I was on duty, but as far as action was concerned it was the same old story – no action in these parts and no promise of any. I stirred up a little for myself, though, for in the afternoon I took old No. 75 up for a test hop. I flew it around for about 25 minutes and found that the prop vibrated at anything under 2,500 rpm, so I landed and [taxied] into the line like a bat out of Hades. I turned the engine off about 50 yards out, intending to coast into the line and spin the plane into position. Imagine my surprise, embarrassment, and chagrin when I suddenly looked out the left side of the cockpit and saw a plane in front of my wing. I hit the brakes, and my beloved No. 75 was on her nose. I missed the other plane but damaged one blade of my prop. Yes, my face was red! And I set them up for the "mechs" in their bar that evening.

Fortunately for Bill's "No. 75" P-40, its engine was not running when it nosed over, limiting the damage to one bent propeller blade. If the Allison had been turning over, the sudden contact with the ground not only would have bent all three propeller blades but also stripped the gears in the propeller hub and possibly damaged internal components in the engine as well. Bill came down with a cold the next day, and by the time he was fit to fly again a few days later, the "mechs" had fixed his P-40 and it was back in service as well.

As February entered its final week, the evacuation of Rangoon was well under way. Pilots returning to Kunming reported that the city was practically deserted, and AVG groundcrew were leaving in trucks piled high with food and supplies, headed for the airfield at Magwe about 200 miles north up the Irrawaddy River. The Rangoon docks, buildings and even Mingaladon airfield were being mined so they could be blown up just before the British fled the city.

Back in Kunming, four pilots of the "Hell's Angels," including Bill, were ordered to fly a reconnaissance mission on February 23. It would be far from another boring flight, as Bill recounted in his diary:

February 23
On duty as spare pilot, so didn't get out to the field until 9 a.m. Olson, Jernstedt, Hedman and I left on a photo mission down into Indochina about 11. Stopped to refuel at TAMPA [Mengtze] and continued on over our objective. Hedman and I got separated from the lead element near the objective, so we decided to go back to TAMPA. Apparently we didn't

figure the winds correctly, for we couldn't find TAMPA! We looked until our gas was pretty low, and finally with about ten gallons left we decided we would have to either bail out or try a forced landing. Fortunately, we spotted a valley and picked out a field. I landed first, wheels down and no damage; Bob also landed wheels down but hit a small ditch and damaged his prop.

A crowd of Chinese farmers gathered, and we tried to find out where we were – no luck, though. We spent the night in a small farming village about six miles away. Had a good meal and amused the natives very much by our attempts at speaking Chinese and our awkwardness with chopsticks. Our bed was a grass mat on some boards and was slightly inhabited by fleas.

February 24

Strange, awakening in the attic of a Chinese farm house, and we were met in the courtyard by the magistrate of the neighboring large village of Miloh. He couldn't speak English, though. He had brought three sedan chairs carried by coolies, so we mounted these after breakfast and went out to the planes. He pointed out our position on a map, and I radioed it in to operations. A huge throng of natives was on hand this morning, and the "chien jang" had posted some of his soldiers to keep [the crowd] away from the planes. We were only 80 miles or so away from Kunming, but roads are bad here and no help arrived this day.

We journeyed to Miloh, ten miles, in our sedan chairs. An English missionary woman, Miss Graves, was here. She acted as interpreter for us. We had a dinner in our honor in the evening, with a couple of local big shots. I like Chinese food, but a steady diet is not so good, and I think we could use the rice wine for gasoline. After the dinner was over, we went to a Chinese play in our honor. We had big wicker seats right in the middle of everything. It was two acts – they lasted two hours. Another hard bed, but no fleas tonight.

February 25
Bob [Hedman] and I walked around the village in the a.m. and were much stared at. Had breakfast with six or eight people, and it was almost as big an affair as the preceding night's dinner. After breakfast a truck arrived with our prop man and two mechanics [Leo Schram and W. R. Seiple]. Bob and I journeyed out to the planes on our sedan chairs and the two trucks went out along the road as far as possible, then transferred the gasoline drums and prop to bullock carts and coolies. This took some time, and at 6 in the afternoon we were all set, but figured we couldn't make it [to Kunming] by dark. We decided to stay with the planes that night and take off in the morning. We unloaded the guns to lighten the ships, as the field was pretty short for takeoff. The boys who brought the gas etc. had brought canned food and blankets, also. We had a good meal out of cans, and all turned in pretty early. I started sleeping on a cot, but the wind got so cold that I finally wound up sleeping – or trying to sleep – in the cockpit of my plane.

February 26
Breakfasted from cans again this morning, much to the amazement and amusement of a large group of natives who had already assembled to be witnesses to the day's proceedings. We waited around for a wind to spring up to aid our takeoff. At 2 o'clock we decided to wait no longer, so we taxied down to one end of the field and in turn, Hedman first, took off with not much room to spare. It only took us 30 minutes to get back to the field, and what a ribbing we took from the boys. It was good to be back in civilization, as it exists in Kunming, again. And, needless to say, we were both in need of a shave, shower and some clean clothing. Had an American dinner for a change and got to bed fairly early, after a discussion with Olson.

Bill was back with no harm done to him or his P-40. He would have two more forced landings with similar results over the next 60 days. The "Hell's Angels" squadron log entry for February 26 added this postscript:

> We are glad nothing transpired and that Flight Leaders W. N. Reed and R. P. Hedman are back with us again, both of which are liked very much in the squadron by all.

In Bill's conversation with Squadron Leader Olson, he learned that change was in the wind for the "Hell's Angels." With the loss of Rangoon just days away, it was assumed that the Japanese ground offensive would continue up through Burma. The Chinese Army had established a defensive line at Toungoo, the AVG's stomping grounds during training, and was hoping to halt the enemy there. The "Hell's Angels," now thoroughly rested after two months in Kunming, would be moving south soon to be in position to support the Chinese.

The following morning (February 27), Bill set out as Olson's wingman for a flight to Loiwing (Leiyun), about 300 miles southwest of Kunming and just inside China's border with Burma. Again, Bill's flight got lost. But this time he and Olson managed to spot a railroad line and follow it to the airfield at Lashio, Burma, where they arrived with just a few gallons of fuel remaining. While the planes were being refueled, Bill chatted with his friend Paul Frillman, the AVG chaplain, who was leading a truck convoy north from Rangoon. Then Bill and Olson made the short hop north to Loiwing, the site of CAMCO's aircraft manufacturing plant, so Olson could discuss arrangements for moving the "Hell's Angels" there.

They spent the night at Loiwing, and during the evening Bill had a long talk with members of the 1st PS who had just arrived from Rangoon. Among them was Bill's old USAAC buddy "Kirk" Kuykendall, who was sporting a nasty scar on his forehead earned in a dogfight with enemy fighters over Rangoon a few weeks earlier.

Olson and Bill took off for Kunming late in the afternoon of February 28 and arrived after a bumpy flight in time to attend a fancy dinner with Generalissimo Chiang Kai-shek, Madame Chiang and Chennault. Bill reported in his diary that he was quite impressed by Madame Chiang, whom he described as being "very brilliant, and a wonderful speaker." It did not hurt that she was quite nice-looking, too.

Bill packed his cross-country bag in the storage compartment of his P-40 on March 1, but the weather delayed his departure back to Loiwing for two days. In the company of four other "Hell's Angels," he finally got off on the afternoon of March 3. He expected to stand alert duty for a few days, but instead he flew on to Lashio with several others the next morning to cover the departure of the plane carrying the Generalissimo from Lashio to Kunming. Once the Generalissimo was safely on his way, Bill and Ed Overend were ordered back to Loiwing with instructions to return to Kunming the next day. While at Lashio, Bill was given an excellent bottle of sherry by some AVG mechanics who were taking a convoy of trucks up the Burma Road. He uncorked the bottle in the Loiwing club that evening with this remark:

> I rather hate leaving this club. It's the nearest thing to civilized living I've known since leaving the States. Orders are orders, though, and maybe we'll get some more action. Action seems to make the days go by much more swiftly, which is a thing much to be desired.

Bill, Overend and "Fritz" Wolfe made the flight back to Kunming on March 5 in one hour and 25 minutes. Once on the ground, Bill received some disturbing news:

> Found that the Generalissimo and the Madame left on CNAC and that the five escorting planes had been expected back for some time. We waited anxiously for news of them. One of them had my plane, No. 75, which I hadn't taken to Loiwing with me. Finally, in the afternoon, we got a report of three of them down at Wenshan in crash landings and one down at Yenshan in a crash landing. No one hurt, though. Oley and I both moaned

because both of our planes were cracked up. The report of the fifth man came in the evening, and he too had made a crash landing and wasn't hurt. There was general cursing and gnashing of teeth, for we can't spare one plane, much less five. Navigation around these parts is tricky.

Bill's assignment the next morning was to fly "Tex" Blaylock, the AVG's line chief, to Wenshan in the AVG's two-seat BT-9 trainer to inspect the damaged P-40s there. He found the small field near the China–Indochina border where the planes had put down and landed on his second attempt. Blaylock felt that two of the P-40s were repairable and could be flown out. Bill's "No. 75" had come in wheels-up, but it must have been one of the repairable planes for a photograph taken on the flightline at Kunming several months later clearly shows "No. 75" parked there.

On his return to Kunming, Bill learned that the "Hell's Angels" would be transferring to Magwe, Burma, in the next few days. Finally, renewed action was at hand. But first, Bill would get another reminder of how "tricky" navigation could be in these parts:

March 10
Hedman, Fish, Brouk, Overend and I left Kunming about noon and started for Lashio and Magwe. About one hour and 10 minutes out, Hedman in the lead turned 180 degrees. I knew where we were at that time, but in the subsequent turnings I got lost, too. All five of us stayed together for a while, but finally Fish, Overend and I picked a valley and decided to attempt forced landings. Fish tried first wheels down, but he went right over on his back. He got out and waved, so after looking a while more, Overend tried one with his wheels down. He, too, went over on his back, and when I flew by to look I saw that his cockpit and canopy were buried. I landed immediately, wheels down like a conceited fool, and luckily I stayed right-side up. I had to dig Overend out, but he was alright. We stayed with three Americans – Hall, a sanitary engineer; Wetzell, an Army captain; and Haas, a Lt Col Medical. Had dinner with

above-mentioned and two Chinese nurses, and some Chinese engineers. Almost got a tiger cub, but his owner didn't want to let him go.

March 11
Up early, and after a makeshift sort of breakfast, Overend and I set out to the island, where he and I landed. We picked up Willie Fish in a small village, and the three of us went out to the planes. Had to cross the Nam Ting River, and we finally got to the planes and stripped all of the guns we could off the two planes. Fish's plane was too far from any road, so we let it go. Finished our work a little after noon, and then proceeded to Kunlong, which was 25 miles down the valley – and what a valley this is. We went swimming in the Nam Ting. There are plenty of leopards and tigers around here – also monkeys and beautiful jungle fowl. At Kunlong, which is a camp for the Chinese who are building a roadbed for a railway, we found Brouk and Hedman. They both landed safely in a sandbar along the river. We all stayed with the man in charge of the same – an American named Wright, and two Chinese engineers.

March 12
In company with most of the staff of the camp, 20 coolies and curious natives, we set out with gasoline for Brouk's and Hedman's ships. It was a good three to four miles' walk, and plenty hot. Finally reached the planes, and they looked strange and out of place along the shore of a river and nestled down amid towering jungle-covered mountains. "Duke" [Hedman] and I measured the stretch of beach for a runway by pacing. It was plenty long. They finally got off all right, and the rest of us started back to camp. It was well into the afternoon, so we decided to stay another night at the camp. Lashio is 90 miles away, but the road is over two ranges of mountains. Wright is a pretty interesting talker. Played some bridge after dinner and went to bed early. Don't think I would like it very long in a place like this. It's really in the middle of the jungle, and I imagine that

it would get lonely as all get-out. Besides, I don't like the boiled bread they eat here – all it is is an aborted dumpling.

March 13
One of the Chinese engineers gave us the loan of his car and his driver. We started late in the morning. The drive to Lashio took us a little over five hours. The road was very beautiful. That is if you don't mind looking out and down several thousand feet to the river. Most of the trip was through the mountains, which were densely covered by all sorts of jungle growth. Saw many brilliantly plumaged jungle fowl and lots of strange vegetation and flowering trees. Got to Lashio late in the afternoon and found orders that I was to fly the ship Hedman brought in to Magwe the next day. Duke was called back to Kunming. Overend and Fish were to drive down [to Magwe]. We all stayed at the RAF mess for the night, though we met Cross, Blackburn and Farrell at the airport and joined them for dinner at the CNAC hostel.

Neither Bill's diary nor the "Hell's Angels'" history record the fate of the P-40 he landed on the island in the river. It apparently was undamaged, but perhaps the field where it sat was too small and/ or too remote to make its recovery possible. In any case, Bill flew Hedman's "No. 92" P-40 through soupy weather to Magwe, about 250 miles south, the next day. Most of the "Hell's Angels" were at the base by then with about a dozen P-40s, and the RAF had 40 to 50 Hurricanes and Blenheims there as well.

Bill's most productive mission with the AVG was just a few days hence.

8

"A pretty good day's work"

Compared to Loiwing or even Kunming, conditions were pretty grim at Magwe. The airfield was about three miles south of the town and within easy range of Japanese bombers coming north from Rangoon or west from Thailand. It had only a few rough buildings, with no dispersal pens or revetments to protect the aircraft based there.[1] Pilots and groundcrewmen found lodgings in an abandoned house that also served as the radio station. But mostly it was hot and dusty. Bill noted in his diary that one saving feature of Magwe was that watermelons were in season and plentiful. He took baths in the nearby Irrawaddy River.

Bill saw his first action at Magwe on the morning of March 16, when he flew one of five P-40s escorting RAF Blenheim bombers on a mission against river traffic on the Irrawaddy about 120 miles south of Prome. The P-40s went down to strafe after the bombers dropped their loads, shooting up a river steamer, a barge and some smaller craft on their way back to base. That afternoon Bill drove with "Oley" Olson to Yenanyuang, a town about 20 miles north of Magwe. Prior to the war, an American colony had been located at Yenanyuang, the site of significant oilfields. The Americans had been evacuated, but Bill and "Oley" were able to take advantage of the swimming pool, golf course and dinner club that they had left behind.

On their drive home, "Oley" outlined his plan to lead a two-plane strafing raid on enemy airfields in the Moulmein area and asked Bill if he wanted to go with him. Bill agreed, but the following morning "Oley" pulled out of the mission and turned it over to Bill. He chose Ken Jernstedt, a friendly former Marine from Oregon, to fly the second P-40.

Moulmein was on the east shore of the Gulf of Martaban, about 100 miles east of Rangoon. The distance was too far for the P-40s to reach non-stop from Magwe, so the planes would stage through the old AVG Kyedaw training base at Toungoo to refuel, both outbound and on the return flight. Toungoo was still in Allied hands, but it was even more exposed to air attack than was Magwe, so all the aircraft had been pulled out and just a skeleton crew remained at the airfield. Bill takes up the story in his March 17 diary entry:

Late in the afternoon Jernie and I mapped out our strategy and took off for Toungoo (our old Point A). Arrived there all right and found that the place had been bombed twice just prior to our arrival. The landing strip hadn't been touched, but the town was ruined. Talked to two Chinese generals and one US general. Told them our mission and got some additional information on what we should look over. Saw a pile of casualties (about 50 to 75) in a field. Jernstedt and I went to bed early after going over our strategy once more.

March 18
We took off half an hour before dawn, climbed on course to 20,000 feet and headed for Moulmein. At 20,000 feet we were in the sun, but the land was still quite dark. Hit the Gulf of Martaban just right but encountered an overcast, which drove us down to 7,000 feet. Saw no shipping in the gulf and proceeded on south of Moulmein out of sight and hearing of land. At last Jernie and I turned in overland south of Moulmein, and at 4,000 feet started back to the north toward the main drome at Moulmein, where we hoped to surprise them and catch some planes on the ground. We had proceeded in this direction only three or four minutes,

however, when just below us I spotted a satellite field lined with 30 or 40 planes.

I immediately signaled for attack and dove, with Jernie following. We each made six passes on this field, and it was a complete surprise, for as far as I could see there wasn't even any ground fire to oppose us. After the sixth pass, though, we both headed north, and in another few minutes we were at the main field. Once more an attack signal, and the low-angling dive with all guns blazing at a field loaded with heavy bombers. This time we met pretty heavy antiaircraft, though, and as I pulled up and turned for another dive I saw Jernie crossing the field with little black mushrooms of smoke bursting all around him. I made one more pass and set another plane on fire, but the antiaircraft fire was pretty heavy and too damn close, so I continued on north across the bay and followed the railroad and road looking for troop movements, which was the main part of our mission. On the way back I strafed a boat, a Jap staff car, and some boxcars.

Arrived in Toungoo just five minutes after Jernstedt, and after leaving our information with the army headquarters there, we went back to Magwe. We left five fires at each field and destroyed at least 15 more planes. I'll bet we ruined plenty of others, too. A pretty good day's work, so Jernie and I took the rest of the day off.

AVG mechanics at Magwe inspected the two P-40s and found just one bullet hole in each of them. They believed the hole in Jernstedt's plane was the result of a ricochet from his own guns. The British headquarters at Toungoo called Magwe the following day to report that the group captain commanding British air forces in Burma had confirmed 15 Japanese aircraft destroyed in the Moulmein raid. Bill was credited with eight and Jernstedt with seven. That meant Bill would receive $4,000 in bonus money for his work – the most any AVG pilot ever earned for a single mission. Later, the inclusion of these eight credits in Bill's AVG service record would lead to confusion when he rejoined the US Army Air Force (USAAF), because the latter listed them as aerial victories.

The Moulmein raid and several other strikes by the "Hell's Angels" at different targets in southern Burma apparently stirred the Japanese to retaliate. Bill nearly paid the ultimate price after the air raid alarm sounded at Magwe about at 1330hrs on March 21. He wrote in his diary entry for that day:

> The planes all took off (six of them) while I was on my way back from lunch. We heard that a few Japs were headed our way, so those of us who had been to lunch got in a trench on the field. There were a few, too! Twenty-seven bombers hit the satellite field, which is a mile or so from the main field, and blew it sky high. Then a bunch of Model os [actually Ki-43 "Oscar" fighters of the 64th Sentai] strafed the main field where we were. After they left, Overend and I walked out and started inspecting the damage done by the strafers. It wasn't much, but imagine our embarrassment when we were just about to look over a transport and someone looked up and saw 17 bombers and seven fighters just off the edge of the field. We ran until we heard the sound of the bombs falling and then fell flat. We were then about 25 yards off the field. This wave was followed by ten more bombers and six more fighters. They dropped quite a load, too. About five Blenheims fully loaded with bombs blew up on the field to add to the confusion. Swartz, a pilot, was badly injured on the ground. Fauth, a crew chief, was so badly injured that he died in the night, and Sieple also was injured.

The damage from the raid was extensive, and the intercepting AVG fighters were unable to mount much of a defense. The air raid warning system was knocked out, and pilot Frank Swartz, mentioned in Bill's account, later died. But the Japanese were not finished. They followed up with morning and afternoon air raids the next day that left Magwe in ruins. The "Hell's Angels'" squadron log stated only six Hurricanes and four P-40s remained undamaged by the end of the day. Fortunately, no one else was killed or injured. At Toungoo, two divisions of Chinese troops were surrounded by the Japanese and Kyedaw airdrome was in enemy hands.

It was time to leave. Chennault ordered the "Hell's Angels" to evacuate the base and the town at Magwe. Bill was not one of the pilots chosen to fly the last P-40s out, so he left in a truck convoy that spent March 23–25 making its bumpy way up the Burma Road to Loiwing, with overnight stops at Mandalay and Lashio.

The squadron's first week passed quietly at Loiwing. The weather was bad, with low clouds in the sky mixing with heavy dust boiling up from the airfield. Bill and the other pilots took turns on alert duty, tensing up every time the telephone rang in the operations room. But fighting spirits remained high – outside, over the front door, someone had posted a sign that read *OLSON & CO. EXTERMINATORS – 24-HR. SERVICE.*

Reports came in that Toungoo had fallen on March 30, and heavy bombing raids on Lashio and Mandalay soon followed. But Bill's spirits brightened considerably when the AVG's Beech 18 utility plane touched down at Loiwing on April 3, delivering a big batch of mail from Lashio. Bill's take was four letters, one each from his mother and sister Dort, plus two from friends back home. He wrote in his diary:

> First real mail I have had since November. The pilot of the Beech said he stole the mail from British headquarters; otherwise we probably wouldn't have gotten it at all. It was a real thrill, though, and I read them all over several times. Mom sent some pictures of most of the girls [his nieces], and of the snowdrifts in Marion. Certainly looked good.

The enemy's air assault on Loiwing began on April 8 with a strafing attack, but Bill was not part of the initial combat:

> My day off today, damn it! Slept at the club last night, and had to get up at 9 a.m. because of an air raid alarm. Nothing developed, and the next alarm came about 1 p.m. I just went across the road from the club on a hill. About 15 minutes passed, and I saw eight or ten planes come across the field; I thought they were ours, but on looking through the binoculars I saw they were

Jap Model o planes – the best fighter the Japs produce [again, actually Ki-43 "Oscars"]. Then our planes hit them. I couldn't see it all, but I did see some good dogfights. On going to the field after the fight I found that the boys had knocked down ten planes – seven of them fell within sight of the field. I looked at three holes where Jap planes had gone in. We didn't lose anyone in the fight, and only one plane picked up any bullet holes. One Chinese guard on the field had five bullet holes in him but was still alive. Four British Hurricanes were up but didn't contact the enemy. They had no radio contact. I felt sorry for them – several of the pilots are Americans.

Bill got his next crack at the enemy on April 10. The day started badly when five Ki-43 "Oscars" of the 64th Sentai surprised Loiwing with a strafing attack at dawn while Bill was still on his way to the airfield. The AVG received no warning of the raid, and Bill could only watch as the Japanese fighters shot up roughly 20 P-40s and Hurricanes parked on the field. When the raiders departed, Bill continued to the field and was surprised to find that while about nine of the P-40s had been damaged, none had caught fire nor had any of them been destroyed. Bill's assigned P-40 had been shot up pretty badly, though, so he was given another plane – "No. 59" – to fly that day.

Bill's flight was scrambled in the afternoon on the report of another raid heading toward Loiwing. His flight of seven had reached 23,000ft among scattered cumulus clouds when Bill noticed drops of oil were beginning to blow out from under the panel in front of his windshield that covered the engine's oil tank filler. Apparently, a mechanic had not secured the cap on the oil tank properly and it was beginning to leak.

Just as the black oil began smearing on his windshield, obscuring his forward vision, the P-40s found themselves face-to-face with nine Ki-43s and a wild dogfight began. Unable to see much, Bill went on instruments and commenced a power dive to get out of harm's way. He dropped several thousand feet and made a sharp turn as he pulled out of a dive. A quick look through a clear spot in his side canopy revealed two enemy fighters had followed him down, so Bill turned into them and opened fire on the closest one. He took two deflection shots at the Ki-43 in front of him.[2] Bill described the final moments of the engagement in the following extract from his diary:

> He pulled up sharply as if he might be hit, and I pumped another burst into him and then ducked under him. Had to open my canopy then – visibility like in a Link Trainer. Landed OK but could only claim a "probable," as I didn't see him crash.

A press photographer was at Loiwing and he captured Bill's landing in "No. 59" on film. Oil covers the plane down the port side of the fuselage from the cockpit back. He also photographed Bill with oil covering his helmet and face, as well as down his left shoulder, arm and pants leg. Bill is a mess, but he's alive and unhurt. For some reason, his April 10 claim of one enemy fighter probably destroyed was not recorded by the AVG. Other members of the "Hell's Angels" received credit for four confirmed kills and one probable, however.

After the drubbings they received on April 8 and 10, the Japanese refrained from further raids on Loiwing for the next two weeks. Almost daily reconnaissance flights by high-flying observation aircraft kept the tensions high in the "Hell's Angels'" alert shack, however. The squadron was down to a handful of P-40s by this time, as most of its planes had been written off due to accidents, bombings and air combat. The few remaining fighters would roar off at each report of enemy aircraft approaching, only to return to base with their guns unfired.

The AVG had in fact recently begun receiving new P-40Es from the USAAF but these were assigned to the 1st and 2nd PSs. The E-model Warhawk had more firepower with six 0.50-caliber wing guns and better visibility from the cockpit due to a redesigned fuselage, but its performance was similar to the AVG's older P-40s. Eventually, some of the other squadrons' P-40s were transferred to the "Hell's Angels" as the AVG's P-40E strength grew.

To ease the tension in the alert shack, "Oley" Olson established the new position of "operations officer" in the radio shack and gave the job to Bill. He described the new duties in his diary:

It's a newly inaugurated office, and a much needed one. The job is to stay at the radio shack and receive the reports that come in from the warning net. When these reports seem to indicate that enemy planes are coming into our area, the alert crew has to be notified. Up to now, all reports from the net have been going to the alert shack. Now, just those that need attention should get there.

It is an indication of the trust that the squadron commander had in Bill that Olson gave him such an important responsibility. This was an additional duty, and Bill continued to take his turn on the flying schedule as well.

Even with the improved communications between the warning net and the alert crews, morale was beginning to flag among the AVG personnel. On April 11 Chennault spoke to the pilots at Loiwing and told them a change was in the works that would replace the AVG with a USAAF fighter group. Rumors of this change, and the possibility that the AVG would be inducted en masse into the USAAF, had been floating around for months. Now it seemed all the more likely, and no one was happy about it. Bill, like most of his comrades, had become fixated on the end date of his AVG contract, and the assumption that he would be going home at that time. Now he confided in his diary, "I don't think any offer would keep me here at the end of my year." He did, however, concede that, "I may come back if the war lasts long enough." He need not have worried about that.

Another factor that was affecting the morale of the AVG pilots was the nature of some of the missions they were being ordered to undertake. Japanese ground forces were now advancing rapidly north through central Burma, and the retreating Chinese generals thought it would inspire their troops to fight if they saw Chinese aircraft overhead supporting them. These so-called "morale missions" would need to be flown at low altitude so the Chinese soldiers could see the markings on the P-40s, but this would place the fighters within range of enemy small-arms fire on the wrong side of the combat lines. On other occasions the P-40 pilots were ordered to provide escort for notoriously unreliable RAF Blenheim bomber formations attacking Japanese-held airdromes. The AVG pilots had signed up to protect the Burma Road from enemy air attack and were happy to do that, but they did not like the idea of needlessly placing themselves in harm's way, especially with the close of their AVG commitments now just three months away.

The burden of these missions fell primarily to the 1st and 2nd PSs, since the depleted "Hell's Angels" currently were tasked with providing air defense for Loiwing. But Bill and his squadronmates were supportive of the complaints voiced by pilots from the other two squadrons. Bill wrote in his diary on April 18:

> Our group ran into its first real clash with the higher-ups today – chiefly Colonel [or now General] Chennault.[3] Had a meeting after duty hours, and he says, in effect "Yours is not to reason why." It was all brought about by three men refusing to take a mission two days ago. Most of the group sympathizes with them, so it's really a test for the group.

Bill was keyed up when he awoke before dawn on April 21. The night before, Olson had assigned him to lead wingman Bob Raines in an attack on Magwe, where the Japanese had recently occupied the former AVG air base there. Perhaps with some luck, Bill could repeat his success at Moulmein. He was to get some excitement that day, but not the kind he had envisioned. He reported in his diary:

> The planes weren't ready for the mission this a.m., so I decided to check out in a new P-40E, or "Kittyhawk." Took off early and flew around the vicinity of the field, for it was very hazy. Up about a half hour when an order came to fly down and patrol

Lashio. I had no map but decided I could find it all right. That was my big mistake, and about an hour later I landed in a big pasture about 40 miles south of Lashio. I didn't damage the plane, but I walked ten miles before I found someone to aid me. Spent the night with an outlying RAF aircraft detector system contingent. One of the RAF boys used to work at Collins Radio in Cedar Rapids. Had dinner at the local big shot's house and fared pretty well. A typical British bore, though, even if I was very grateful to him and his wife for the good chow. Slept – or did I? – between two British army blankets on a rope mattress. War is Hell!

April 22

A very nice morning, but my hosts of the RAF are facing an acute food shortage. Plenty of tea and porridge, but from breakfast on it's going to be rough. No gas, or "aviation spirits" as they say, so no chance to get away this morning. Had two of the eight remaining eggs for lunch, and went out to the plane to see if any of the Shan villagers had gotten over their curiosity and started tampering with it. They hadn't, and at about 4 o'clock Buck Rogers, one of our crew chiefs, was stopped on the road up to Lashio, and he brought his truck over and gave me enough gas to get home. He was going back from Namsang and told me that Brouk ["Hell's Angels'" Flight Leader Bob Brouk] was strafed on the ground at Namsang yesterday and hit in the legs a few times. The weather piled up, and I was forced to stay another evening. Listened to the gramophone awhile and then retired. I couldn't stand listening to the chatter of the C.O. of the outfit any longer.

Bill flew the P-40E back to Loiwing without any further problems on April 23. There, he learned that Brouk had been evacuated to Loiwing for medical treatment in the AVG's Beech 18 utility plane, and Rogers had reached Lashio safely in his truck.

As April neared its end, everyone could see that Loiwing's time as an operational AVG base was running out. The Japanese advance was closing in on Lashio and its airfield, and when they fell it would place enemy aircraft just 60 miles away. As R. T. Smith wrote in his diary, that was just "too damned close," because the air raid warning net would not be able to provide sufficient warning of incoming attacks. Still, Chennault hesitated to pull the AVG out of Loiwing because he wanted to continue running missions over the front lines for as long as possible. Bill apparently took part in one of those missions on the morning of April 25, but he left no record of the flight. Bomb-carrying P-40Es of the 2nd PS caught a Japanese convoy of trucks on the Burma Road and worked it over while the "Hell's Angels" provided top cover. Later, two enemy observation planes were shot down, but Bill was not involved in the scoring.

Japanese bombers returned to attack Loiwing on April 28, doing heavy damage to the airfield and the town. Chennault ordered the AVG to move to Mangshih, a remote airfield about 80 miles north of Loiwing. Mangshih was a nasty place – muddy airfield, poor accommodation in a dirty hotel, and infected with malaria. Bill made no diary entries during his short stay. On May 1, he returned to his diary:

Weather still pretty lousy, but we finally got our orders to move to Kunming as soon as we could get away. None of us need any urging to get out of this hole. We went out to the field during a thunderstorm, and after a delay occasioned by General Chennault coming in on an Army transport, we all took off. Raines got stuck in the mud, and Paul Greene had to land with engine trouble; so that left 19 or 20 of us. The clouds were about 300–500 feet off the tops of the mountains all the way, but we got there alright. On landing I found that Ajax Baumler, an old Army pal of mine, is here.[4] He is going to be attached to our group as soon as he gets well. He made the mistake of going into the men's bar and saying Army pilots could do as well as the AVG had. One of the boys really worked him over. It was good to get back to such civilization as we have here and enjoy clean clothing and such luxuries as showers and a barber shop again. Bob [R. T.] Smith and I spent too much of the evening saying hello to the boys in the bar, and I didn't get to bed at any reasonable hour.

May 2
Spent most of the day in bed and not feeling too well either. Managed to get the room straightened out. Ajax and Kirk [Kuykendall] came over to the room, and we had a good visit. Kirk told me he is still a little shaky about tangling with the Japs due to the fact that one shot his cap off and furrowed his "noggin" a little. Also he told me he was going to get married as soon as he got home. Think I'll wait until after the war.

The "Hell's Angels" and the 2nd PS soon got back to their familiar duty pattern of daytime alerts, night alerts and days off. The squadrons flew several combined missions to attack the Japanese advance on the Salween River front. The 1st PS operated out of Paoshan, near the border with Burma, in early May before it, too, pulled out for Kunming. By May 13 all three squadrons of the AVG were back at Kunming.

Two days later, Bill sat down to write a letter to Neil Martin's wife. It was a task he had been putting off for nearly five months. He mentioned Neil often in his diary over the months, but it shows how deeply he felt his friend's loss that he could not bring himself to write to his family for such a long time. Apparently, Mrs. Martin's letter to David Harris, who had flown with Neil in the USAAC, requesting information about her husband prompted Bill to break his silence. He wrote to her:

Dave Harris was kind enough to show me the letter that he received from you a short time ago, and I wanted to write to you at that time; but that was down in Burma and the situation was pretty hectic. That this letter should have been written long before goes without saying, and I did make several attempts to write to Neil's mother; however, each time that I started to write I found myself at a loss for words to express my feelings.

Bill spent several paragraphs recounting their friendship and describing Neil's death in combat on December 23. He closed with these words:

> I took care of Neil's personal effects that he had taken to Rangoon with him, and after inventory I placed them in our head office in Rangoon for shipment to Texarkana. I am enclosing the snapshots that I have of Neil. They were all taken in Toungoo, Burma, in the period from September to December. I have the negatives to all of them but the one of Neil and I in the rickshaws, and that was taken with his camera, which he set and placed on the ground with the shutter on automatic release. I hope these pictures and this letter reach you safely and soon, and that they help clear up any details you have not been informed about by this time.
>
> In closing I ask you to forgive me for not having done this very thing long ago, and I invite you or any of Neil's relatives or friends to write me and ask any questions concerning him or to request that I send them any of the snapshots I have. I promise that I will answer all letters and fill all requests – that is, if I am still here. Again I plead inadequacy of my expression in telling you how much Neil meant to me. Perhaps if fate is kind, one day I shall come back to the States and have an opportunity to visit you and Neil's parents. Until then I remain, sincerely, William N. "Bill" Reed

Bill took time that same week to write a letter to his nephew Dick, who had completed his USAAF flight training and was now a second lieutenant flying P-38 Lightnings with the 63rd FS/56th Fighter Group (FG) at Farmingdale, New York. He took a decidedly lighter tone in this letter:

> Dear "Nephie," Mom sent me a picture of you in your new Army regalia – You certainly looked big, and from all reports you have picked up a little weight since I dropped you in San Antonio last July. A fellow doesn't get too much opportunity

to exercise in the flying game, and from medical testimony it seems that the more quiet and reserved individuals, who refrain from too much physical exertion, are, oddly enough, the ones least susceptible to "black outs." I remain about the same – the old 165–170. I may have lost a little bit. For the last two months I have been down Burma way – a little "big game" hunting you know. Got mighty tired of living out of a suitcase in any old place [I] happened to be, but now that I'm back here I rather miss the excitement and uncertainty we used to have. We have some here, and I expect plenty some of these days.

How does pursuit agree with you? I have a friend at Farmingdale who is an engineer with the Republic Co. there. You might look him up and have a beer with him some time. His name is Eddie Israel. I suppose you have lined up some of that N.Y. society stuff. Give 'em Hell, Nephie, but don't get too involved 'til I get back. As for coming out this way, I hope you wait until I get home before you make any decision one way or the other. If all goes well, I may see you in July or August. That's not so far away, really, but it actually seems an eternity. Of course, the whole situation is rather uncertain yet, but I hold out hope.

I wonder what you are flying these days. Mom said you had some time in the 36's [Curtiss P-36 fighter, a predecessor to the P-40]. I'll wager plenty that you got a kick out of them. I know I used to like them very much. Probably now, though, you are in something pretty hot. I wouldn't mind getting assigned to a duty station such as you are in when I get back, though there is some possibility that if I get a long enough vacation I may come back over.

I haven't had any letters from you for a long time. Suppose you have been plenty busy since graduation. Had a letter from Emma the other day – the first one in a long time. She said that you still kept her informed as to my whereabouts etc. I once asked you to write your candid opinion of her, and with no sparing of horses. In one letter a long time ago she told me that you were "tops" and that you used to fly in from Houston on occasional weekends. How about a letter, Nephie?

Have you met any of my classmates? Knocking around much in the Air Corps you should meet one occasionally. A couple of them are in this outfit – "Kirk" and Probst, and one, Lacy Mangleburg, was killed over here last December. All told now, we have lost 20 or 21 pilots. I wonder how those boys they are turning out now are making it? They get the best training in the world, though it's nice to get a little experience under one's belt. Alertness is the prime essential in pursuit flying.

Well, Nephie, you take it easy now, and no flying through hangars or under bridges or "stuff like that there." Sometime in the future I see you and I buzzing over Marion at zero altitude and really giving the folks a show, but let's save most of our tricks for the "flannel bellies" or the boys on the other side. Say hello to the boys for me. I was stuck for a day or two in a little Chinese town, and another guy and I bought seven bottles of beer for $42.00 gold. How's that? There isn't any liquor over here at all, which is just as well. I go on duty at 4 a.m. and get home about 6:30 p.m., which makes a pretty long day of it. I may be heading for India on a trip one of these days, and I may write you next from Chungking. Be good, Nephie, and keep your nose in the blue! Good luck, Bill.

Just as Bill had predicted in his letter to Dick, the excitement picked up at Kunming when he was assigned to take part in a mission into French Indochina on May 16. He wrote:

Today six of us went on a reconnaissance mission down into Indo China – Dupouy, Haywood, Raines, Older, Laughlin and I. Found a freight train coming up the track from Hanoi. It didn't blow up, but we riddled it with .50s and .30s so that it wouldn't run under its own power again. That's the first locomotive strafing I've done, and it's fun. Our object is to stir up the Japs in Hanoi. I say that's like poking a stick at a hornet's nest, but the powers that be don't consult me so often. Got back about 2 p.m. and had lunch. Just finished when someone reported that one of the P-40Es had spun or dived in over by the bombing range. Sure enough we spotted some smoke over that way, so Older and I drove over. We were the first ones except a crowd of Chinese. I never saw such a complete wreck. There wasn't a big enough piece to ever tell that it had once been an airplane. Couldn't identify the pilot, but later found out it was [Tom] Jones. It was pretty nasty, and I won't go chasing wrecks again. He was on my boat coming over. A nice kid – married and has a baby girl he had never met.

May 17
[R. T.] Smith and I represented our squadron on a mission down to Lao Kay in Indo China. There were four Kittyhawks [P-40Es] with bombs and four Tomahawks [P-40s]. The Second Squadron Kittyhawks were going to strafe and bomb the train we wrecked yesterday. When we got down there, though, the train had been moved. So [Lewis] Bishop, leading the Second Squadron, started back to Lao Kay where he said over the radio he was going to bomb the station. Smitty and I had seen a train coming up the tracks about ten miles from Boa Ha, though, so he and I peeled off and went back and strafed it pretty thoroughly. I saw the engineer or fireman jump off after the first pass. When we got through it was smoking and steaming, but again I was disappointed because it didn't blow up. When we got back we found that Bishop had been knocked down over Lao Kay by antiaircraft fire. He bailed out and fell right into the town. He was married and had a baby he's never seen. That makes three pilots lost in five days.

The two shot-up trains were the last damage Bill inflicted on the enemy while serving in the AVG. He later confided to a newspaper reporter that an RAF pilot had told him to expect the boiler of a steam engine to explode if he ever strafed one, which accounted for his disappointment when the two engines he hit gushed steam but did not blow up. Bishop's fate remained unknown at the time, but later it emerged that he was captured by the Japanese and imprisoned in French Indochina. In 1945 he was placed on a train bound for a new Prisoner of War (PoW) camp in Manchuria, but he managed to escape and eventually made his way back to Kunming, and freedom.

Excitement also picked up on the ground at Kunming, but it had nothing to do with air combat. It had been decided that the AVG would cease to exist on July 4, when the USAAF's 23rd FG would assume responsibility for combat operations in China. However, only a handful of inexperienced USAAF fighter pilots had arrived in Kunming so far, and there was little chance that the full unit would reach China in time to take over from the AVG. So, on May 21, Chennault and Brig Gen Clayton Bissell of the USAAF's Tenth Air Force called a meeting for the personnel at Kunming to attempt once more to convince them to join the Army.

Bissell's haughty attitude irked the AVG troops – pilots and groundcrew alike – and they were not impressed with the terms he offered. They had honored their AVG contracts and were proud of the combat record they had compiled since the start of the war. But they were weary from the strain of fighting what appeared to be a losing battle, despite their individual successes. Most, including Bill, were fixated on the July 4 departure date. No thanks, Gen Bissell, you can carry on without us.

On May 24 and 28 Bill took part in two flights over the Salween River front that had far more significance than he could have guessed at the time. The Chinese Army, with the help of close-air support from the AVG, had stopped the Japanese advance on the Burma side of the river by this time. These missions – one an escort, the other a patrol – promised little chance of action, so Bill's friend R. T. Smith took his camera along. Smith had purchased a Leica camera in February from an American civilian in Chungking. The camera's F2 lens and 1/1000th of a second shutter speed made it ideal for shooting air-to-air photography, and R. T. used it to take a selection of formation photos as each mission was returning to base. The scattered cloud conditions and angle of the sun were favorable. The then-rare roll of Kodachrome film, which R. T.

had hoarded for months waiting for this opportunity, performed perfectly.

One can only imagine R. T. flying along in the narrow cockpit of his "No. 47" P-40 as he juggled the camera and the aircraft's controls while trying to click the shutter when the other P-40s were properly "posed" – and then wind the film forward for the next shot. Somehow, he succeeded masterfully. Those color photographs – the only ones ever taken of AVG aircraft in flight – have been published hundreds of times over the years, helping to bring the story of the AVG to life for at least five generations of aviation history enthusiasts.[5]

With June came the onset of monsoon season. Chennault moved the 1st and 2nd PSs north to Chungking to protect the capital city from expected air attacks, leaving the "Hell's Angels" at Kunming on alert duty. As near as can be determined, Bill performed a flight test with R. T. Smith on June 1 and false-alarm alert scrambles on June 6, 10 and 19.[6] Bill had stopped writing in his diary in late May, so the alert flights cannot be verified. He and the rest of the "Hell's Angels" spent the last two weeks of their AVG service sweating out the weather and making arrangements for their trip home. The discovery of an excellent restaurant in downtown Kunming serving Cantonese food perked up the evening on several occasions.

END OF THE AVG

Dissolution day for the AVG was at hand. The departing AVG personnel were not provided with transportation home by the US government and had to make their own arrangements. Hoping to get a jump on the other "AVGers" who were leaving on July 4, Bill joined R. T. Smith, "Oley" Olson, Parker Dupouy and Tom Haywood in reserving seats aboard a CNAC DC-3 that was scheduled to fly from Kunming to Calcutta that day. The rest would be flying to Dinjan, in upper Assam, on USAAF transports and making their way homeward from there as best they could.[7]

The flight out on Independence Day was uneventful. Bill and his traveling companions, flush with cash from their lucrative

AVG contracts, checked into Calcutta's Great Eastern Hotel and then headed directly to Firpo's restaurant for steak dinners. They spent several days touring around the city and enjoying the fare at Firpo's each evening while they researched options for the trip home. They learned that the troop ship *Mariposa* was due to arrive in Karachi, India (now Pakistan), in about a week with some 5,000 US Army troops aboard. It would be proceeding to Bombay to pick up cargo and passengers before returning to New York. Passage would cost about $200 each, but this sounded like the best of limited options for getting home.

India is vast. The distance from Calcutta to Karachi is roughly 1,350 miles and to Bombay about 1,000 miles. Bill and his companions chose the shorter route and boarded a first-class compartment on the train to Bombay for a two-day rail trip across the country. The weather was hot and humid with frequent downpours as the train chugged westward. Ever resourceful, the boys had brought along a large wash tub, which they filled with ice to maintain their supply of cold beer and perhaps provide a little cooling for the compartment as well. They replenished their supply of ice as the train made numerous stops along the way.

On arrival in Bombay the group rented a suite of rooms at the Taj Mahal Hotel. This would be their home for the next three weeks as they sampled the city's hot spots while they awaited the *Mariposa*. Other AVG personnel drifted into Bombay as the departure date drew nearer. Then when the ship arrived, they learned that others had traveled to Karachi to catch the ship and were already on board when it steamed into Bombay harbor.

The Bombay passengers boarded the *Mariposa* in early September. In addition to the AVG contingent, there were about 70 Chinese flying cadets on their way to the US for flight training, plus a number of civilians who were mostly missionaries returning home. If Bill was expecting accommodations aboard *Mariposa* to be as comfortable as those on MS *Bloemfontein*, he was bound to have been disappointed. The cargo hold on board the 18,000-ton ship had been converted into cramped sleeping quarters featuring three-tier bunks. It looked like a long month ahead. On the plus side,

American-style food prepared by US Army cooks was plentiful and tasty. Boredom overtook the passengers after the first few days at sea, leaving mealtimes as the highlights of each day.

Eventually, *Mariposa* reached Cape Town, South Africa, where it stopped to take on fuel, water and provisions. The passengers had a few days to stretch their sea legs before the voyage resumed. Back at sea, *Mariposa* rounded the tip of southern Africa and turned northwest toward New York. Now the tension ratcheted up because German U-boats were on the prowl in the Atlantic Ocean, and *Mariposa* was traveling alone with only its 20-knot top speed and a few small deck guns to protect it from the threat of a torpedo attack. As R. T. Smith observed, "If our ship had been sunk, about half of the old AVG would have gone down with it."

Somehow, *Mariposa* avoided the attention of any U-boats, and 30 days after leaving Bombay the ship entered New York City harbor on a beautiful early September day. Bill and the other passengers lined the rails as the city's skyline came into view. Soon they were watching the Statue of Liberty pass by, and before long the ship had docked. Most of the passengers quickly dispersed for homes across the United States, but Bill and R. T. Smith were not quite ready for the party to end. The two young men had become fast friends when they met in San Francisco prior to shipping out for China. They rarely flew together in the AVG because they were assigned to different flights within the "Hell's Angels" squadron, but they enjoyed each other's company while off-duty, especially during the last few months in China. Their bond grew tighter during the trip home, and they were both eager to blow off some steam in the big city before heading home to Iowa and California, respectively. They caught a cab to the Hotel Pennsylvania, checked in and made quick calls to their families to let them know they had arrived safely.

Bill and R. T. spent the next three days in New York, sightseeing during the daytime and hitting hot spots such as the Stork Club and the Copacabana at night. They attracted a lot of attention with the distinctive Chinese insignias on their uniforms and their all-American good looks, meeting several beautiful women, including one that R. T. would marry less than a year later. Finally, with their bankrolls running low and their parents' impatience to see them running high, Bill and R. T. decided it was time to go home.[8]

Bill traveled first to Providence, Rhode Island, where "Nephie" Dick Reed was now flying P-40s in the 317th FS/325th FG. Dick arranged a ten-day leave, and the two headed for home, with plans to arrive in Marion on Friday, September 11. They got as far as New York but then got lost in Grand Central Station and missed their train to Chicago. After spending the night in the city, they caught a westbound train for Chicago the next day. On Saturday morning, September 12, 1942, Bill and Dick boarded a train bound for Union Station in Cedar Rapids, Iowa. Bill's 14-month round-the-world AVG adventure was coming to an end. A hero's welcome awaited him in Marion.

9

"I might have stayed over there"

It was noon on Saturday, September 12, 1942, and the town of Marion, Iowa, was in a state of high excitement. A parade was forming along seven blocks of Seventh Avenue, the main street, with color guards, three fancy drum corps, the Marion High School and Loras College marching bands, a formation of local Civil Defense troops, several American Legion squads, Boy Scout troops and local children with decorated bicycles all finding their places in line. Camera crews from three major newsreel companies — the equivalent of today's major television networks – were getting set up near the city park. In the park behind a raised platform and on cables hung across Seventh Street in the business district were banners proclaiming in bold lettering, "*Welcome Home BILL REED.*"

All was in readiness for what promised to be the biggest event in recent memory for the citizens of Marion. The sun was shining, and the temperature was just right as several thousand people began to gather along the parade route. For nine months they had been reading in the local newspapers about the exploits of a scrappy group of American fighter pilots that was giving the Japanese a bloody nose in the skies over China. The stories held special interest in Marion because one of the most successful of those pilots was one of their own, as the editors of the *Marion Sentinel* and the *Cedar Rapids Gazette* were careful to remind them each time another report about the AVG – now known as the "Flying Tigers" – hit the front page. Now the day had come that Mrs. Mayme Reed of 1314 Fifth Avenue had been longing for since July 1941 – her youngest son, Bill Reed, was coming home.

In September 1942, it was rare to encounter a combat veteran of the current war anywhere in the United States. The nation was fully mobilized for the war effort, but most servicemen were still in training. Naval battles had taken place in the Pacific, yet most of the participants remained in the combat zone. The fighting in the Philippines had ended, and the vast majority of Americans who fought there were either PoWs or dead. The Marines had invaded Guadalcanal in August, and the fighting there would continue for many months before they secured the island. The massive effort to take on Axis forces in Europe and North Africa was still in the planning stages. It was a big deal for a community to be welcoming home a combat veteran, and Marion, Iowa, was pulling out all the stops to honor its very own "Flying Tiger."

Bill started the day in Chicago with his nephew and best friend Dick Reed. They were a day behind schedule, and the event organizers were beginning to sweat. When the train had pulled into Union Station in Cedar Rapids on Friday afternoon without the Reed boys on board, the event committee sent a representative to Chicago by plane to try to find them. The man met three incoming trains from New York but failed to make a connection. After taking the overnight train from New York, the Reed boys caught the Northwestern train bound for Cedar Rapids and would arrive there in late afternoon. They were unaware of the scope of the celebration that awaited them.

The Bill Reed Day schedule called for the parade to start at 1400hrs, followed by an event in the park at 1530hrs. Then at 1900hrs, a banquet at the Marion Country Club would cap the day's festivities. But as the clock wound closer to 1400hrs, the event promoters had to face the grim reality of the railroad schedule. Bill would not be arriving in time. The parade would have to start without its star attraction.

At the strike of the hour, parade chairman Allen McElwain, commander of American Legion Post 298, gave the order to start the parade. As the *Marion Sentinel* newspaper reported, "The parade itself was something to talk about. With but a short time to develop it, A. R. McElwain got together an impressive street show." The throng lining the sidewalk waited restlessly for a view of their returning hero, but in the end had to settle for a look at the governor of Iowa, George A. Wilson, and Marion Mayor John Mullin waving furiously at the crowd from an open car. The parade wound its way on a loop through central Marion, starting eastbound on Seventh Avenue and heading through the business district as far as 13th Street, then north two blocks, west on Ninth Avenue to 11th Street, south back to Seventh Avenue and east to the corner of Seventh Avenue and 9th Street, where the parade disbanded. Most folks moved to the city park for the next phase of the celebration. The parade was over, and still there was no sign of Bill.

The following extract is from the *Marion Sentinel* story reporting on the day's events:

The program from the bunting-decorated bandstand in the city park began, and newsreel cameramen from three great movie services had their cameras in focus. Benne Alter, the announcer imported from the radio station in Cedar Rapids, was master of ceremonies. The high school band played, the Rev. Frederick Nelson of the Congregational Church prayed, and a squadron of planes dived low over the speakers' platform in honoring salute – not knowing that the honoree was still missing.

The band played again, and the announcer tried to appease the restless crowd with radio's best wit. The governor was there and ready to speak, but was not put forward. And the band played on.

And then, all of a sudden, a car dashed up the street, its occupants hurried to the stand, there was a faint handclapping that gradually swelled into a tremendous, cheering ovation, and Flying Tiger Bill Reed, after 14 months of fighting in the Orient, was back home.

Bill's train had pulled into Union Station at 1530hrs – on schedule – and was met by a small contingent from the Marion Chamber of Commerce, along with an officer of the Iowa State Patrol. As Bill and Dick descended from the train, a group of 74 men from Draft Board No. 1 was down the platform boarding the train on the way to basic training. The two young men in uniform passed the draftees unnoticed. The state patrolman bundled them into his car and roared out of the station, siren wailing. According to one report, the car made its way from central Cedar Rapids to the Marion City Park in seven minutes flat.

Bill paused to speak quietly to his mother as he ascended the platform. When the cheering died down, Governor Wilson rose to address the crowd. His remarks went on for quite a few minutes, considering that everyone in the audience had come to hear Bill, not the governor, speak. Wilson did get in one witty quip when he said, "We have no native tigers in Iowa, but we are proud to have grown at least one 'Flying Tiger' who traveled all the way around the world to show what that means. But, after all, the spirit of the 'Flying Tigers' is the spirit of Iowa. It is part of our tradition." Another speaker that afternoon was the Reverend George A. Stemm, an instructor and administrator at Loras College who had taken an interest in Bill during his collegiate career. He described Bill as "the type of manhood that, under God, will bring to this country the peace that we all desire."

Then it was time to hear from Bill. To make it as easy as possible on him, the organizers had arranged for Alter, the radio announcer, to conduct an interview rather than calling on Bill to give a speech. It would have come as no surprise to those in the audience who knew Bill personally to see that he was fully capable of exhibiting, as the *Marion Sentinel* put it, "clear thinking, his breadth of view, and his ability to clothe his thoughts in good English. No one ever need fear to present him to any audience." As future events would show, this assessment of Bill was right on the money.

In response to Alter's questions, Bill explained how he came to join the AVG, his trip to Asia, his actions in combat, his opinions of Japanese aircraft and pilots, and his experiences interacting with the Chinese. He paid tribute to two of his friends who had been killed in action – his AVG buddy Neil Martin and a close high-school friend, Don Goodyear of Marion. Goodyear was a USAAC flyer who had lost his life when the aircraft carrier *Langley* was incapacitated by Japanese bombers on February 27, 1942, while trying to deliver a load of P-40s and their pilots to the hard-pressed island of Java – the carrier had to be scuttled by its destroyer escorts. Bill credited Madame Chiang Kai-shek with conceiving the idea of the AVG and lauded Gen Chennault for his leadership of the group. Bill also made it known that he would be buying War Bonds with a sizable portion of the money he earned while serving in the AVG, and urged the audience to consider similar purchases. Finally, Alter asked Bill how his hometown looked to him after 14 months away and his around-the-world travels.

"This is the most marvelous country between here and China, no matter which way you go," he replied.

The event closed with introductions of friends and family, most notably Mayme Reed. She stepped forward when her name was called to receive a tremendous cheer from the audience, but as might be expected no photographer caught a picture of Mayme with a smile on her face. Then, after a rousing rendition of the national anthem by the band, the crowd dispersed with the satisfaction of finally having seen and heard from their "Flying Tiger" hero.

It was a short walk to the Reed home from the park. Once there, Bill and Dick had some time to catch up with Mayme and the rest of the family before freshening up for the evening event. Bill put on a clean shirt and selected a dark tie to go with his distinctive dress uniform, which was a mix of Army-issue summer belted blouse and pants with CAF rank, wings and decoration ribbons.

Only 200 tickets were available for the banquet at the country club, and these had been snapped up quickly at a cost of $1 each (about $15 in today's money). Louis C. Ross, president of the Marion Chamber of Commerce, presided over the banquet. A five-foot-by-seven-foot blowup of a photo showing Bill in the cockpit of a USAAF plane was mounted behind the speaker's table. Guests of

honor joining Ross and his wife at the head table included Bill and
Dick, Mayme, Bill's sister Marion (Dick's mother), Father Stemm
and Father Dan Coyne (Bill's football coach) from Loras College,
Governor Wilson and Mayor Mullin. At the end of the table,
"Mick" Forbes was seated between pioneer Cedar Rapids aviator
Dan Hunter, who was now a lieutenant colonel in command of the
Iowa wing of the Civil Air Patrol, and Lt Cdr Truman Jones, state
naval recruiting officer. Among other family and friends attending
were Bill's sisters Isabelle and Dorothy, his brother Edward and
Aunt Em Van Buskirk, his father's sister.

After Ross made opening remarks, short speeches followed
by Dick, Mayor Mullin, Lt Cdr Jones, Father Coyne and Father
Stemm. To give an example of Bill's daring during his younger days,
Stemm had related a story about Bill and a friend encountering
an unattended railroad engine with its steam up one night in
downtown Dubuque. Bill, calling on his father's long experience
as a railroad engineer, suggested that they take the engine for a
ride. Stemm could not say how far they got, but he did recall the
students were called on the carpet by the college dean the next day.
When Bill began his talk, he admitted that though he thought he
knew how to run the engine, he was not able to get it to move
before the train crew chased him from the cab.

As in the afternoon, Bill spoke with easy grace to the audience.
He said he was happy to be home and went on to repeat some
of the experiences and observations he had mentioned earlier in
the day. In expressing his respect for the fighting ability of the
enemy's air force, he said he believed the American people had
underestimated Japan as a military power prior to the war. The
evening ended with four vaudeville acts by a Des Moines troupe
followed by a hearty singing of "God Bless America." Bill Reed Day
had been memorable from start to finish, even if Marion's war hero
had missed his own parade.

Bill was looking forward to taking a few weeks off in Marion
before he got serious about making plans for the future. He fully
expected to rejoin the USAAF, but first he wanted to relax and
have some fun. For months, Bill had been looking forward to

long talks over the dinner table with his family, scouting up what few buddies were still around for a night on the town, doing some fishing with his brother-in-law and perhaps figuring out his relationship with "Mick" Forbes. It did not work out that way, however, because duty called in the form of the federal War Finance Committee. The committee's job was selling War Bonds, and it needed Bill's help.

WAR BONDS SALESMAN

With the outbreak of the European war in September 1939, it quickly became obvious that the United States would play a key role in the conflict – whether the nation became actively involved in combat or not. Once they maximized their own industrial capacities, the warring nations needed everything from warplanes, tanks and trucks to ammunition and even food to continue to fight. Orders began rolling in from the Allied nations for American products, and the nation geared up to fill those orders.

Meanwhile, the leaders in Washington, D.C., finally recognized the need to expand and modernize the military forces of the United States in light of the growing world conflict. On September 16, 1940, Congress passed the Burke-Wadsworth Act by wide margins in both houses, imposing the first peacetime draft in the history of the United States. Selective Service came to life. The registration of men between the ages of 21 and 36 began a month later, and soon recruits were flowing into military training bases all over the country, trading work clothes for service uniforms and tools for weapons. The jobs they left behind would need to be filled by other workers, pushing the nation toward full employment.

The economy was now booming for the first time in more than a decade, and with the military buildup taking hold, it might have seemed that the troubles caused by the Great Depression were over for the United States. But it was not that simple. High levels of employment while production was being diverted to the war effort meant Americans had more money to spend but fewer items to buy. Without corrective action, prices would begin to rise in a spiral of inflation that could drag the nation's economy back down. At the same time, the government needed money to pay for the military buildup without taxing American citizens beyond their willingness and ability to pay.

The solution to these problems was surprisingly simple. Rather than taxing its citizens, the US Government would borrow money from them. This would have the dual benefit of removing money from circulation, thereby limiting inflation, while also providing the government with the funds it needed to bolster the armed forces. The loans took the form of War Bonds, which were debt securities that yielded a small 2.9 percent return after a ten-year maturity. They were sold at 75 percent of their face value in denominations beginning at $25. For people on a limited budget, stamps could be purchased in smaller denominations and pasted into books that could be redeemed for a bond when filled.

The War Finance Committee supervised the sale of War Bonds, and the War Advertising Council promoted bond purchases by private citizens. War Bonds were not necessarily an easy sell, considering they offered a rate of return below market value. But many Americans remembered the Stock Market crash of 1929 and remained wary of investing in stocks, although they offered the possibility of a higher rate of return. And besides, after December 7, 1941, the nation was at war, and buying bonds represented a moral and financial stake in the war effort for Americans of all ages and income levels.[1]

Heavy advertising, appealing to patriotism and the safe nature of the investment, proved effective in driving bond sales. One of the government's best strategies was the use of famous celebrities to make the sales pitch for bonds. Operating in cooperation with the War Advertising Council, the Motion Picture Industry's War Activities Committee began organizing bond tours in which popular Hollywood stars traveled the country to speak at public events, luncheons, dinners and in factories. The first of these, titled the "Stars Over America" tour, was just taking hold when Bill returned from China. In fact, a banner in the Marion park on Bill Reed Day advertised upcoming tour stops in Iowa. During the

month of September 1942, seven touring groups totaling 337 stars
would make 353 appearances throughout the nation, selling more
than $800 million worth of War Bonds.[2]

The phone at Mayme Reed's home began ringing within a day
of Bill's arrival in Marion. It seemed that everyone wanted him to
speak at their events. How could he refuse? Bill's first appearance
promoting War Bonds came just one day after he returned home.
Sunday, September 13, was Pershing Day, and the US Navy had
arranged a mass enlistment of 24 recruits during a celebration in
Memorial Stadium in Cedar Rapids. The event also included a
pitch for War Bonds, and Bill was the day's main attraction. The
Cedar Rapids Gazette published this account:

> Mayor Frank K. Hahn took the microphone to introduce the
> man who more than anyone present needed no introduction –
> Bill Reed. As the uniformed flyer marched into the coliseum
> at the head of a V formed by Legionnaires, the band struck up
> the Army Air Corps song and the crowd rose to shout and clap
> its welcome. If a boy were made to order for the part, he could
> fit the popular conception of a hero no better than Bill Reed.
> Handsome, modest, visibly tickled pink to be home and a little
> overwhelmed by his welcome, he has captured the hearts of
> crowds as completely as his air successes in China and also has
> captured their imaginations.
>
> He marched briskly to the platform, head high and perfectly
> poised, as the crowd outdid itself for him, and not a few
> spectators ducked their heads to hide their tears. Master of
> Ceremonies Fred Henson interviewed the 25-year-old flyer,
> bringing out many of the interesting experiences which
> Reed had recounted the day before in Marion. When asked
> whether dogfights in the air or public appearances were more
> nerve-wracking, Reed grinned and replied, "If I'd known what
> was going to happen when I got home, I might have stayed
> over there."
>
> Following Reed's talk, Orville Rennie, the manager of the
> Paramount Theater, launched the bond and stamp sales contest

as members of the drum corps passed among the crowd and sold stamp corsages and bonds in 15-minute periods for the army, navy and marine corps.

Monday brought a new speaking assignment for Bill. This time his job was to give a pep talk to workers for the LaPlante-Choate Manufacturing Company, which made crawler tractors and other construction equipment at its plant in Cedar Rapids. He would give numerous similar talks in the coming months, as the encouragement of factory workers was considered equally important to the war effort as the sale of War Bonds. Speaking from a platform on the plant floor while workers were on their lunch break, Bill lauded them for their recent increase in production and described the importance of their work to the troops overseas.

"You have no idea how much it helps the men out there fighting when they hear or read of the tremendous production job being done in the United States," the *Cedar Rapids Gazette* quoted Bill. "Although I never saw any LaPlante-Choate constructed machinery in action, I saw a lot of it crated on the docks of cities all over the country on my way home. I saw crates of material from other Cedar Rapids plants, too, and I'm afraid I made a pest of myself all the way home bragging about Cedar Rapids and the fact I lived so near here and knew a lot of people here.

"Speaking of knowing people, I see 20 or 30 fellows here from Marion. I wish I had time to visit with everyone but I don't have time. Since I got home I have had one opportunity to kiss my mother – and that's about all." After Bill's talk, the president of the CIO workers at the plant presented Bill with a carton of cigarettes with best wishes from the local union. This was a generous gesture, considering that cigarettes were rationed at the time. There is no evidence to suggest that Bill was a smoker, but surely someone in the Reed family made good use of the gift.

The rest of the week included a trip to Anamosa to visit family, a meeting in Des Moines and an appearance with Dick at Loras College in Dubuque, along with speeches to the Cedar Rapids Lions and Hi Twelve clubs and a presentation at McKinley High

School, also in Cedar Rapids. Finally, on Sunday, September 20, there was enough time for the Reed family to gather in Marion's Thomas Park for a reunion picnic before Dick had to return to duty in Rhode Island.

Bill's introduction to the "Stars Over America" tour came the next day in Des Moines. It is not surprising that its organizers in Iowa were quick to enlist Bill in the bond drive. Orville Rennie likely told his boss, G. Ralph Branton, general manager of the Tri-State Theater Corporation, about Bill after hearing the self-assured, handsome war hero speak in Cedar Rapids. Branton had strong ties to Hollywood, and within the week he had arranged for Bill to join one of the "Stars Over America" touring groups.

Accompanied by his mother, "Mick" Forbes and two others, Bill arrived at the Hotel Fort Des Moines in time to take his place on the speakers' platform in the Grand Ballroom before the start of the Stars and Bonds Luncheon. According to a story in the *Des Moines Register*, Bill was the top attraction, despite the presence of bond-tour celebrities including movie stars Claire Trevor, Ralph Bellamy, Richard Arlen (a star of the epic 1927 World War I flying movie, *Wings*), Walter Abel and Peggy Diggins, plus big-band vocalist Dorothy Cordray.

The event started with a sumptuous meal that included such delicacies as "Victory Veal with Doolittle Dressing," "Parisienne Bomb-de-Terres," "Flying Tiger Red Cabbage," "Old Glory Salad" with "Free French Dressing" and "Commando Cream Pie" for dessert. The program followed a now-familiar format, with Governor Wilson making opening remarks before Bill was introduced by the toastmaster and gave a talk. He spoke smoothly without notes, telling the audience about his experiences in the AVG with a "spontaneous and sincere" smile on his face, according the report in the *Des Moines Register*. "There was no groping for words, no hesitation. He innately seems to know the right thing to say and the right thing to do on any occasion," wrote reporter Betty Hoyt. The audience especially liked his comment that he wanted to get back into combat flying and would be unhappy if he were assigned to a more prosaic job, such as transport duty.

Actor Ralph Bellamy was particularly impressed with Bill, and he wrote later:

I was immediately captivated by his singular ability to stand before people and state so simply and clearly and with such sincerity and purpose what this war was all about.

When Bill finished his remarks, toastmaster Arthur Brayton introduced Mayme Reed, who was sitting at another table with "Mick." Bill rose from his seat and walked to Mayme's table to escort her to the platform and a seat of honor next to Claire Trevor. The audience rose as one to applaud the gesture.

Then the Hollywood stars took over to sell bonds. Bellamy – who had operated a repertory troupe in Des Moines in the late 1920s – served as master of ceremonies in selling the stars' talents. One man bought $50,000 worth of bonds to hear Trevor recite a poem. Arlen sold his necktie ("loud enough to serve as an air-raid warning," according to the *Des Moines Register*) for $30,000, and the Iowa-Des Moines National Bank paid $80,000 to hear Bellamy sing a corny song from one of his movies. At one point, the actor tried to stand on his head for $100 but fell into the footlights.

To close the luncheon, the lights went dim in the ballroom and the last message from Corregidor before the island fortress fell to the Japanese was rebroadcast. A silent prayer and the national anthem followed. Then Bill and the movie stars departed for a tour of ordnance plants in the Des Moines area. The total bond sales raised by the event, including a dance featuring the Claude Thornhill orchestra that evening, was $350,000.

It is natural to speculate what "Mick" Forbes was thinking as she saw Bill ascending into celebrity status. A picture of Bill and "Mick" in the *Des Moines Register* described her as his "girlfriend," but she had been waiting since high school for that status to upgrade. He had given her a jade ring from China a few days earlier, and she understood it to be a pre-engagement gesture – whatever that meant. Now she was seeing him mixing comfortably with movie stars, politicians and business tycoons. During a photo session for the Stars and Bonds Luncheon, she could not help but notice how Claire Trevor, a petite blonde with a "1,000-watt smile," glommed onto Bill and hooked her arm around his elbow as the cameras clicked. Did "Mick" and Bill have a future together? All she could do was watch and wonder.

It was already clear to the War Advertising Council that spotlighting returning combat veterans would be a powerful tool in the effort to convince American citizens to buy War Bonds. The veterans who, like Bill, could tell compelling stories and express heartfelt patriotism were irresistible to the civilian public, especially when accompanied by a cadre of glitzy Hollywood entertainers. Shortly after appearing in Des Moines, Bill agreed to join the "Stars Over America" tour full-time. This was a posh assignment for a guy who had spent the previous year in such rugged outposts as Toungoo, Magwe and Kunming. Bill would be traveling in first class on the train, eating in fine restaurants and staying in the best hotels.

Bill met up with his troupe on Wednesday, September 23, 1942, in Omaha, Nebraska. There, Bill was reunited with Walter Abel, who had shared the spotlight with him in Des Moines a few days earlier. Abel was a respected character actor on Broadway and in the movies. Also in the troupe were The Ritz Brothers (Al, Jimmy and Harry), a popular vaudeville song, dance and comedy team that began performing in 1925 and made the big jump to movies in 1934. Their forte was precision dance numbers, with a heathy helping of slapstick comedy mixed in. But the star attraction – in addition to Bill – was fashion model and movie starlet Jinx Falkenburg.

If ever someone fit the term "cover girl," it was Jinx Falkenburg. Tall and tanned with the slim, athletic figure of the tennis champion she was in her teens, Jinx was a classic brunette beauty of 23. Her all-American face and figure had graced the covers of magazines such as *LIFE*, *Redbook* and *Saturday Evening Post*, and in 1940 she had appeared in advertisements and on billboards after she was chosen as the first "Rheingold Girl" by a New York brewing company. She also was a rising star in Hollywood, and her current movie was the aptly titled *Lucky Legs*. Jinx's role in the War Bond appearances was primarily to look beautiful and feed punchlines to the Ritz Brothers.

She freely admitted to having limited talents in singing and dancing, but she was enough of an actress to pull this off due to her self-deprecating sense of humor and her natural charm.

When Jinx Falkenburg met Bill, she was already romantically involved with the man she later would marry, a New York newspaper reporter named "Tex" McCrary. But there is little doubt Bill made a strong impression on her. When she wrote her autobiography a decade later, the only detail she included about her participation in the "Stars Over America" tour was the fact that Bill was a member of her troupe. But a decade later, during an interview on television, she had this to say about Bill:

> He was one of the most outstanding young men I know I've ever met. I never was so impressed with anyone as I was with Bill Reed; and when we toured the country selling War Bonds together, he in his Flying Tiger uniform, and he would stand up in school rooms or in town halls or in auditoriums, wherever we spoke everyone just sat and listened intently to this boy, and would always be so moved by his spirit and his belief in what he was doing.

Did romance blossom between Bill and Jinx during the short period they spent on the tour? Rumors to that effect persist to this day, and it is certainly possible. Putting two attractive and charming young people out on the road together sounds like the setup for one of Jinx's B-movie plots. However, neither of them left any direct evidence to support the rumors. Whatever the case, they only had about a week together before Jinx and the Ritz Brothers left the tour to depart for a month-long trip to entertain troops in the Panama Canal Zone. The two said goodbye in Denver at the end of September, but Bill and Jinx would meet up again two years later under far different circumstances.

Meanwhile, a romance definitely had entered in Dick Reed's life. He married Mary Bourquard in South Orange, New Jersey, on September 26, 1942. Surely Bill would have attended and perhaps served as best man had he not been committed to the bond tour. John H. Porter, one of Dick's best buddies, stood in instead. A farm boy from Ohio, Porter would not survive the war. In fact, he never made it overseas. Porter was landing a P-47C Thunderbolt at Mitchel Field, Long Island, New York, when the plane skidded on the icy runway, hit a revetment and burst into flames. He was killed in the wreck. Several years after the war, Dick honored his best man by naming his son for his friend.[3]

BACK IN MARION

Bill returned home in late October 1942 after completing his commitment to the War Bonds tour. He would continue to honor requests to make personal appearances promoting bond sales and war production throughout the remainder of his time in the United States.

Bill's friend Orville Rennie invited him to the Paramount Theater in Cedar Rapids for a private showing of the new movie *Flying Tigers*, starring John Wayne. Bill gave a thumbnail critique to a newspaper reporter who also attended the screening, saying the movie was good entertainment with plenty of action and was no more exaggerated than most Hollywood offerings. "They've tried to glamorize the Flying Tigers, and it just can't be done," Bill said. "The Flying Tigers weren't glamorous – it was just hard work."

Back in Marion, Bill's first priority was to buy a car, and he was soon making the rounds in a snappy 1941 Plymouth convertible with whitewall tires. In it, he kept the long-delayed promise to go fishing with brother-in-law Joe Dumbolton, and he drove to Sioux Falls, South Dakota, to visit his sister Isabelle and her family. While there, he hunted pheasant with another brother-in-law, Gilbert Rathburn. Bill returned to Marion in time to participate in the Armistice Day observance there on November 11.

Then Bill met up with R. T. Smith, and the pair set off on a road trip to California. Their route took them first to Texarkana, Arkansas, where he paid a courtesy call to the family of his dead AVG buddy, Neil Martin. "Perhaps if fate is kind one day I shall come back to the States and have an opportunity to visit you and Neil's parents,"

Bill had written to Neil's wife from China back in May. Now he was taking that opportunity. The next stop was San Antonio, Texas, where Bill renewed friendships with pilots from his training days at Randolph and Kelly fields and applied for reinstatement in the USAAF. It is likely he had some speaking engagements with the cadets in flying schools there as well. From San Antonio, he and Smith headed west across New Mexico and Arizona, arriving in Los Angeles on December 3. They rented an apartment on Wilshire Boulevard in Westwood with the intent of having some fun before they got serious about addressing their futures. Not much is known about the month Bill spent in Los Angeles, except the contents of a single note he wrote to Mayme around Christmas:

> Just a note to let you know that all is well. Am really enjoying a swell rest. May go to work for Paramount next week while I wait for my reinstatement papers to go through. I took my physical yesterday out at Santa Ana and passed with flying colors. According to the results I am in better shape than I ever was.

Bill did, in fact, spend time on the set of a Paramount movie titled *China* on January 3, 1943, just before his return trip to Marion. The movie told the story of a pair of American adventurers in China at the outbreak of World War II, and it starred Loretta Young, Alan Ladd and William Bendix. Bill served as a technical advisor for *China*, although flying was not central to the plot of the movie. His Paramount friends in Iowa, Orville Rennie and Ralph Branton, already had dreams of launching a movie career for Bill after the war.

Bill was not back in Marion long before he received his reinstatement orders from the USAAF. "2Lt William N. Reed, serial number O-398589, should report immediately to I Fighter Command at Mitchel Field, on Long Island, New York." He had gotten his wish to go back into fighter operations.

PART THREE

Back to China

10

"I felt a hit in my engine"

It was January 1943, and Bill Reed was heading back into the USAAF. But he had to attend to a few details first. He retrieved his China souvenirs – among them several teakwood chests, two hand-embroidered robes, hand-carved ebony and ivory elephants and two silk "Flying Tiger" banners – from the front window of the Boston store in downtown Marion, where they had been on display, and placed them in storage. He arranged for brother-in-law Joe Dumbolton to take care of his Plymouth and he stripped the CAF decorations from his uniforms. He left for Chicago on the weekend of January 9–10, 1943, and from there he flew to New York.

While in Chicago, he called his sister Leota Shesler and learned that she and her family were having money problems. In typical Bill fashion, he solved this by arranging to buy War Bonds valued at $500 from the Sheslers so that they would have cash to pay their bills. It was not the first time Bill stepped in to help members of the family with money woes, and it would not be the last.

He arrived at Mitchel Field on Monday, January 11, and checked in at I Fighter Command headquarters. He spent the next few days processing back into military life. Although he was now back to the rank of second lieutenant, he was told that his promotion to major had been approved, which meant he would be skipping the ranks of first lieutenant and captain. Bill also learned that his duty station would be the new fighter training base at Millville, New Jersey.

It had been six months since Bill had piloted an airplane, and he lost no time getting back into a cockpit. He had to wait two days for the weather to cooperate, but on Wednesday, January 13, Bill was able to take his first flight. He reported in a letter to Mayme:

> Flew a P-40 yesterday, for the first flying I've done so far. I didn't spin in, so now I think things will be all right. Tomorrow, weather permitting, I'm going to try to check out in one of the P-47s. They look like a big piece of machinery – and are – 14,000lb.

Bill's buddy R. T. Smith was also at Mitchel and destined for Millville, and the two of them made a foray into New York City on Wednesday night. Through Bill's connection to actor Walter Abel, they managed to meet and enjoy the company of famed restaurateur Vincent Sardi and noted actress, writer and stage producer Katharine Cornell. Then on Saturday Bill went to Philadelphia for a brief stopover on his way to Millville.

Millville Army Air Field, about 40 miles south of Philadelphia, was a brand-new facility that must have reminded Bill of his days on the raw field at Selma, Alabama, in 1941. Spread over 14,000 acres of former forest and farmland, including a spot where members of the Millville Flying Club previously operated a grass-covered airstrip, the base had four concrete runways and facilities – hangars, shops, barracks and other buildings – to support the operation of 125 single-engined fighter planes.

Millville served dual purposes. Its primary job was to provide gunnery training for fighter pilots preparing for combat tours overseas, and it also provided air defense for Philadelphia and the surrounding areas, should that be needed. Air-to-ground gunnery practice took place on a target range just south of the runways, where pilots could strafe and bomb full-scale replicas of ships, bridges, tanks, trucks and railroads. Air-to-air gunnery practice, in which fighter pilots shot at a banner towed behind a utility aircraft, took place on ranges over nearby Delaware Bay and the Atlantic Ocean off the New Jersey coast.[1]

One of the first men Bill met at Millville was another Bill – Capt William L. Turner. Like Bill Reed, Bill Turner was a combat veteran, credited with shooting down three Japanese planes over Java and New Guinea during 1942.[2] The two got off to a rocky start when Bill was assigned to the training squadron that Turner commanded. As a captain, Turner outranked Bill, who was still a second lieutenant while he awaited his promotion to major.

In later years, Turner liked to tell how his new subordinate projected a lax attitude when attending to his duties, to the point where Turner decided he would have to talk to Bill about it. As one of the very few pilots in Training Command with combat experience, it is not much wonder that Bill was not taking his new assignment seriously. Another factor was the continuing requests for him to speak to civic groups about his experiences in the AVG. The USAAF was eager for him to honor those requests, which required him to travel off-base often. But Turner apparently was unaware of these factors.

On February 4, Turner was walking toward his office when who should he spot coming the other way but Bill Reed with a shiny new major's oak leaf insignia on his collar. His promotion had come through that morning. Turner snapped off a salute to his superior officer and promptly canceled plans to chew him out. Instead, the pair had an amicable chat comparing notes about their combat experiences, and a solid friendship formed.[3]

Within a few days, Bill was reassigned as Millville's assistant director of training. His new boss was none other than Maj R. T. Smith, whose promotion to major predated Bill's by a short period. The two buddies would partner in developing a syllabus for the training program at Millville and then monitoring its application. Their first task was to familiarize themselves with the Republic P-47 Thunderbolts that the trainees would be flying. To do so, they spent quite a few hours in the air during early February, flying the new fighter to learn its strengths and weaknesses. They could not teach new pilots how to fight in the P-47 until they determined that for themselves.

Bill was not impressed with the Thunderbolt. Built to meet the USAAC's 1940 specification for a "super fighter" – 400mph top speed, 40,000ft ceiling and heavy armament – the P-47 was huge by contemporary standards. Its wingspan exceeded 40ft, it weighed upwards of seven tons fully loaded and its engine was a turbo-supercharged Pratt & Whitney R-2800 radial pumping out 2,000hp. The P-47s at Millville were mostly early B-models, which the USAAF already had determined to be unsuitable for combat. Bill agreed with that assessment, finding the planes were slow climbers with heavy control loads, a propensity for aileron snatching and marginal spin recovery. Engine unreliability was another problem.[4] All these issues and more would be addressed in subsequent models of the Thunderbolt, and it would go on to become the most-produced and one of the most effective American fighters of the war. But in a letter he wrote that spring, Bill referred to the P-47 as the "Repulsive Scatterbolt," an unflattering nickname that reflected his low opinion of the plane.

Regardless of Bill's opinion of the P-47, training proceeded at a rapid pace. During February, the 353rd FG began rotating pilots through Millville for gunnery training in preparation for their deployment to England. The training must have been effective, for the 353rd would go on to post an outstanding combat record with the Eighth Air Force.

Bill stayed busy on the weekends at Millville by sampling the night life that Philadelphia had to offer, often in partnership with R. T. Smith. He met a nice English girl named Doris Head and had several dates with her before Doris made the mistake of broaching the subject of marriage. Their relationship went no further. Bill also made the acquaintance of a pretty young woman named Mary Patch. He met her at a nightclub in New York but quickly found out that her husband was playing in the band at the club. Despite that complication, Bill and Mary kept in touch for nearly two years. On another February weekend, Bill went to South Orange, New Jersey, for a visit to "Nephie" Dick's wife, Mary, who was four months pregnant at the time. Bill would not be seeing Dick during the visit, however, as the younger Reed had shipped out with his squadron for overseas duty the previous month.

POSTING ABROAD

The chattering of the teletype at the 325th FG headquarters in Hillsgrove, Rhode Island, on New Year's Day 1943 spat out news that everyone in the outfit had been expecting for weeks. Special Order Number One from Headquarters Boston Air Defense Command ordered the group with its three squadrons – the 317th, 318th and 319th FSs – to proceed by rail without delay to Langley Field, Virginia, in preparation for a move to a combat theater.

The timing could have been better for 1Lt William R. "Dick" Reed[5] of the 317th FS. Married just three months, Dick and his wife Mary had learned recently that their first child was on the way, the birth expected in early July. Eager as Dick may have been to get into combat, leaving now would mean missing the bulk of Mary's pregnancy, the birth of their child and the first months of the baby's life. But orders were orders, so on January 2 Dick packed his bags and met his buddies for the bus ride to the South Boston railroad depot, where they would catch a troop train bound for Norfolk, Virginia. After traveling all night, the train pulled in to the Norfolk station at 1100hrs the next day, and the men rode buses to nearby Langley Field. Meanwhile, Mary prepared to move to her parents' home in New Jersey, where she planned to stay until Dick returned from overseas.

At Langley, Dick learned that the 325th was being re-equipped with new P-40F Warhawk fighters for its combat assignment. This plane was an upgraded version of the Tomahawks and Kittyhawks that Bill had flown in the AVG, featuring a Packard-built Rolls-Royce Merlin engine that provided slightly better performance at high altitude. Otherwise, the P-40F handled and performed similarly to the earlier P-40 models.

The other news was that the USAAF planned to load the 325th FG pilots and their aircraft onto an aircraft carrier, which would deliver them offshore of their overseas destination. Once in position, the P-40 pilots would fly off the carrier and land at their new base. This plan was disconcerting to Dick and the others, none of whom had ever boarded, much less taken off from, an aircraft carrier. It was not unprecedented, however, as P-40s had previously been delivered successfully by carrier to locations as diverse as Midway Island, Iceland and North Africa.

After six days of its pilots practicing short takeoffs on a runway marked with the outline of a carrier deck, the 325th was pronounced ready. An unusual – and loud – sight greeted the residents of Norfolk, Virginia, on January 8 when Dick and the other pilots taxied their P-40s down the main street of the town to the harbor area for delivery dockside to USS *Ranger* (CV-4). Then, one by one, the P-40s, with pilots still in their cockpits, were craned onto the deck of the big ship.[6]

Delivering the P-40s by aircraft carrier made good sense. With an effective range of 1,150 miles, the planes could not cross an ocean in flight, and delivering them by ship in crates required reassembly at their destination – an inefficient use of time. On the other hand, there was a risk that the entire 325th FG could be lost at once if an enemy submarine were to sink *Ranger*. Security was paramount ("Loose lips sink ships"), and it was only once they were at sea that the pilots learned of their destination – Casablanca, Morocco, on the west coast of North Africa. The ocean crossing passed uneventfully, and the pilots all enjoyed a steak dinner on their last night aboard ship. The next morning, January 19, 1943, 72 P-40s took off from *Ranger* and flew to Cazes airdrome near Casablanca.

Dick did not leave a description of his takeoff from *Ranger*, but one of his squadronmates, Herschel Green, recalled that the US Navy had calculated that the P-40s could get off in 425ft of carrier deck with the ship at top speed heading into the wind. The pilot would set the brakes, advance the throttle to full military power and select 15 degrees of flaps down. When the ship's Landing Signal Officer flagged him away, the pilot would release the brakes and hope like hell the roaring Merlin engine would drag the P-40 into the sky before the plane ran out of deck. "Lady Luck" smiled on the 325th FG, and all 72 P-40s took off safely for the flight to dry land.[7]

A few days later, Dick's squadron moved from Cazes to Tafaroui ("where the mud is very gooey") airfield, a few miles south of Oran, and set up tents for living quarters. Dick wrote his first letter home to Mary on January 26 to give her his new mailing address. He also told her, "Am in Africa as you probably thought. Am roughing it, but don't mind it. Miss you plenty."

Dick Reed's logbook showed he had 429 hours and 10 minutes of flight time when he arrived in North Africa. He may have thought that was plenty of experience to prepare him for flying combat missions, but the Twelfth Air Force had other ideas. In the two months since arriving in North Africa as part of the Operation *Torch* invasion, the Twelfth's five other fighter groups had learned some valuable – and painful – lessons during their initial encounters with the Luftwaffe. The plan now was to pass along these lessons to the 325th pilots before they entered combat. Lt Col Phil Cochran of the 33rd FG, a highly experienced P-40 pilot just back from the front in Western Tunisia, arrived to brief the new pilots. He explained the importance of using the "finger-four" formation, in which four planes flew in roughly line-abreast so the pilots could watch each other's tails and be in position to turn into any enemy aircraft attacking from the rear. He also urged them to fly at 8,000–9,000ft altitude, where enemy small-arms fire could not reach them and their P-40s had a maneuverability advantage over German fighters.[8]

So far, Dick's war had provided a prime example of the old US Army axiom, "Hurry up and wait." Other than a few practice flights, his first month in North Africa had produced little to write home about. This changed on February 18 when the commanding officer of the 317th FS was reassigned and Dick was appointed as the new CO. This came as quite a shock to everyone, including Dick, because he was still a first lieutenant and squadron commanders usually held the rank of captain or major. But Dick adapted quickly, as he reported in a letter to Bill not long afterward:

> Mary probably told you about my getting the squadron. I must say, I was really a surprised individual. Really enjoy it though, now that I am accustomed to the new position. Lots more work than before, but it keeps my mind more occupied and gives me less time to be lonesome. Am getting plenty to eat – have a good sack fixed up in my tent, so I sleep pretty well and there isn't a thing that I need, with the exception of a bath and a shave which is no exception over here. Mind you now, I don't go completely without them. It's just a little longer between the times when I can get them.

By this time the 33rd FG had suffered substantial losses, including many P-40s destroyed on the ground at Thelepte, its exposed air base near the front in western Tunisia. In order to make good the losses, the 325th was ordered to turn over two dozen of its P-40s to the 33rd. This left the 325th with only enough planes to equip two squadrons. When the group received orders on April 5 to move two squadrons to the frontline airfield at Montesquieu, in Algeria, Dick and the other two squadron commanders drew straws to see which squadron would have to remain behind. Dick drew the short straw and had the frustrating experience of watching the 318th and 319th FSs take off to join the war while his squadron waited at Tafaroui so its complement of P-40s could be brought up to strength.

Five more weeks would pass before Dick received orders to lead his 317th FS to Montesquieu and join the others. The Germans in North Africa surrendered on May 13, 1943, bringing the campaign to a close before Dick's squadron had had a chance to fly a single mission. Dick need not have worried himself about it, however. The action was just getting started for the 325th FG.

With the end of the fighting in North Africa, the Allied leaders immediately began preparing for their next move – the invasion of Italy. The first step was to eliminate the threat posed by the

Italian-held island of Pantelleria, a 42-square-mile rock off the coast of Tunisia that bristled with observation posts, direction-finding radios, fortified artillery posts and a large airfield with underground hangars carved into a rock cliff. Taking Pantelleria would clear the way for Operation *Husky*, the invasion of Sicily. Another part of the plan involved neutralizing Axis air units on the island of Sardinia to prevent them from assisting in the defense of Sicily. Dick Reed and his 317th FS would fly missions against targets on all three islands.

Group Mission No. 26, on May 19, would be the first time that all three squadrons of the 325th FG would take part in the same operation. Dick Reed would be leading his 317th FS into action for the first time, too. The orders called for the P-40s to escort Martin B-26 Marauder medium bombers sent to attack Decimomannu airdrome on Sardinia, just north of the port city of Cagliari.

Dick arrayed his squadron in four-plane flights around the bomber formation as the strike proceeded north to the west coast of Sardinia, then turned onto a southeast heading toward the target at 13,000ft. To everyone's disappointment, the target was obscured by clouds, which made the results of the bombing questionable. Defending Messerschmitt Bf 109 fighters surprised the Americans near the target, and several large dogfights broke out. Dick's flight was not involved in the action, although he was close enough to see an aircraft fall in flames from one of the dogfights while he was maintaining escort position near the bombers. All of Dick's P-40s returned safely to the base at Montesquieu.

Later, as Dick was walking from his plane toward the operations tent for the mission debriefing, he encountered 1Lt Herschel Green. As Green recalled the day in his book, *Herky*, Dick greeted him with, "Hey, Herky. Did you see that big dogfight that broke out just as we turned east over the coast? I never saw anything like it. There were about six or eight airplanes, and they all were going in all directions. It was spectacular." "Yes, I saw it," Green replied. "It was me and six 109s."

During the debriefing, Dick was able to confirm the 317th's first aerial victory for 1Lt "Herky" Green. In a discussion later, Dick and his pilots decided that the Germans had been able to surprise the 317th because the Americans were flying their four-plane formations too tightly, requiring wingmen to concentrate too much on maintaining position on their leaders when they needed to be watching the sky behind them. The next time out, Dick's squadron would loosen up its formation.[9]

The following day's orders sent Dick's squadron to Pantelleria for a strafing mission against the airfield there. The P-40s dove to just above the waves as they approached the island and spread out in a line-abreast formation when they crossed the beach. Streams of tracer bullets arced toward them as the P-40s flashed across the airfield with guns blazing, but few targets presented themselves to Dick and his pilots. They limited themselves to a single pass over the target and stayed low as they withdrew over the sea on the far side of the island. Some pilots reported that the enemy's coastal artillery fired at them, the shells throwing up big columns of water when they hit. Fortunately, none of the P-40 pilots flew into the water spouts, which could have been disastrous for them. Again, all planes returned safely to Montesquieu.[10]

Dick shot down his first enemy plane on May 21. The mission was a follow-up strike by B-26s against Decimomannu airdrome, with P-40s providing escort. Dick's squadron was assigned high cover and was at 16,000ft when Bf 109s attacked over the airdrome. Dick provided a terse description of the action in his Combat Claim Report:

> When four Me-109s dove for the bombers I went after one, and shot several bursts as I followed him down. When he crashed I was nearly on the deck.

Dick described what happened next in a letter to Bill:

> Got in on another one after that, but three of us were loading him up with lead when he went in, so we drew to see who got him, and I didn't. Got a lot of satisfaction out of it anyhow. I was on his tail, my wingman was above and inside shooting down at

him, and the other one had a belly to shoot at – some deal – we were right on the water when the old boy just flipped over and went right in.

By the end of May, Dick had completed eight combat missions and was recommended for his first Air Medal in recognition for shooting down the Bf 109 on May 21. But when he wrote to his mother on June 5 he never mentioned being in combat, preferring to tell her about an "Arab celebration" that he and other officers attended at the invitation of a local French official. He was obviously taking a page out of Bill's book when it came to writing letters to his family. Dick completed 12 more missions in June, and the 325th FG moved to a new base at Mateur, in Tunisia, on June 21. Shortly after that, Dick was granted several days of rest and relaxation leave, which he spent in the famous Egyptian coastal city Alexandria.

Also during June, the 325th FG adopted distinctive markings for its P-40s by painting black and yellow squares on their tail surfaces. As the 325th's successes mounted, the press coined the nickname "Checkertails" for the group, and the moniker has lasted to this day. Dick's assigned aircraft was P-40F-15-CU 41-19895. Its camouflage colors were Olive Drab over Neutral Gray. In addition to the checkered tail, its markings included a large, white 10 on the fuselage (denoting the commander of the 317th FS) and the name "*Queen Mary*" (for his wife) on both sides of the engine cowling. Other markings included the names of Dick and his crew chief, SSgt J. M. Nixon, below the windshield on the port side, and a string of white mission markings – one for each combat flight Dick had completed – on the starboard side.

The number of mission markers on "*Queen Mary*" stood at 27 when Capt Dick Reed led 16 P-40s of his squadron away from Mateur on the afternoon of July 10, 1943. Their destination was Sicily, where Allied troops had just started coming ashore in Operation *Husky*. As the P-40s flew eastward, they picked up a formation of North American B-25 Mitchell medium bombers that they were to escort in an attack on Trapani Milo airdrome

at the western end of the island. The other two squadrons of the
325th FG took their positions toward the front of the formation,
while the 317th FS covered the rear.

Dick had no way of knowing it, but back in New Jersey his
wife, Mary, just then was going into labor. She would deliver their
daughter, Dianne, the following day. But by that time Dick would
be concentrating on saving his own life rather than contemplating
the arrival of his first-born child into the world.

As the strike formation neared its target from the seaward side,
Dick noticed that the B-25s he was covering were drifting away
from the rest of the bombers. Just then, he spotted some 25 Bf 109s
queuing up for an attack. He was unable to contact the rest of the
main body of P-40s, so he ordered three flights of the 317th to stay
with the bombers while he led his flight of four in an attack against
the enemy fighters. Dick picked out one of the Bf 109s and went
at it head-on. Unfortunately for him, his P-40 took a hit from the
heavy cannon carried by the Messerschmitt before he could bring
his own guns to bear.[11] Several months later, Dick described the
action to a newspaper reporter:

> I felt a hit in my engine and it started to smoke. I tried to
> throttle [back] but nothing happened. Then I knew that the
> engine had been hit and it probably would catch fire. I bailed
> out at 2,500ft at about 5:30 p.m. I was mad, too, because I
> missed a good steak supper and ice cream they had at the base
> that night.
>
> I felt the chute open and then one of the German pilots tried
> to machine-gun me. I felt something hit the chute. The pilot
> must have figured he got me or received a call of conscience,
> because he didn't come back. He just about got me at that,
> because my heart almost stopped.

Once his heart rate returned to normal, Dick checked himself
over and realized he was uninjured. He continued to drop in his
parachute until he landed in the sea about five miles off the coast
of Sicily. With his "Mae West" life jacket keeping him afloat, Dick

released the inflatable dinghy from his parachute pack, pumped it up and hoisted himself into the tiny craft. It was getting dark by this time, so he settled in for an uncomfortable night afloat. While lying there in the darkness he watched night bombers make another raid on Trapani. When dawn broke, Dick spotted a lighthouse on a tiny island not far away and began paddling toward it. He reached land at about 1030hrs and went ashore to find the island was nothing more than a rock poking out of the sea with an unmanned lighthouse on it. He tried opening the lighthouse door, but it was locked, so he entered through a window. He pulled the dinghy into the lighthouse and turned it over to use it as a bed.

Dick sat on his lonely rock for seven days, subsisting on the emergency rations packed in the dinghy. His water supply soon ran out, and his thirst began driving him crazy. He began going swimming five or six times a day to convince himself that he was not thirsty. He could see fishing boats in the distance from time to time, but none of them came near the island until July 18. Then, seeing a boat approaching, Dick launched his dinghy back into the water and began paddling toward the vessel. He was hoping to convince the fishermen on the boat to give him water and to agree to bring him supplies at the lighthouse until the Allies captured Sicily.

On reaching the boat, Dick gave the men 500 lira from his emergency kit and got the water he wanted, but he also got some bad news – the Germans had forbidden fishermen from approaching the lighthouse island, so they would not be able to supply him. With no other options, Dick allowed the fishermen to row him ashore, where Italian soldiers immediately took him into custody and escorted him to their headquarters. There, clad only in his shorts, Dick got a real "tongue lashing" (his term) from an Italian captain before being sent on to the local jail, where the local police treated him well for six days before American paratroopers captured the area and freed him.

Dick then hitch-hiked across Sicily to an American-held airfield, where he caught a flight back to North Africa. He was reunited with his squadron at Mateur on July 27, 1943. Three months later, Dick Reed was awarded a Distinguished Flying Cross (DFC) for the "skill, aggressiveness and skillful leadership" he displayed during the July 10 mission.

Dick returned to flight operations just three days after rejoining the 317th FS. Now flying P-40F-10 41-14496, he led 20 Warhawks of his squadron, along with 16 more from the 319th FS, on a fighter sweep over southern Sardinia on July 30. They reached the target area and cruised for an hour at 9,000ft before the action started. Keeping a sharp eye for trouble, Dick's pilots got their reward when they spotted about 30 Bf 109s approaching from the rear near Sassari. A huge dogfight broke out, and 12 more enemy fighters soon joined in. Fighters were twisting and turning all over the sky, occasionally one falling in flames. This time Dick got his revenge, as he described on his Combat Claim Form:

I approached an Me-109 from the rear, both of us climbing. I fired a long burst, and saw him roll and dive. I turned sharply away and lost sight of him.

Capt Bunn Hearn, Jr., Dick's wingman, reported seeing the Bf 109 crash, which confirmed the victory for his CO. The mission was the most successful yet for the 317th FS. Only one P-40 was missing when the unit returned to Mateur, its pilot later reported a PoW. In return, the 317th was credited with shooting down no fewer than 21 enemy planes, although actual German losses were not that high. Later, the squadron was awarded a Distinguished Unit Citation for the mission.

With the invasion of Sicily well in hand, the 325th FG increased its attacks against airfields and industrial sites on Sardinia. Dick continued piling up missions, completing ten operations in August and seven more in September. He had a close call during a mission on August 26 when he flew through power lines while strafing. His P-40 was badly damaged, but Dick managed to nurse it back to a crash landing at Mateur. His luck held, and he walked away from the wrecked plane unhurt.

Dick and his squadron got a break from combat on September 22, 1943, when the 325th FG turned in its aging P-40s and began transition training in the P-47 Thunderbolt. Along with the new planes – the same type that Bill Reed had been flying in New Jersey – the 325th got a new job. The group was transferred to the newly formed Fifteenth Air Force, where its primary assignment would be escorting heavy bombers on long-range missions over southern Europe. Training on the big P-47s took two months, hampered by bad weather and slow deliveries of the new planes. In early November, the group moved from muddy Mateur to the airfield at Solimon, in Tunisia, where it could fly from a paved runway. Although Bill Reed had a low opinion of the P-47, Dick's pilots soon learned to appreciate their powerful new fighters, which were upgraded versions with better performance and reliability than the ones Bill flew in Training Command.

By early December, the Allies had invaded southern Italy and were developing air bases on the Foggia Plain, an area on the eastern side of the Italian "boot" roughly opposite Rome. The groundcrew of the 325th FG departed North Africa for their new base at Foggia Main on December 1–3, and the pilots followed in their P-47s on December 9.

The first P-47 mission was an escort of bombers attacking targets in Greece, and no opposition was encountered. The next five operations were similar "milk runs," and Dick finished his combat tour of 50 missions by the end of the month. Dick, now wearing the oak leaves of a major on his uniform like "Unc" Bill, left Italy for home in January 1944 with a proud record to show for his year spent overseas. His decorations included the DFC and the Air Medal with nine Oak Leaf Clusters. He arrived in the US a month later and saw his new daughter, Dianne, for the first time on February 24, 1944.

Maj William R. "Dick" Reed spent the rest of the war in Texas, flying in Air Training Command. He separated from the USAAF on December 15, 1945, at Randolph Field.[12] Dick had done his fair share of fighting and brought home deep insights into air combat earned the hard way. Imparting his knowledge to new pilots heading off to battle was an important contribution to the war effort. Besides, he had the welfare of his wife and child to consider now, too.

Maj William N. "Bill" Reed had a different view of training command. To his way of thinking, it was a waste of his time for him to be training new combat pilots when he was fully capable of doing more fighting himself. Unlike Dick, Bill had experienced the frustration of being on the losing side of a campaign. He – and the entire AVG – had fought well, but the Japanese nevertheless had pushed the Allies out of Burma on his watch. He wanted another crack at the enemy.

Bill was determined that his training assignment at Millville would be short term. It was not long before he was offered an assignment in Alaska's Aleutian Islands. He was quick to turn that down. A plan was forming in the back of his mind – he would figure out a way to return to China and resume flying for Gen Chennault.

"Some scheme afoot in Washington"

Bill Reed's prospects for returning to combat took an upward turn when orders arrived at Millville in March 1943 transferring him to the USAAF School of Applied Tactics for a special course in fighter tactics and administration. This was good news, not only because the course would help prepare Bill to take on the responsibilities of a combat command, but also because the school was located in Orlando, Florida, providing him with a respite from New Jersey's dreary winter weather.

In Florida, Bill found himself on yet "another camp where the place is still unfinished" where "the darn quarters at the school are a mess," as he described Orlando Army Air Base in a letter to his mother. After a short time roughing it on the former civilian airfield, Bill was able to move into town and take up residence in the San Juan Hotel, which boasted 250 rooms with private baths. He appreciated Florida's warm weather, and he was pleased to reunite with several other ex-AVG pilots, most notably Maj Charlie Bond, commander of the school's 81st FS.

As Bond described the course Bill was taking, "realistic combat tactics and techniques were taught to members of newly activated fighter groups of the rapidly expanding USAAF."[1] The school worked its pupils hard. The first phase of the course involved classwork, which began at 0715hrs and ran all day. When the flying started in the second phase, Bill often did not get home until

1900hrs. And requests for speeches still came in for Bill. While in Florida, he spoke to several civic organizations, including the Lions Club and Red Cross in nearby Kissimee.

Early April found Bill back at Millville. The training program there, particularly the ground gunnery practice, continued to be hampered by rain and wind. But Bill was able to get out on the skeet-shooting range several times and reported in a letter that he was getting pretty good at it. Shooting skeet was considered good practice for fighter pilots, because the shooter is required to lead the target to hit it, similar to what a pilot must do when trying to shoot down an enemy aircraft in flight.

A major change had taken place at Millville while Bill was away. R. T. Smith had received a transfer to California, and in his place as director of training was Lt Col Bill Schwartz, who had transferred from the 353rd FG to take the job. Bill did not adjust well to his new boss, as he described in a letter to Mayme on April 6:

> In my absence a new director of training was appointed to take Bob Smith's place. He is Col. Schwartz, and to say he is an eager guy is a gross understatement. Everyone is hopping around here, most of them not knowing what they are doing, but looking busy just the same. I am the assistant director, and so far he has not told me exactly what he wanted me to do. I have already had one good argument with him, and I think that soon I will be on my way out of here. I will be glad to get out, too.

Bill was right. Within a few weeks orders arrived sending him to Mitchel Field and shortly after that on to Westover Field, in western Massachusetts, as a combat instructor. But before Bill left for his new assignment, he made a quick trip to Washington, D.C., where Gen Chennault was attending meetings at the War Department. Bill's goal was to meet up with Chennault to request an assignment to China, but he missed the general by about five minutes and had to return to Millville empty-handed. Meanwhile, the war was reaching deeper into his family and friends back in Marion. Laurence Martin joined the USAAF, hoping to follow his half-brother Dick Reed and Uncle Bill into flight training.[2] And Bill's old flame "Mick" Forbes announced plans to join the US Marine Corps.

Bill arrived at Westover Field during the third week of May 1943. Westover, like Millville, was a replacement training center for P-47 pilots preparing to go overseas. Also like Millville it served a secondary purpose, providing air defense for the New England area. Bill had this to say about his new surroundings in a May 27 letter:

> It's a swell field, but I can't say much for the surrounding towns. Springfield, Mass., and Chicopee Falls are the two nearest towns. Am sitting around here now waiting to get a flight up. Still flying the P-47, and still don't think much of it.

Three weeks later Bill got a new assignment at Westover when he was appointed the CO of one of the fighter training squadrons there. This was Bill's first military command, and like Dick had found out several months earlier when he assumed command of the 317th FS in North Africa, taking on the added responsibility of command was a major adjustment. Bill described his new job to his mother in a June 6 letter:

> Have really got my troubles now, for they have made me c.o. of the "Fighting" 320th Squadron. What a job. Guess it will be easier when I get things running smoothly. This is a squadron in the parent group[3] of the New York Wing, and as such it's not a normal squadron. In the first place, it has about three times as many pilots and personnel as it should, and they are constantly moving large bunches either in or out. I have a swell bunch of kids working with me. A few of them knew Bill II [Dick]. I usually get up at 4:30 and am here on the flight line until dark. You can bet that I just eat supper and then flop in my bunk.

Got my first sunburn of the season yesterday while out in the command car talking some of my trainees in on their first P-47 ride. The weather hasn't been too good for flying, but has improved considerably the last few days.

The "swell bunch of kids" working for Bill in the 320th FS included his operations officer, Capt George Parker, whom Bill described as "a honey."[4] Parker's experience in the South Pacific early in the war and his months in training duties paid off a year later when he got a combat assignment to China. As a member of the 5th FG, Parker shot down a Japanese fighter on July 13, 1944. His luck would run out nine days later, however, when he was killed in an accident while taking off from a remote Chinese airfield.[5] Another member of Bill's staff was 1Lt Armit W. "Bill" Lewis from Colorado. He, too, would get a combat assignment to China, serving there again under Bill Reed and becoming one of his closest friends.

Bill's July 6 letter to Mayme reported that the 320th FS "is shaping up nicely," but there was even bigger news to pass along:

There is some scheme afoot in Washington to get all the ex-AVG members back with Gen. Chennault for some special work in China. Think I'm going to Washington in the next couple of days on it. If I'm to go over, and it's definite that I will sometime anyway, there isn't anyone I'd want to be with half so much as Chennault.

Shortly after writing the letter, Bill was granted a short leave to visit his hometown. While in Marion, he sold his Plymouth convertible that brother-in-law Joe Dumbolton had been taking care of for him on the assumption that he would be getting an overseas assignment soon. On arrival back at Westover on July 24, he learned that plans were afoot to give him a new job as air inspector for the 326th FG, a step up from his current position. But those plans never came to pass. Instead, Bill got what he really wanted: orders sending him back into combat. His destination – Maj Gen

Claire L. Chennault's Fourteenth Air Force in China. The "special work" was about to begin.

Bill Reed's second departure for the Far East might have been considered a comedy of errors, had there been any humor in the fact that he was heading back to the war. After clearing out of Westover Field, he made his way to New York and took a room in the Hotel Pennsylvania while awaiting transportation. While there, he wrote to Mayme requesting her to buy a strongly built box to ship items to him such as extra uniforms, gloves and flying boots, as he would be traveling overseas by air this time and his baggage allowance would be limited. Bill expected to be in New York for several days, so he sent out a load of laundry for cleaning. Then the phone rang, and he was told to get himself out to La Guardia Field on the double to catch a plane bound for Miami. Not only was he unable to retrieve half of his laundry, he also left his toilet kit in his hotel room by mistake.

Bill's flight arrived in Florida on August 10, and he reported to the First District headquarters of the Miami Area, Army Air Forces, where he was assigned to a room in the Hotel Floridian. While in Miami, he took care of some final details, including setting up a $250-per-month allotment to his mother's bank account and drawing field equipment. He had time to make a quick deep-sea fishing outing and then set out with a friend on August 12 for a final steak dinner in downtown Miami.

Waiting for Bill and its other passengers on the tarmac at Miami Airport the next morning was a four-engined Douglas C-54 Skymaster, USAAF serial number 41-20138. The plane would carry 26 passengers from Miami to Karachi by flying south to Brazil, then east across the Atlantic Ocean, the African continent and the Middle East. Bill's companions on the trip were several officers who, like him, ultimately were bound for combat assignments in China. He bonded most closely with Lt Col Irving L. "Twig" Branch. Born in Iowa in 1912, Branch had been a USAAC pilot since 1935 and spent the early part of the war on anti-submarine duty over the Atlantic. His new job would be to help organize and later command a B-25 medium bomber group that was forming in Karachi. Another fellow traveler, Capt Bill Dick, would later command one of the B-25 squadrons in Branch's group.

A week of long days in the air was ahead. Under the command of a pilot named Roberts, the C-54 took off from Miami at 0535hrs and landed at Borinquen Field in Puerto Rico almost five hours later. After a 30-minute stop to refuel, the plane again took to the air and flew for a further five hours to Atkinson Field, in British Guinea, to stop for the night. With an average speed of 200mph, the C-54 had covered roughly 2,000 miles in the first day of the trip.

Bill had restarted his diary in Miami, and as it was in his AVG diary, Bill's writing is clear and colorful. He reported this impression of his first stopping place on the journey:

> Found Atkinson Field a most delightful place with fine barracks, a good officers mess, and a fine club. Wrote four or five letters, and Col. Branch and I had a couple of beers while we listened to a colored boy play a little "boogie woogie" on the piano. The place here is literally hacked out of the jungle, and the air is filled with the voices of myriad unseen insects. Already I can feel that unmistakable tingle that speaks of adventure in the offing.

The passengers and crew turned in early because the next day's flight was set to depart at 0140hrs. Bill and Branch grabbed the front seats in the cabin and quickly dozed off to sleep after takeoff. The C-54 crossed the Equator at 0420hrs, and Bill noted in his diary entry for that day that it was his seventh crossing, "so I was an old 'shellback' amongst a bunch of 'polliwogs'." The plane continued south across the mouth of the Amazon River and landed in another jungle airfield near Belem, Brazil, at 0600hrs. The men ate breakfast while the plane was being refueled, and they took off again at 0805hrs. This time their destination was Parnamarim Field in Natal, Brazil, the jumping-off point for Africa. Bill got a diversion on this leg, as he reported in the diary:

Read awhile, then went forward to look over the control room, etc., of the C-54. Had a long talk with Captain Roberts and discovered a few mutual acquaintances. He let me fly the ship for a while, and I was amazed at the ease of control of a ship which grossed some 63,000 pounds. Quite a change from the 8,000- to 14,000-class ship I'm used to flying.

The plane landed at 1255hrs and was not scheduled to leave until that evening, so Bill had time to do some shopping at the post exchange before going to dinner with Branch and two of his friends who were stationed at Parnamarim. When they learned their departure had been delayed until the following morning, they found lodgings and went to bed. The next day, August 16, was an exciting one as the C-54 headed out across the Atlantic. Bill noted in his diary:

After a brief sleep, punctuated by weird dreams of gigantic tigers (not the flying variety) I was up before dawn, packed and ready to go. Didn't get away, however, until 07:50. Our destination this time was Ascension Island, a distance of about 1,500 miles, and all over water. Rather a small little spot to be aiming at from 1,500 miles, for Ascension Island is only five miles wide and eight miles long. Little to worry about with modern radio navigational aids. Quite a bit of excitement about 11:00, though, when the starboard outboard motor started missing and the wing tank on that side sprung a leak.

Our new skipper (Captain Tahey, who we picked up in Natal) came back and instructed everyone in the procedure for abandoning ship if he had to put it down in the Atlantic. We were just about halfway between Natal and Ascension Island. I was put in charge of one of the lifeboats, as was Col. Branch – there are four lifeboats in all. Lt. Sullivan, an M.D. from Chicago, was really excited, and the colonel and I kidded him about it the rest of the trip, which proceeded without further incident. The C-54 landed at 2:15 p.m. making it a trip of six hours and 25 minutes.

Ascension Island, as Bill put it, proved to be "a rocky, mountainous little island cast up out of the sea by some past volcanic activity." There was a relatively large contingent of USAAF, US Navy and US Coast Guard artillery personnel stationed at the lonely outpost. After dinner, the travelers watched an outdoor showing of the movie *Reveille with Beverly* and went to bed early. Bill's lodgings for the night was a tent he shared with four lieutenant colonels and a civilian. Despite the close quarters, and the fact that the island is only a few degrees south of the Equator, Bill spent a chilly night under two blankets.

The travelers awoke before dawn and dressed quickly to ward off the cold. A short bus ride after breakfast took them to their plane, which departed for Africa at 0710hrs, just as the sun was coming up. Again, the flight was almost entirely over water, so Bill read a book for part of it. He was not impressed by what he read, however, despite the book being a bestseller. Indeed, it remains to this day one of the most popular first-person accounts written by an American fighter pilot during the war:

I have already finished one book, *God Is My Co-Pilot*, which was written by Col. Robert L. Scott, who came to China about a month before I left, and the book is as great a compilation of lies and overstatement as it has ever been my displeasure to read.

The C-54 landed at Accra, on the Gold Coast of West Africa, at about 1300hrs. Bill spent a busy afternoon there:

After checking into my room, my first move was to go up to the Post Exchange, reputedly the best in Africa, and buy myself a new shirt and pair of trousers. We have been living out of our musette bags since leaving Miami. Certainly did feel good to shave, shower, etc. and climb into some clean clothes. From here three or four of us went over to the staff officers' club and rolled for the drinks. The club walls were lined with some copies of

Petty and Varga [pinup] drawings drawn or painted by one of the enlisted men. He really had the touch, and it gives the club a very unique appearance.

After dinner, Bill declined the opportunity to go into town and instead went to his quarters to read his new book, *Count Bruga*, by Ben Hecht, before going to bed. "It's back to mosquito nets again – I imagine for another year," he confided to his diary.

A predawn takeoff at 0415hrs started August 18, a Wednesday. It was a cloudy day, so the passengers could not see much of Africa as they headed for Maiduguri, near Lake Chad. Instead, Bill played cards most of the way before they arrived at 1415hrs. Bill's diary entry for the day read as follows:

The camp is seven miles from the field. Rode out in an old Ford over roads that were really something. The natives here are a pretty sorry mess, but they seem happy enough. Heard some of them "giving out" on the drums, and they had that real boogie woogie beat. Shot a few baskets with the colonel [Branch] and then a good shower. Walked over to a little native shop and looked over their wares. It's too early to begin accumulating things this trip, I decided.

The C-54 left Maiduguri at about 0140hrs on August 19 and landed at Khartoum, the capital of Sudan, at 0815hrs local time. An hour later the plane was back in the air and soon headed across the Red Sea toward to port city of Aden, where it landed at 1355hrs. Servicemen were prohibited from going into the city from the airfield at night, so Bill contented himself with watching the movie *Stage Door Canteen* in a half-constructed hangar before going to bed. "It's easy to see that all the corn doesn't come from Iowa," Bill wrote in his diary.

It was an early start on Friday, August 20, the last day of the journey. Bill's C-54 took off at 0520hrs and flew east into the dawn until it landed at Misera, a British airfield on a desolate island in the

Arabian Sea, at 1050hrs. After an hour's stop, the plane proceeded
to Karachi Army Air Base and landed at 1815hrs local time. Bill's
diary records his first impressions of his new duty station:

> After going through the quarantine area and being passed, we
> climbed aboard an Army truck and were driven about 15 miles
> to the city of Karachi, where we were to stay for the night at
> the Mohatta Palace. This edifice proved to be a very imposing
> and elaborately decorated palace which had been converted
> into a barracks or hostel. As we were all tired etc., we decided
> to stay in this evening – so we unpacked, had dinner, then
> engaged in a lengthy poker game which lasted into the wee
> hours. Most relaxing, but not too lucrative. Finally hit the hay
> after a refreshing shower and shampoo, and slept on the outside
> of the sheets, as rumor has it that the place is infested with
> bedbugs. Sometimes I wonder why I don't stay home and mind
> my own business!

The Bill Reed who arrived in India on August 20, 1943, was a
different guy from the Bill Reed who had left Asia a year earlier.
As an AVG flight leader, Bill's job had been to fly missions
and take care of some minor administrative tasks. He had gained
valuable combat experience, learning not only how to succeed
in air combat but also how to cope with the inevitable losses of
friends and colleagues. But he had not played a leadership role
in the AVG. During the past year he had grown into a public
figure and a field-grade officer while developing the instincts
and skills of a military commander. Now, he was comfortable
with himself and with the USAAF's expectations of him. He was
ready to lead.

Bill learned on his first full day in India (August 21), however,
that the China-Burma-India (CBI) Air Forces Training Unit,
to which he was being assigned, was not ready for him. Bill
was awakened at 0800hrs that morning by Lt Col Branch, and
after breakfast they caught a GI bus to the airfield at New Malir
Cantonment, on the edge of the nearby Sindh Desert. They were

31

32

33

34

36

37

38

39

40

41

42

43

44

45

46

47

48

49

50

51

52

53

54

55

63

64

65

66

67

68

69

eager to get their orders and move into some permanent quarters. On checking in, they learned that they were not expected for another month or more! Surprised, but not disheartened, the pair searched out Lt Col T. Alan Bennett, whom Bill had known in I Fighter Command in the US. When they reached Bennett's office, who should Bill find there but his old friend from Millville, Capt Bill Turner. By then it was lunchtime, and during the course of the meal Bennett and Turner filled in the new arrivals on what was happening at Malir.

Much had changed in the CBI theater during the year that Bill had been away, although the tactical situation on the ground in Burma and China was little different. The Japanese essentially held all of Burma now, having pushed north of Myitkyina into the shadow of the Himalaya Mountains in Tibet shortly before the AVG disbanded. In China, the Japanese held the northern provinces, all the port cities and the Yangtze River valley as far west as the pivotal city of Hankow (Wuhan). British forces were regrouping in eastern India while the Chinese Army was desperately retraining, both with the long-term goal of retaking Burma to clear a land supply route from India into China. In the meantime, a steady stream of cargo aircraft passed back and forth over the famed "Hump" route between airfields in the Assam Province of eastern India (now Bangladesh) and those in China's Yunnan Province in order to keep a trickle of ammunition, aviation fuel and other supplies flowing into China.

What had changed was the Allies' commitment of air power to the CBI. When Bill left China in July 1942, the entire complement of USAAF combat units had numbered four understrength P-40 fighter squadrons and one B-25 medium bomber squadron in China, plus two bomber squadrons in Assam. The RAF had had no aircraft in China and one squadron of twin-engined Wellington bombers plus a small number of war-weary Hurricane fighters in India.

Now, a year later, the picture was much different. Allied air strength included 12 RAF fighter squadrons providing air defense for Calcutta and Ceylon.[6] The USAAF had grown even more, establishing the Tenth Air Force with ten squadrons in India and

the Fourteenth Air Force in China. The latter organization, under
the command of Gen Chennault, numbered five fighter squadrons,
four heavy bomber squadrons with B-24 Liberators, one B-25
squadron and one photo-reconnaissance squadron.[7] More units
slated to fly in China were training at Malir, and that is where
Bill came in.

As Al Bennett explained to Bill Reed and "Twig" Branch, they
would be serving in a unique new outfit known as the Chinese-
American Composite Wing (CACW). The CACW was considered
a "composite" not because Chinese and Americans would be
serving together, although that was indeed the case, but because it
combined bomber and fighter units under a single command. The
first two P-40 fighter squadrons and one B-25 bomber squadron
had been training at Malir for about three weeks. Eventually, the
CACW would grow to eight fighter squadrons and four bomber
squadrons.

The CACW was born amid serious political and social tensions
that marked relations between the United States and Chiang
Kai-shek's National Chinese government throughout World War
II. While Chiang continually pressed the US for more military
aid, Washington's established war policy was "Europe first," with
the goal of defeating the Axis powers in Europe being the highest
military priority. Chiang, meanwhile, was not doing himself any
favors. By August 1943 he had allowed the CAF to deteriorate to
the point that it could no longer be considered an effective combat
force. Its rocky history contained only a few proud moments
among the various beatings that the Japanese had meted out since
the war began in 1937. Obsolete aircraft and indifferent leadership
were the chief culprits. Even the presence of Claire Chennault as
the director of training could not turn the tide.

Late in 1938, Chennault had hired a contingent of foreign pilots
to serve as flight leaders in the CAF, while filling other formation
slots with Chinese pilots. Although not especially confident of
success, he tried the idea in order to use a group of Vultee V-11
and V-12 single-engined monoplane bombers that China had just
purchased. Immediately, one of the most ancient and constant of

Chinese considerations arose, that of "face." Nothing was more important to the Chinese than saving face, or pride. Losing face was to be avoided at all costs, and the Chinese considered Chennault's plan a great blow to their pride. The Chinese pilots went on strike, refusing to be led by foreigners, and the bombardiers walked out in sympathy. A pep talk by Chennault eventually resolved the situation, but the Vultees only flew a few missions before they were caught on the ground by the Japanese and destroyed. Chennault had learned a valuable lesson about Chinese culture.

In the 20 months since the Pearl Harbor attack of December 1941, the air war in China had been fought almost entirely by American pilots. What remained of the CAF was deployed in rear areas, its pilots getting familiar with new American P-40, Republic P-43 Lancer and Vultee P-66 Vanguard fighters supplied through the Lend-Lease program. Meanwhile, arrangements had been made to give Chinese air cadets their flight training at the USAAF's Luke and Thunderbird fields in Arizona. Many of those cadets were now completing their training and returning to China as American-style, combat-ready pilots.

The USAAF found itself in a bit of a bind in the summer of 1943, and the problem would contribute to the creation of the CACW. While American aircraft manufacturers were fully geared up for the war effort and turning out a steady stream of new airplanes, Air Training Command was having a difficult time producing sufficient numbers of airmen to fly them. In the month of July, the five major manufacturers of fighter aircraft rolled out 1,576 new airframes from their factories. Curtiss-Wright alone was completing 11 P-40s per day.[8] However, the growing scope of air operations around the globe was soaking up new pilots and crewmen faster than the training scheme could turn them out. As a result, many fighter pilots were being sent overseas after having completed just half of the 60 hours of operational training called for in the syllabus.[9] And fully trained or not, very few of these pilots were being sent to the CBI.

The US could provide combat aircraft to expand the air war in China, but the Chinese would need to supply many of the aircrew to fly them. Now the major concern became how to make sure that once equipped, the Chinese actually would fight, for thus far the air force and particularly the army had exhibited a persistent reluctance to do so. Many Americans believed Chiang was hording his forces, looking past the present conflict to the day when he would engage the Chinese Communists in a civil war.

The obvious solution was to devise a way to place the Chinese airmen under Chennault's command. He had a plan. On January 21, 1943, he wrote a long memo to Gen Joseph W. Stilwell, the American theater commander in the CBI:

> . . . I have given careful consideration to the matter of super-vising and commanding Chinese Air Force units in China. As a result of more than five years' experience in training and controlling Chinese air units, I herewith submit the following suggestions:
>
> The supervision and control of Chinese air units by foreigners in an advisory capacity never produces the best results.
>
> Chinese air units will be effective in combat only if provided with flying equipment equal to or superior in performance to that of the enemy.
>
> While there is a considerable number of experienced aircrews, both bombardment and pursuit, available in China, the majority of those crews will need carefully planned refresher courses. For several years the Chinese have not had sufficient numbers of airplanes to maintain pilot and crew efficiency. Nearly all the older pilots will require special training in tactics most suitable for the new types of airplanes which will be furnished to them.
>
> Special attention will have to be given to the organization of tactical units and to other necessary features such as communications, supply, housing, mess, and transportation.
>
> While it is believed that supervision and control by foreigners acting in an advisory capacity cannot produce the best results, it is believed that excellent results could be commanded by a

foreign officer assisted by a staff of officers from all nationalities having combat units operating in China. In this way, the facilities, supplies, and personnel now available in China would be made available equally to all operating units. Plans for the offensive and defensive employment of combat units could be coordinated and put into execution with the least delay and greatest effectiveness.

In Chennault's final paragraph was the germ of an idea that would blossom later into the CACW. Six months after writing the memo, Chennault's Fourteenth Air Force remained understrength, but a solution to the problem was beginning to take shape. On June 30, 1943, Chennault sent the following cable to Gen H. H. "Hap" Arnold, chief of the USAAF:

An OTU [operational training unit] for Chinese Air Force at Karachi has been staffed by American and Chinese personnel and is now prepared to train Chinese personnel from the states commencing August 5, 1943. Imperative that commitments to the Generalissimo be kept and that following plan be adhered to: organize and train two Chinese fighter groups and one Chinese medium bombardment group of four squadrons each. Two fighter squadrons and one bombardment squadron may train simultaneously; training period six weeks, first class starts August 5th.

In order that these Chinese units operate efficiently and be employed to advantage tactically, organizations of groups and squadrons necessitate the assignment of American officers and enlisted supervisory personnel as an integral part of each unit. This requires that American personnel reach Karachi at the same time, or prior to arrival of Chinese personnel. All personnel referred to must be furnished as same are not available Fourteenth Air Force.

First contingent requires forty U.S.-trained Chinese P-40 pilots plus American personnel as outlined. First contingent of medium-bombardment squadron required twelve U.S.-trained

B-25 pilots plus American personnel. All thirty-six Chinese pilots now available can be utilized to advantage.

Best interest will be served if Chinese B-25 pilots ferry aircraft to Karachi utilizing ATC [Air Transport Command] flight leaders. Plans call for twelve B-25s [to] arrive Karachi by July 25 for maintenance before start of training. All other personnel, both Chinese and American, arrive prior to August 5. Immediate attention should be given to the requirements of the above plan.

This was the "scheme" to send ex-AVG members back to China for "some special work" with Chennault that Bill had reported in his July 6 letter to Mayme. Following approval of Chennault's plan, Brig Gen Howard Davidson was assigned the job of organizing the CACW under the code name "Lotus." Davidson worked fast, and on July 5 he reported satisfactory progress on the Lotus project. Meanwhile, the first group of pilots and technicians Chennault had requested was gathering in Miami for shipment to the Far East. Led by Al Bennett, this contingent of 24 Americans arrived in Karachi on July 31. None of them were ex-AVG pilots. In fact Bill would be the first of only two AVG veterans ever to serve in the CACW.

Eventually, the CACW would comprise two fighter groups and one medium bomber group, each with four squadrons. The CACW would be a provisional unit of the CAF but fly under operational control of the USAAF's Fourteenth Air Force. Unique to the CACW was its mirrored command structure – American and Chinese officers would co-command at each level, from wing commanders all the way down to individual flight commanders. Most of the staff functions, such as intelligence and engineering, were also duplicated. The intention was that the Americans would withdraw from the CACW when the Chinese were deemed ready to assume full command, but this did not happen until after the war ended.

Training of the first CACW units began as planned on August 5 with a morning meeting held in the big hangar at Malir for all fighter and bomber personnel. Bennett commanded the 3rd FG, and he was to be joined by his Chinese counterpart in October. The group's first two fighter squadrons were the 28th and the 32nd, the latter commanded by Bill Turner and the former by Capt Eugene Strickland, a West Pointer whom Bill had known at Westover Field. The 1st Bomb Group's American commander was Col John Hilger, a veteran of the Doolittle raid on Japan in 1942, but he would soon give way to Bill's travelling companion, Lt Col "Twig" Branch. Since the squadron Bill was slated to command would not be forming until mid-October, he was assigned to assist his buddy Turner in preparing the 32nd FS for combat in China.

12

"Time we stopped fooling around"

Bill spent a leisurely first week in India, sharing a room with "Twig" Branch and Bill Dick in officers' quarters at the Killarney Hotel in downtown Karachi. During the day, they would rent bicycles and tour around the city. One day they stopped at a bank to change some US money to rupees. On another morning they bought some material and took it to a tailor shop to be fitted for making bush jackets. They also visited a British gymkhana club and signed up as honorary members, so they could take advantage of the tennis courts and the men's bar. But in general, Bill was not impressed by Karachi, as he recorded in his diary:

> This place is not as nice as the other cities in India. Guess that's because it isn't as large as they were and, though it is a fairly important seaport, it doesn't rate with the leading Indian cities. The people don't change much, though – either the natives or the British who infest the land. I don't believe I can ever come to appreciate or like these provincial British, though I will continue to enjoy their "gymkhana" clubs. There is the most appalling lack of sanitation and cleanliness. I had to laugh at the colonel [Branch] when we were riding along on our bicycles. He rode along with his nose all wrinkled up as if he had just stepped on something filthy. The odors that assail the nostrils on the streets are terrific.

The evenings would start with drinks and dinner at the hotel. One evening Bill ran into Capt Hollis Blackstone, one of his flying school classmates who had just finished a combat tour in China with the 23rd FG. They compared notes on others who had gone through training with them and concluded that quite a few of them were now dead. Bill was especially sad to learn that his roommate at Randolph Field, Johnny Hampshire, had been killed in action in China about three months earlier. At the time of his death, Hampshire was the leading fighter ace in China, with 13 confirmed victories. After dinner, Bill and the others usually repaired to the Karachi officers' club, a short walk from the hotel. There, Bill generally got caught up in a poker game, some of which lasted into the wee hours.

The soft life could not last, of course. A call to the hotel on August 25 notified seven officers, including Bill and his roommates, that they were to report to the airfield at Malir the following day to receive their assignments with the Chinese-American Operational Training Unit. They packed at the hotel the following morning, caught a ride in a truck out to the field after lunch and checked into their new quarters there. Again, from Bill's diary:

> I share a room with five other majors. They are all much older than I am, but all seem to be nice guys. We sleep on little folding cots. The buildings are made of yellow bricks and stucco, and have cement floors – pretty good quarters. The latrines are at a goodly distance from the quarters – nothing like a nice hike early in the morning. The Malir area is about 18 miles from Karachi and is in desert country. As far as the eye can see building after building – the British must have planned to move a whole army here at one time.
>
> Had supper with Bill Turner. Here we eat from mess kits, which we wash before and after eating in four barrels of boiling water behind the mess hall. After supper I set up my bed and made it up. Then went to an outdoor movie with Bill – some

old Wild Western movie. Finally back to my bunk and crawled in in the dark. No electricity here. Have a feeling I'm going to like it here, though.

On Friday, August 27, Bill got his first chance to fly since arriving in India. He woke up too late for breakfast and made his way over to the flightline to get acquainted with some of the pilots who would be working with him in the coming weeks and months. They gave him a bit more information about the CACW, which he recorded in his diary:

> This outfit is regarded as one of the top-priority projects by the higher-ups. It could be called the real beginning of a new and potentially great Chinese Air Force. It is what the original AVG had hoped to be, but it was rather an abortive attempt. I have no doubt that this, too, is General Chennault's idea. It is a good one, and there is no doubt what it will succeed if it gets the proper backing. This makes the second time I've been in on the ground floor, and I'm glad of the opportunity.
>
> Browsed around the operations building and finally borrowed a plane (an AT-16) and went for a ride to look over the area. Found that it would be very easy to get lost around here. The country is much like west Texas – sand and sage brush.

Later that day in a meeting with Col Bennett, Bill learned that he would be appointed commanding officer of the third CACW fighter squadron after the first two completed training. For now, he would assist Bill Turner with his squadron. The following day, he expressed in his diary admiration for the Chinese pilots he had met:

> They are really an eager bunch – clean cut and hard working. Bet they will prove to be good fighters, too. This time I am going to really learn their language. If I am going to lead them, into battle, I want to be able to give them definite commands and have them executed.

It was a noble goal, but there is no evidence Bill ever succeeded in mastering Chinese.

After an uneventful weekend, flying activity picked up for Bill during the week of August 30. In addition to the AT-16 (a Canadian-built version of the ubiquitous AT-6 Texan two-seat trainer), the CACW had six Hawk 81-A-2 fighters that had been flown by the AVG and later by the 23rd FG in China before being retired to training duties. In fact, it is possible that Bill had flown one or more of them before while serving in the AVG. These fighters, referred to as "P-40Bs" by the CACW, were supplemented by several war-weary P-40Es and P-40Ks ferried in from China and Assam. All of these aircraft needed refurbishment, which Chinese technicians were doing with American supervision. As the work was completed on each plane, it had to be flight-tested. Bill slow-timed a P-40 on August 30, although the overcast monsoon sky limited flying to altitudes under 1,500ft. He described the last day of August in his diary:

> I had more fun today working on the line than I've had since leaving the States. Didn't actually accomplish much, but learned a little more about Curtiss Electric props. Got in one test hop in a P-40K. Still used to gliding at 115–120 (a hangover from P-47s), but don't have any trouble landing them [P-40s]. Don't care much for their gunsight, though. Not enough ceiling to "wring them out." That will come later. Got my first mail today, too – a letter from Private Mick Forbes [she was now serving in the US Marine Corps] and one from Mary Patch in Vineland, New Jersey. Should be getting some from home one of these days.

Bill made the final entry in his diary on September 2, 1943:

> Still haven't much work to do, but I am reporting to the line every morning as usual. Things are getting pretty bad when a fighter pilot has to stoop to flying a PT-17 [open-cockpit biplane trainer]. Took Kebric[1] up and let him fly around a bit. Played

[football] this evening, and I am ashamed to report that our team lost. We have too many triple-threat men (stumble, fumble or fall) on our team. We have a lot of fun, though, and the exercise is the main thing.

Went over to the fighter squadron barracks and wrote letters. Bill Turner wandered in about 10:30, and we had quite a "bull session" with the boys. [Turner] was in Java and New Guinea. Broke it up at midnight, and I wandered back to my barracks. The sky was clear as a bell, and the stars were brilliant. Strangely enough, the wind isn't blowing. Maybe the monsoon season is over.

It is unfortunate that Bill discontinued his diary, as his excellent writing skills and keen observations are a delight to read. But he did continue to write letters home to his family members. He told them on September 15 that the weather was getting hotter with the end of the monsoon, so he was getting in a lot more flying. He also said he had learned to ride a motorcycle and was enjoying it. On the social side, he reported attending dances at the officers' club in Karachi and taking a nurse from Philadelphia on a date. Bill was still Bill.

The training of the first two CACW fighter squadrons took longer than expected, stretching into October due to organizational growing pains and a shortage of aircraft. The CACW headquarters, meanwhile, was formally activated on October 1, 1943, with Col Winslow C. Morse as the American commander. Morse had served as CO of the USAAF's proving grounds at Eglin Field prior to coming overseas.

With CACW headquarters taking shape and the first round of training winding down, the second trio of CACW squadrons was activated on October 9, 1943. As promised, Bill was assigned as CO of the 7th FS. One of Bill's roommates at Malir, Maj Howard "Snatch" Cords, would command the 8th FS, which would train with the 7th. The two men had formed a close friendship over the preceding six weeks – a relationship that would allow close coordination and cooperation as they trained their squadrons and, later, led them into battle. The squadron activations were primarily a paper move at this point, however, as no facilities or aircraft were yet available to begin training.

Finally, on October 15, graduation ceremonies took place for the first three CACW squadrons. Soon they would be departing for China. First, however, they faced the tasks of preparing and flight-testing 24 new P-40N Warhawk fighters and 12 B-25 bombers to ready them for service in China. That process would take nearly two weeks before the Malir flightline and training aircraft would be available for Bill's 7th FS and the other two outfits.

The first meeting of the 7th FS, held in conjunction with the 8th, also took place on October 15. Majs Bill Reed and "Snatch" Cords led the gathering, which was rather small since at this point the 7th FS consisted of just three American officers, and the 8th FS had four. Bill's subordinates were two first lieutenants who had previously served as flight instructors: John T. Hancock, from New Jersey, acting operations officer and B Flight commander; and Floridian Donald J. Burch, A Flight commander. Burch would go on to experience a particularly eventful combat tour.

Fortified by a supply of beer and nuts, the officers discussed problems they would be facing in the weeks ahead, along with various procedures that were already in place. The squadrons would be dealing directly with wing headquarters, which would require them to submit daily progress reports on each pilot in English and Chinese. The flight training would operate on a schedule of half-day flying and half-day ground school, weather permitting. It was to stress the good points of the P-40N and emphasize mutual support in two-ship elements, as Bill had learned from Chennault two years earlier. All pilots were to be briefed prior to each flight. American personnel would take charge of training Chinese groundcrews.

Two days later, the first 15 Chinese pilots of the 7th FS arrived, and Bill convened a meeting of American and Chinese flying personnel in the operations office. Most of the Chinese pilots were combat veterans who had been involved in providing air defense for the Chinese capital at Chungking, but the younger pilots were fresh out of flying school in the United States. Speaking through an interpreter, Bill explained that they would be spending the next six to eight weeks learning to work together as they molded themselves into an effective fighting force. The 7th FS unit history described other points that Bill covered:

> He outlined our table of organization as six American pilots and twenty-four Chinese pilots. Our emphasis will be on tactical formation with mutual support. Our missions will include skip- and dive-bombing, bomber escort, aerial and ground gunnery, and altitude missions. He stressed our limited time and our difficulties; thus the necessity for complete cooperation. The plan of operations was explained.

Bill was most interested to meet his counterpart as squadron commander, Capt Hsu Jie Hsiang (now spelled Xu Hua-jiang). Little did Bill know that Hsu was every bit as much a veteran fighter pilot as he was. In fact, Hsu had already begun flying in combat when Bill was finishing up his studies at Loras College in 1939.

Hsu was born just a week before Bill, on New Year's Day, 1917, in Fujin, a county in the northeast corner of Manchuria. He was a 14-year-old schoolboy when Japan invaded Manchuria in 1931 and subsequently created the puppet state of Manchukuo. Like many Manchurians, young Hsu had no wish to grow up under Japanese rule. He fled his homeland to join his father, who was working in Shansi (Shanxi) Province at the time, and completed his schooling there.

In 1935, Hsu was accepted into the Chinese Military Academy in Nanking. After completing his recruit training the following year, he transferred to the Central Aviation Academy (CAA) in Louyang for flight training. After fighting between the Chinese and Japanese resumed in 1937, the CAA was forced to move several times, and Hsu completed his pursuit training at Kunming in May 1938. His first operational assignment was with the 21st PS/4th PG, flying Russian-built Polikarpov I-15 and I-16 fighters. Promoted to warrant officer in early 1939, Hsu transferred to the 17th PS/5th PG and saw his first combat during the Battle of

Lanchow. By the time the squadron moved to Peishiyi that summer to provide air defense for the capital city of Chungking, Hsu had been awarded a Star Medal for one aerial victory. On September 13, 1940, Hsu had the misfortune to be flying an I-15 biplane fighter when the IJNAF debuted its new A6M Zero-sen fighter in combat over Chungking. He was one of 13 Chinese pilots shot down during that encounter, suffering a minor head injury. After that, the CAF instituted a strategy of avoiding combat to conserve its dwindling supply of aircraft.

Nearly two years later, in September 1942, Hsu joined a contingent of Chinese pilots sent to Karachi, India, to ferry new American-built P-66 fighters up to China. Shortly thereafter he was promoted to a division leader in the 32nd FS/3rd FG, and in March 1943 he was appointed commander of the 7th FS/3rd FG – the position he still held when the squadron's pilots were sent to Malir for retraining as a unit of the CACW.

Hsu was immediately impressed by his American counterpart, both in respect to Bill's combat record and also his demeanor. But it took the two men some time working together before they bonded. Hsu described this period many years later for an oral history:

Reed was a polite gentleman and skillful pilot, and [he] was very friendly to Chinese people. To Chinese people he was a person who was adept with pen and sword. After I became leader of the 7th Squadron, I worked with him in many missions. One day he asked me through an interpreter: "I like Chinese people and would like to be friends with all Chinese people. But it seems you don't like me. Every time we work together, your attitude is rather distanced. Is there something wrong?" I said, "No, it's not that! I'm just a quiet person who does not like to socialize with people, and my English is also poor. That's why we have this misunderstanding." After hearing this explanation, Reed understood me perfectly, and then we cooperated more closely. Prior to each mission, he always discussed the mission with me and provided me with data such as flight routes and charts. He also fully respected my opinions. We usually had a thorough discussion before a briefing. I was not only a close colleague with Reed at work; we were also good friends in private.[2]

Together, Bill and Hsu would build the 7th into the top-scoring fighter squadron in the CACW. Key contributors to their success would be the small cadre of American enlisted technicians who would supervise the maintenance of the unit's aircraft and other equipment: H. S. Smith, first sergeant; G. V. Masselos, line chief; C. P. Marchall, H. C. "Jug" Nunley, M. P. Paige, J. A. Rogers, E. F. Holewinski and C. W. Cimbalas, crew chiefs; J. N. "Moose" Rumen, armament chief; N. P. Nardelli, J. C. Lowry and C. E. McAdams, armorers; W. L Whisenant and S. F. Sosh, communications; K. H. Keene and T. J. Jebeles, supply; W. H. Dora, instruments specialist; D. J. Winchell, sheet metal; and C. M. Grace, clerk. Officers joining the squadron in the coming few weeks included 1Lt William H. Ramsey, adjutant; 1Lt Charles Lovett, intelligence officer; 1Lt Clarence Davis, engineering officer; and WO Roswell Davis, supply officer.[3]

Things started slowly because the war-weary P-40s assigned for training were all under repair at Karachi air base. In addition, afternoon temperatures were now reaching 130 degrees Fahrenheit with the end of monsoon season, so most work could take place only in the mornings. Lectures, mostly given by Bill and 1Lts Hancock and Burch, covered topics such as the table of organization, field procedures, radio procedures and operational procedures for the P-40 in preparation for cockpit checkouts. Translations of notices and operations orders were completed as well. The Chinese also gathered flying clothing and equipment as they became available. When the first P-40K was delivered on October 20, cockpit checks began. Apart from a lecture on the local flying area given on Saturday morning, there were no activities during the weekend of October 23–24.

Flying began on Monday, October 25, when Bill took Capt Hsu up in the squadron's AT-16 for a familiarization flight around the

Malir area. Other flights followed throughout the day and again on Tuesday. But the squadron still could not begin P-40 flights until the first two squadrons departed for China, making the maintenance facilities available for the 7th and 8th FSs. Mechanics in the 7th were sent to help those working on the senior squadrons' P-40Ns, while mechanics of the 8th continued making repairs on the P-40 trainers.

More lectures continued throughout the week, and excitement started to build when the Chinese staff were invited to sit in on a briefing for the pilots who were about to leave for China. Meanwhile, five more Chinese pilots joined the squadron, along with 34 enlisted technicians, including mechanics and armorers. Finally, on October 28, the 28th and 32nd FSs took off for China, and the new squadrons now had Malir all to themselves. P-40 flying began the next day when Bill slow-timed the first one delivered to his squadron.

P-40 checkout flights for the Chinese pilots began on Saturday, October 30. Tensions were high, as few – if any – of these pilots had flown a P-40 before, and the Warhawk was not forgiving of poor takeoff and landing technique. Capt Hsu went first, followed by his vice commander, Lt Yang Y. K., and the assistant operations officer, Lt Lee C. K. All three completed successful flights, though Bill noted that all three landed with excessive speed and had to abuse their brakes to get stopped on the runway. Capt Yieh W. F., the operations officer, went last. He overshot his landing and went off the end of the runway but did not damage the P-40 – a mistake he repeated when flying resumed on Monday.

As the rest of the Chinese pilots continued to check out, the problem of excessive speed while landing persisted and would take several weeks of practice to overcome. The first damage to one of the squadron's P-40s occurred when a pilot skidded off the end of the runway with his wheels locked and blew out both tires. Then on November 2 the squadron lost its first P-40 when Lt Lee C. K. bailed out after his engine caught fire about ten miles south of the airfield. He was unhurt and hitched a ride back to base on a camel. Another P-40 went down two days later with an engine failure just short of the runway, again with the pilot unhurt, and the following morning the squadron had just one P-40 plus the AT-16 in flying condition. Still, the pilots were able to log 11 hours of flight time during the day.

The squadron was working hard, and Bill decided it was time to let off a little steam by having a party. The gathering, held at the Allies Café on the base, featured dinner and drinking. Before long, the Chinese began making toasts according to their "Gombei" tradition, which required everyone to drain their glass at each toast amid much laughter and shouting. As the squadron history noted after the party, "It is safe to say that if Chinese–American friendship is not now cemented it never will be." The parties continued on a weekly basis after that. Another motivator freely exploited by Bill and Capt Hsu was competition with their sister squadron, the 8th. Both units kept careful track of their flight hours and number of flights, each trying to outperform the other.

Perhaps reflecting his experience in the AVG, Bill eschewed many military traditions when exercising leadership of the Americans in his squadron. He had no interest in segregating officers and enlisted men, who worked closely together during duty hours and socialized in the evenings. Nor was he a stickler when it came to appearance, caring little about his men keeping their shoes shined, their trousers creased and other such fixations of the military during peacetime.

Capt Hsu reflected on the budding relationship between the American and Chinese personnel, recalling that although they were housed in separate facilities, the officers shared an officers' club. As he reported in the oral history:

> Every Friday night the club would allow American officers to play poker for money. But there were limits on the amount of money that was allowed to be involved and the number of games. They often had to end a poker game on that day, and bets could not be accumulated for the next week. Because of our separate living spaces, the personnel of the two countries

did not have much contact with each other, except during [duty hours] or at large meetings. Generally, our living conditions were inferior, and the Americans had access to much more in the way of material things than we did.[4]

After a week of checkouts, the squadrons went to a seven-days-per-week flying schedule in an effort to speed up their training. By this time all the Chinese pilots had at least six hours of P-40 flight time. The training syllabus called for each pilot to complete ten hours of P-40 familiarization flying, followed by 11 hours of formation flying, seven hours of ground gunnery, 11 hours of shadow gunnery, six hours of air-to-air gunnery, two hours of bomber escort practice and seven-and-a-half hours of navigation and dive-bombing. In addition, they needed to complete 60 hours of ground school, covering topics including emergency procedures, navigation, air tactics, practical aircraft maintenance and gunnery and bombing techniques.[5]

With the squadrons having been told that they should be ready to leave for China by Christmas, they needed to get a lot more flying in if they were to meet the deadline.

Training flights accelerated, but accidents continued to dog the squadron as the pilots began practicing formation flying. On November 10, 1Lt Burch was leading a three-plane flight when his engine's oil temperature started to climb. He peeled away and came in for a forced landing, and the Chinese pilots with him came in too. The squadron history reported:

Lt. Tan followed him and ground-looped in [P-40] 999, damaging the right wing and aileron, and Lt. Chao followed Lt. Tan in and forgot to put his wheels down, bellying in on the runway in the ex-sacred cow – [P-40] 059. It was one of those things that don't happen. If Lt. Tan hadn't ground-looped in front of Chao the tower would have caught him. In any case let's hope we are pulling our "boners" now and getting them out of our system before we get into combat.

It was Bill's turn to have the next problem. He was flying in the squadron's ex-AVG Tomahawk when the oil cap came off and Bill got soaked in hot engine oil. This was all the more notable since it was exactly what had happened to him in a similar aircraft on April 10, 1942, during a scramble at Loiwing while he was flying with the AVG. Then on November 22 Lt Yang C. F. ground looped a P-40E, damaging both wings, wingtips, ailerons and flaps. With that accident, Bill lost his patience and gave his pilots a stern lecture, as reported in the squadron history:

> After the accident Major Reed held a meeting and told the squadron that it was time we stopped fooling around and got to work. Our combat duty is coming uncomfortably close and he did not feel that the pilots were showing the proper application to their jobs. They all took it very seriously, and we should see some improvement. The pilots have been improving, but there is still a lack of realism of the seriousness of our task. For the Chinese-trained pilots who have been fighting in China this is a "rest," and the others have a tendency to follow their lead.

Bill got a pleasant surprise about this time when who should show up at Malir assigned to the 7th FS but 1Lt Armit W. "Bill" Lewis, his friend from Westover Field. Lewis, a colorful character who had brought along a "Zoot Suit" (a high-styled man's suit with high-waisted, wide-legged, tight-cuffed, pegged trousers and a long coat with wide lapels and wide padded shoulders) to wear on special occasions, would serve as C Flight commander.

Arriving with 1Lt Lewis was Capt Thomas F. Hackleman, who would serve in the key position of squadron operations officer. Hackleman, who hailed from Springfield, Ohio, and was married with a young daughter, brought considerable flying experience to the squadron. He had learned to fly in the Civilian Pilot Training Program and enlisted in the USAAC in April 1941, receiving his wings the day after the Pearl Harbor attack. Since then Hackleman had been flying from various airfields on the US East Coast in I Fighter Command.[6] Another American pilot, 1Lt Wilbur W. Walton, was assigned shortly afterward.

Bill now had his full complement of American officers, enabling the 7th FS to speed up the training of its Chinese pilots. But it did not last long, as the squadron diary reported on November 29:

> Today was a very sad day for the 7th. Capt. Hackleman, our operations officer, was killed in a crash on the mud flats about five miles south of Landhi Field. He was on a formation flight, with Lt. Chang L. M. leading Lt. Lin flying on his wing, Capt. Hackleman leading the second element and Lt. Hu number four. They were flying at about 300 feet over a low cloud bank. As they went into a climbing turn Capt. Hackleman suddenly dived into the cloud and disappeared, and a few seconds later they saw black smoke come up through the clouds. Lt. Chang immediately brought the formation back to the field and reported the incident. We went out and located the scene of the crash. As yet we have not recovered the body. Capt. Hackleman was a capable officer and a good pilot. We have lost a valuable member of our squadron and a good friend. The cause of the accident is undetermined.

Capt Hackleman's badly mangled body was recovered the next day, and 1Lt Hancock was appointed to take his place as operations officer. On the morning of December 3, the squadron personnel went to the cemetery at Malir for Hackleman's funeral. The squadron formed up outside the chapel and marched in for a brief and simple service. Bill served as a pallbearer, along with 1Lts Hancock, Burch, Lewis and Walton, plus Capt Ray Callaway of the 8th FS. That afternoon the squadron got back in the air to complete 26 missions of dive-bombing, ground gunnery and formation flying.

Hampered by the chronic shortage of aircraft and other equipment, the training fell behind schedule, and on December 7 – the second anniversary of the Pearl Harbor attack – Bill told the squadron that its departure date had been set back. At that time, the Chinese-trained pilots averaged only 25 hours of P-40 time and the US-trained pilots just 15 hours, while the training syllabus required each pilot to have 60 hours for graduation. That evening, Col Morse, the CACW commander, backed up Bill's lecture of two weeks earlier with another lecture to the Chinese officers and enlisted men. He did not mince words, according to the squadron history:

> He told them that there was a notable lack of discipline and application to the task at hand, and there must be immediate correction of both. He said that while the Americans were here they were giving the orders, and any Chinese who did not see fit to cooperate would be sent back to China. It was pretty strong.

Morse did not spare the Americans from criticism, either. He followed up the next morning in a meeting called for the squadron commanders and operations officers of the two fighter squadrons and one bomber squadron then in training. Again, from the squadron history:

> He told us that a good bit of the laxity around here could be traced back to us. We were instructed to publish daily schedules in advance and to furnish base operations with a copy. We were told to issue clearances for all flights. We must have an operations meeting each morning before 0830. We must get our flights off on time, and if we don't that fact will be reported by the airdrome officer who will be furnished with a copy of our flying schedule. We must start using the Link [the training device that simulated flight], although we are to do no "beam" work as there are no beams in China, but will practice homings. We must segregate our bulletin boards, and we must have the Chinese operations officer put out the same as we do, in Chinese. With the exceptions of the clearances, we have been doing all of this ever since we started operations.

Perhaps to speed up the training process, CACW headquarters reorganized the squadron into three flights: Lts Burch and Tan would command A Flight; Lts Hancock and Chang, B Flight; and Lts Lewis and Kung, C Flight. Also, Bill assigned more of the ground school briefings to the experienced Chinese pilots in the squadron, as he had noticed that the young pilots paid closer attention when they spoke, as opposed to having Americans speak through an interpreter.

Some improvements were noted quickly. One in particular was the pre-setting of rendezvous points and altitudes after dive-bombing to improve the join-ups. On the negative side, the start of air-to-air gunnery practice had to be delayed for four days when the B-25 assigned to tow the target banner went down for repairs. The deadline for departure was moved back to New Year's Day, but despite improved attitudes and increased efforts, it looked like a long shot to be ready by then.

Bill got a pleasant surprise on December 11 when R. T. Smith showed up at Malir for a visit. He was in India with the 1st Air Commando Group, which would soon provide air support for British Gen Orde Wingate's second Chindit expedition into northern Burma. Bill mentioned their reunion in a letter to his mother:

Guess who came in the other night. None other than old "R. T." Smith, and you had just inquired about him several letters ago. He's happily married and has a family. A two-year-old boy came with his wife, and he tells me they are expecting another one one of these days. He and I won't be together, but it surely is good to see him again and have him around awhile.

In typical Bill fashion, he went on to give his mother some folksy details about his situation without going into the serious side of it:

A couple of the Chinese boys have some Chinese station on the radio, and it must be Chinese "boogie-woogie" from the sound of it. We were thinking of going to the post theater, but since we are on the early schedule in the morning decided not to. We had a nice Thanksgiving dinner over here with chicken, ham, cranberries etc. and even took half a day off. Of course, I missed the family gathering, but that's not unusual for me the past four years, is it? Well, Mom, I'm sitting here writing this by lamplight, and my eyes are getting tired. Have some nice music on our battery radio set, so I think I will sit back and enjoy some music for a moment or so and then write another letter perhaps. Don't worry much about me, Mom, because I'm in fine health, and am happy and working hard.

The squadron was scheduled to start air-to-air gunnery practice on December 13 but suffered another delay when the B-25 assigned to tow the target banner went out of commission again. Three days later, when the bomber had been fixed, it was reassigned to other duties. The mechanics then set to work modifying a P-40 to pull the banner, but the first time it tried to take off with the banner the tow cable broke. Eventually, the P-40 managed to haul the banner, which measured six feet wide and 30 feet long, aloft enough for the pilots to complete their training requirements. But time was passing.

The training schedule took another hit when a film crew showed up to shoot scenes for a movie about the CACW. Lts Chow, Lin and Burch were picked to "star" in the film. This project had a high priority, so Bill and his squadron had to adjust their schedules to suit the needs of the movie-makers. When the film crew returned for a second shoot, the squadron diary expressed some frustration with them:

This morning the movie men were here again shooting pictures. Their work is important, and they are usually very decent. But it is impossible to turn our airplanes over to them at the snap of a finger. We have tried to cooperate so far, but if they don't stop taking the attitude that they will run to Colonel Morse if we don't do what they ask, they will find our cooperation at a minimum.

Despite the distractions, training flights and classroom lectures continued at an acceptable rate. On December 17, the CACW squadrons were considered ready to take part in a large training exercise, which the squadron history described in some detail:

> This morning we were assigned two tactical missions in conjunction with a wing problem supposing a Japanese invasion of this area to disrupt convoys and the ATC route. Our field was considered captured, and our base shifted to Newabshah, about one hundred miles northeast of here. Briefing was at 0815.
>
> The first flight was simulated strafing of Watyi strip and Landhi Field. Lt. Lewis had the first flight with Lt. Kang Y. K. leading the second. Takeoff was at 0900 with "H" hour over Newabshah at 0930. Watyi was hit alright and Landhi was strafed, although the top cover was forced to return due to engine trouble.
>
> On the second mission two flights, led by Major Reed and Capt. Hsu, were to rendezvous with the bombers at Kurra Lake one hundred miles north of the field, and escort them on a shipping sweep and return. Takeoff was at 1100 with rendezvous at 1130. Our planes were there at 1131, but the bombers never showed up. Fault has not been assessed as yet. In the afternoon operations were called off as the Chinese and Major Reed were attending a party given by Chinese Headquarters.

The first sign that the 7th FS would be moving up to China soon came on December 23, 1943, when ground school was canceled so that all personnel and equipment to be shipped to China by ATC could be weighed. The next day the squadron learned that it had earned a rating of satisfactory in a recent inspection, and 1Lt Hancock went to the Technical Inspectors' office to clear up a minor matter related to paperwork. Christmas fell on a Saturday, so the squadron took the holiday weekend off, with no flying, to mark the occasion. Then it was back to work for the final push to the completion of training.

On the afternoon of December 28, a dark-colored P-40 entered the flight pattern at Malir and came in for a landing. This was not one of the old and worn P-40E/Ks the 7th FS had been flying during training, but factory-fresh P-40N-15 42-106323, the latest version of the venerable Warhawk. Bill would fly P-40Ns throughout the coming year. They were similar in performance to the P-40s he had flown in the AVG, but they had heavier firepower, including the provision to carry a bomb or drop tank under the belly, and the canopy was enlarged to give the pilot a better view out from his seat.

When the ferry pilot shut down the engine and climbed out of the cockpit, he announced that this was the first of 12 new P-40Ns being assigned to the 7th FS. The squadron history noted this memorable event:

> It is a small step but a significant one. We will put five hours of slow time on it, give it a shakedown inspection and boresight it [the process of aiming its six wing-mounted 0.50-caliber machine guns]. One of the reasons that we have not gotten our planes faster is because they are having some carburetion trouble with them. Also they must have the kit boxes that came with each of them secured. And as the planes and equipment belong to the Chinese and must be signed for by them before we can get them, it is a pretty tedious process.

The CACW's executive officer, Lt Col Tom Summers, spoke to the American personnel of the two fighter squadrons at a meeting the following evening to help prepare them for the move to China. As the squadron history reported, "His main theme was that we are going to a foreign country where many will be watching us, and we must act as a unit and not act as individuals." He cautioned them that fighting the air war involved a lot of sitting around waiting for something to happen, so they needed to steer clear of the powerful Chinese rice wine called "Gombei Juice" and beware of Chinese women of the evening. At his conclusion, Summers awarded Good Conduct Medals to 12 enlisted men.

As New Year's Day 1944 arrived, it was clear the squadrons were not going to make their deadline for departure to China. The training requirements were nearly met, but so far each fighter squadron still only had one P-40N on strength. The Chinese and Americans in the 7th FS held separate parties on their day off and then welcomed new American supply, engineering and intelligence officers the next day. WO Davis, the supply officer, went right to work rounding up the last items the squadron would need in China, while 1Lt Davis got busy giving the engineering section a much-needed reorganization. Then the film crew returned January 4 through 6, which required Bill plus 1Lts Lewis, Burch and Walton to take time away from training to make formation flights for the movie cameras.

The formal training program ended January 6, by which time the 7th FS had received six of its P-40Ns, and their carburetion problems had been solved. The squadron history includes this summation of the training program:

The program set up for us called for sixty hours per pilot in a six-week period. This proved unfeasible for us, as it did for the previous squadrons. Our actual flying started about November 1st, and in eight weeks we got in over 1,100 hours' flying. Our Chinese-trained pilots got between 45 and 50 hours, and our American-trained Chinese about 45 hours. After initial instruction, we stressed Chinese-led flights. We concentrated on formation, ground gunnery, dive-bombing, shadow gunnery, navigation, skip bombing and aerial gunnery. Each pilot averaged eight ground gunnery missions, twelve dive bombing, five shadow gunnery and two navigation, skip bombing and aerial gunnery missions. The weak points were aerial gunnery, which was curtailed because of the lack of facilities, and bomber escort, which failed of accomplishment due to the lack of availability of the bombers, which failed to rendezvous on our one scheduled mission.

The Link trainer became available in early December, and each pilot got about two hours in it. Ground school was conducted by American and Chinese squadron officers, OTU personnel and technical representatives. It covered all phases of practical maintenance, tactics, orientation, radio, navigation and intelligence. We feel that our program has been successful and that our squadron is ready for combat.

Time would tell if the last statement was correct.

13

"Stay in there and try a little harder"

A few minutes before 1230hrs on January 14, 1944, the propellers on ten P-40Ns at Malir air base, in India, began to turn as the planes' Allison V12 engines started up. Soon a roar filled the flightline, and then the planes began to taxi toward the runway, with Maj Bill Reed leading the way in Warhawk 42-106322. He would lead the first of three flights, with Capts Hsu and Wang heading the others. 1Lts Burch and Lewis would take turns carrying "Fubar," a small mutt dog the Americans had adopted, in their cockpits. The dog would transfer to a B-25 a few days later for his high-altitude ride over "The Hump" into China.

The final few days at Malir had been hectic, with all personnel confined to the base in an attempt to maintain secrecy about the impending move to China. Pilots received maps showing the route from Malir to Kunming, a distance of approximately 2,200 miles – times and distances between stops were clearly marked. Unfortunately, two of the squadron's Warhawks were under repair, requiring Lts Walton and Yang Y. K. to stay behind until their planes were ready to go.

The first leg of the journey to Kunming took Bill's squadron about 380 miles across the desert to Jodhpur. The 8th FS, also with ten P-40Ns, had left earlier in the day and was still on the field at Jodhpur when Bill landed. Its aircraft took off while the 7th FS's P-40Ns were being refueled and the pilots ate lunch. The next hop was more interesting. After taking off at 1615hrs, the pilots soon saw the peaks of the Himalayas come into view to their left and small, walled cities in the mountains below them. They arrived at Agra near sunset at 1815hrs and flew low across the city, getting a good look at the Taj Mahal. On landing they saw the 8th FS and the 1st Bomb Squadron (BS), with B-25s, had arrived ahead of them.

The three squadrons spent the next day at Agra attending to maintenance issues on some of their planes before making the 464-mile flight to Gaya on January 16. Then it was on to Lal Manir Hat, on the Brahmaputra River, the next day for another overnight stay.

The route on January 18 took the P-40s northeast up the Brahmaputra Valley about 400 miles to Chabua, in Assam (now Bangladesh), which would be their jumping-off point for China. About 45 minutes into the flight one of the 8th FS P-40s experienced engine failure, and the pilot rode it down to a crash landing. The others had no choice but to continue on, and they were relieved to learn the next day that the downed pilot, 1Lt Herman Byrd, was unhurt and would be rejoining them in the near future.

The two P-40 squadrons accompanied the 1st BS's B-25s on this leg, getting in some valuable practice at bomber escort. They arrived over Chabua at about 1600hrs, and it was nearly an hour later before the last plane landed. Again, the plan was to lay over at Chabua for a day to give the planes maintenance, oxygen service and general checkups before pushing on over "The Hump" into China. The oxygen would be essential to keep the pilots functional during the high-altitude flight over the mountains. With an afternoon off, several of the pilots took the opportunity to go on a hunt for water buffalo with Capt Hendricks, the CACW liaison officer at Chabua. Bill described the adventure in a letter to his family:

> Went hunting in Assam, and though I didn't get to shoot anything, I saw a lot of jungle. We were quite a party – about 15 strong – and all around me with carbines and .45s, and a couple of the boys had regular .30-caliber rifles. The native guide took us down the game trail to a place where there were

supposed to be water buffalo. Sure enough, when we got to the clearing we detected some movement in the jungle on one side of us. Suddenly, out popped this immense bull, and he started to charge. We were only 30–40 yards away, and I surely wasn't slow in turning to run, but all I saw was the heels of the other intrepid members of our hunting party. The bull didn't charge very far before he stopped. So about three of us who were nearest to him decided to shoot it out. I was fumbling with the cartridge clip for my carbine, another major was shooting, but in his excitement was just sighting through the rear peep-sight – and thereby shooting into ground about 30 feet in front of him – and another member of the group [Capt. Hendricks] cut loose with a .30-caliber. The darn bull fell down and started shaking. I thought at first that he was just overcome at the comical sight our brave hunting party had presented, but then another .30 caliber hit him and he was through. They estimated his weight at about 8,000 pounds. Some bull, huh?

Bad weather forced the squadrons to lay over in Chabua for a second day, but they were able to depart for the 500-mile flight to Kunming at 0930hrs on January 21. The three squadrons had planned to fly in a single formation, but they never got formed up properly. As a result, 14 Warhawks wound up escorting three B-25s, and the remaining six B-25s had just two P-40s for escort. Two of the P-40s had mechanical problems and had to return to Chabua, along with three B-25s that got lost. Bill and the other pilots reached Kunming at around noon. It had taken them eight days to complete a trip that a modern jetliner can make in six hours.

Their stay at Kunming would be temporary, and Bill wasted no time checking in with Gen Chennault, who maintained his Fourteenth Air Force headquarters there. He told his mother in a letter just two days after arriving:

Talked quite some time with my "Old Boss," and we really had a good visit. Things have changed a lot in some respects, but I still know my way around.

It was the beginning of a close relationship that the two men would develop over the coming months. Several years after the war, Chennault said in a letter to R. T. Smith, "In the A.V.G. I considered Bill one of our good pilots and good reliable boys, but after he returned to me in the Fourteenth Air Force I soon discovered he was a real man among men."

The plan was for the CACW squadrons to move up to Erh Tong air base at Kweilin (Guilin) as soon as possible, but a stationary front over Kweilin made flying there impossible and mired Bill's pilots in a classic military "hurry-up-and-wait" situation. Conditions at Kunming were not particularly pleasant. Lodgings in Hostel No. 7 were acceptable, but the base personnel were not exactly helpful. The P-40s were due for their 25-hour inspections, but with the ground personnel still en route to China there were no mechanics to do the work. Only members of the resident 26th FS/51st FG pitched in to provide minimal servicing of the planes.

After it became clear that the 7th and 8th FSs would not be moving out in the foreseeable future, they were assigned a room in the base operations building where the pilots would spend their days on alert for flying missions. Even this was hardly an improvement, however, as explained in the squadron history entry for January 24:

> This afternoon we were given an alert room in the operations building. We cleaned it out, moved in some tables and benches, and set up shop. It is colder than blue blazes, as some of the windows don't have glass, and there is lattice-work around the top which can't be closed off. Many of the fellows are catching cold.

Three days later, the situation was no better:

> The impossibility of keeping the alert room warm is telling on the pilots. Those who have colds are getting worse, and those who hadn't are getting them. Capt. Callaway [8th FS pilot] has hooked up his radio and we are getting some good comedy in the form of broadcasts from "Radio Tokio."

Bill was one of the pilots who caught a bad cold, as he told his mother in a letter. Catching cold was a big deal for pilots during World War II, because the cockpits of their planes were not pressurized like modern aircraft. That meant that changes in air pressure during climbs and dives played havoc on their ears, even when they were healthy. A pilot with a cold was almost assured of getting an earache if he went flying, and bursting an eardrum was not out of the question. The sub-freezing temperatures in the cockpit at higher altitudes only added to the misery.

Finally, on January 31, the alert room was moved from the frigid operations building to a warmer spot in the barracks. With that change, one officer was assigned to the 51st FG's operations office to be in a position to phone the pilots if any action started. It did not. Meanwhile, 1Lt Charles Lovett, the 7th FS's intelligence officer, put his time in Kunming to good use by collecting information about enemy activities in China and French Indochina that would be useful to the pilots when they reached their forward base at Kweilin. He prepared a map showing the locations of American and Japanese bases, along with the latest intelligence about the numbers and types of Japanese planes operating in the region. And on February 4 the first of the ground echelon began to arrive in Kunming.

Orders to move reached the unit two days later, but the 7th and 8th FSs would not be going directly to Kweilin. Instead, they were instructed to set up shop for the time being at Chanyi (Zhanyi), an ATC field about 85 miles northeast of Kunming. They were not told the reason behind the move, but no one was complaining about getting out of Kunming. A week after arriving at Chanyi, further orders arrived instructing the squadrons to move up to Kweilin. Surely, most of the pilots thought, they would be seeing some action soon.

At 1300hrs on February 12, 1944, a formation comprising nine B-25s, 21 CACW P-40s and five P-40s of the 74th FS/23rd FG took off from Chanyi for the two-hour flight eastward to Kweilin. As the planes approached the latter, Bill got his first look at the city and its surrounding territory, which he had not visited during his service in the AVG. Most notable were the odd, ice cream cone-shaped limestone mountains that rose hundreds of feet above the floor of the Li River (Lijiang) valley. Here, because of its strategic location, Chennault had built three airfields and established the headquarters of the 68th Composite Wing under Col Clinton "Casey" Vincent. The CACW squadrons would operate under Vincent's command while they were in Kweilin.

Kweilin had been a hot spot in the China air war since the summer of 1942. Farther east were advanced airfields at Lingling, Hengyang and Suichwan (Suichuan). From these bases, Vincent's fighters and bombers could reach the Japanese strongholds at Hankow (Wuhan) to the northeast, Canton (Guangzhou) to the southeast, Hong Kong on the coast and Hainan Island in the South China Sea. Of course, that meant enemy aircraft in those areas could reach Kweilin as well, so Bill's pilots in the 7th FS could expect to be performing defensive as well as offensive missions from their new home.

On arrival at Kweilin, the P-40 pilots put down at Erh Tong air base, which would be their home for the time being. When they reached the hostel area where they would live, the pilots received a hearty greeting from their groundcrews, who had arrived from India a few days earlier. For the first time since leaving Malir a month ago, the squadrons were back to full strength.

Bill was pleased to learn that his 7th FS was being paired with the 32nd FS, which was commanded by Bill's stateside friend Bill Turner, and that they would share the orderly room and operations building at the north end of the field. The other two CACW P-40 squadrons, the 8th and 28th FSs, would have a similar setup at the other end of the runway. Pairing the new squadrons with the more experienced ones made good sense. The 28th and 32nd had flown about a dozen combat missions by this time and were beginning to know the score, having shot down several enemy planes but also having lost several pilots and planes. Passing along their knowledge to the new pilots would give them a leg up when they got their first chance to confront the enemy.

Bill was less pleased to learn that two of his P-40s were being reassigned to the 28th FS, which was short of aircraft after losing five during December and receiving only two replacements up to now. He turned over the squadron's two P-40N-5s, keeping its ten P-40N-15s together.

The first full day at Kweilin (February 13) was a busy one for Bill's squadron. 1Lt Hancock made his way to the 3rd FG operations office in the morning to pick up copies of operations orders and other pertinent publications. There, he learned that the squadron would stand alerts on a 24-hour schedule, noon to noon, operating as a separate squadron and using only its own planes. All ten of the squadron's P-40s were assigned tactical numbers, which the mechanics painted in white on their tails. The numbers were "660" through "669," and Bill's plane, 42-106322, got the low number. Five of the squadron's P-40s were taken out of service for their 25-hour inspections, leaving the other five available for alert duty.

At 1610hrs the phone rang in operations, alerting the 7th FS that an unknown aircraft had been reported 80 miles from the base. Bill and four other pilots raced to their planes and hurriedly took off to chase down the intruder. They searched the cloudy sky for about an hour before giving up and returning to base. The first combat mission of the 7th FS had been anticlimactic, to say the least. That evening at about 2100hrs another alert was received, and the men scurried from their quarters to one of the limestone caves where they had been instructed to go for shelter during air raids. This time the intruders turned out to be three B-25s returning from a mission, so the men returned to bed when the all-clear sounded. They had not seen any action yet, but Bill and his men were beginning to feel that they had caught up to the war at last.

LETTERS FROM HOME

When Bill arrived at Kweilin, he was pleased to find nearly 30 letters and eight packages waiting for him. Receiving mail was very important to Bill, as it was to most people serving in the military, and the long intervals between deliveries in remote overseas theaters could be a real drag on morale. But a big haul like this at mail call was a sure-fire boost to the spirits. One of the packages contained a fountain pen, which his mother had sent after repeated requests from Bill. He was also happy to get a deck of cards and a cribbage board from his sister Isabelle. "Mick" Forbes, now serving in the US Marine Corps, was his best correspondent with eight letters in the stack.

Bill sat down with his new pen to write Mayme a letter on February 16. It was obvious why he had wanted the pen, because his handwriting on the letter looks very neat. As usual, his letter was very folksy and omitted any details about combat operations. He told her he had a new head cold, weighed 170–175lb and was, "eating like a horse. A usual day will find me consuming about six eggs, two pancakes, and two cups of coffee for breakfast – for lunch two plates of whatever we've got and the same in the evening, with great volumes of tea with the last two meals. I eat lots of rice. I don't get enough exercise but plan on inaugurating a strenuous athletic program in my squadron when my cold gets better." He went on to mention the letters he had received from "Mick," but was quick to assure his mother, "You're still my favorite girlfriend, and I've looked plenty of them over here and there going both ways."

Earlier that day, Bill had convened a meeting of his flying officers, American and Chinese, to discuss several items on his mind. The weather had been consistently bad since his squadron arrived in China and showed no signs of improving, so Bill was worried that his pilots would lose some of their edge during long periods of inactivity. He urged them to take care of their flying equipment and pay close attention to their piloting techniques whenever they got a chance to fly. He also brought up the need for an insignia for the squadron, since the other three CACW fighter units had already chosen their designs. Eventually, they settled on a design that superimposed a fire-breathing eagle over a 12-pointed Chinese sun roundel, and some of the pilots had patches made that they applied to their flight jackets. Then Bill turned over the meeting to his operations officers, 1Lt Hancock and Capt Yieh, to explain the new system of alert schedules. The squadron's 22 pilots were divided into two sections, which would alternate on alert schedules. With just ten aircraft, two pilots were assigned to each plane, and they would alternate duty days.

The remainder of February was soggy tedium for the pilots at Erh Tong. They got a brief respite when Madame Chiang Kai-Shek and Gen Chow, commander of the CAF, showed up one afternoon to greet their new CACW squadrons. As Bill reported to his mother in a letter, "She looks about the same as I remember her and seemed as nice as ever." In the same letter, Bill described his living conditions:

> We live in hostels run for us by the Chinese government. I get a big kick out of my house boy. He wakes me in the morning, and not being very well versed in the English language, instead of telling me to get up he stands there and tells me to stand up. He is a pretty wise lad, though, and when he found that I like to sleep a little more each morning after he called me, he started your old trick of telling me that it was half an hour later than the actual time.

The ample breaks between flying days also provided time to paint additional markings on 7th FS P-40s, according to the squadron history. "We are having shark noses, flight numbers and CAF [serial] numbers painted on our ships, in addition to the CACW numbers we now have." The 7th FS applied distinct "sharksmouths" that turned up in a sinister grin, and several weeks later the markings were completed with the addition of 12 alternating stripes of blue and white on the rudders of the planes.

Soon the lack of activity began to sap the morale of the men. On one drizzly morning, the pilots arrived at the flightline to find that none of the planes had received preflight inspections, and only two mechanics, both Americans, were present. It was the worst showing yet by the Chinese ground personnel, although they had exhibited a marked lack of discipline at times in the past. Bill prevailed on

Capt Yieh, the operations officer, to speak to the men. Yieh outlined their past delinquencies, went over their duty schedules and made it clear that no further fooling around would be tolerated. It did not help much, as the squadron history for February 27 shows:

> This morning we had a major catastrophe when the planes were being preflighted. A Chinese sergeant was running up [P-40 number] 661 but had only set the left brake. When he ran it up, the right wheel jumped the chock and the plane swung around, hitting the wing of 666 with its wing and tail. Damage to 661 consisted of a badly bent vertical fin and rudder, and a bent left wing and wingtip. Damage to 666 was a bent left wingtip and wing, and a torn aileron. Our sheet metal man says that neither plane will require a wing change and that both should be in [operation] in a few days. It is a commentary that we should have brought our planes all the way here without an accident, and then have two banged up without ever getting into action.

The weather finally broke on February 29, and a mission was scheduled for the following day. The operation – a bombing strike against a concentration of Japanese troops reported near Nancheng (Nanxian) – would not only be the first offensive mission for the three newly arrived squadrons but also the first all-Chinese mission for the CACW. Capt Hsu led off the four 7th FS pilots participating in the mission at 1001hrs, and they rendezvoused with B-25s over the field, then provided escort to the target. No opposition was encountered, and the P-40s stopped to refuel at Hengyang before returning to Erh Tong at 1600hrs. As missions go, the Nancheng strike was routine, but it was a proud achievement for the Chinese members of the CACW. Bill, too, could take pride in the fact that the squadron he had trained was now in the fight. He would not have to wait long before taking his own crack at the enemy.

On the evening of March 3, Bill called his pilots together to let them know about the next day's mission. Everyone was excited to learn this would be their first offensive mission at full squadron strength, and that the objective would be a surprise attack against Kuingshan (Qiongshan) airdrome on the northern tip of Hainan Island. Bill would be leading the squadron in one flight of P-40s, with Lts Chang, Lewis and Tan on his wing, while Capt Hsu would lead the second flight, accompanied by Capt Yieh and 1Lts Hancock and Walton.

Bill and the other seven pilots assigned to the mission were awakened at 0530hrs on Saturday, March 4, and made their way to the group operations office at 0615hrs for a briefing by 1Lt Watson, intelligence officer of the 8th FS. As Watson explained, this would be a combination escort and strafing mission for the 7th and 8th FSs, who would be covering 14 B-25s at low level while a P-40 squadron from the 23rd FG provided top cover. According to the most recent intelligence report, the Japanese had 35 fighter planes and 23 bombers at Kuingshan, and the base was well defended by antiaircraft guns. Therefore, the pilots were instructed to make just a single pass over the target. Pulling off a surprise attack would be paramount to the success of the mission.

The pilots returned to their alert shack and were told to wait for while final arrangements with the 23rd FG were completed. They spent a nervous hour in the shack before getting orders to take off at 1000hrs. Once airborne, Bill rendezvoused his P-40s with the B-25s and took up position on the starboard side of the formation. The 8th FS, led by Maj Cords, was on the far side of the bombers, and the 23rd FG P-40s lined up above and behind the B-25s. They flew a southerly course from Kweilin, and when they crossed the coast of the Hainan Gulf they dropped down to an altitude of 100ft to avoid detection by the Japanese. Then the formation got lucky, encountering overcast with a 100ft ceiling about half-an-hour before they reached the target. By dropping just below the cloud deck, they were reasonably safe from enemy interceptors attacking from above.

The formation crossed the coast of Hainan Island about 16 miles west of Kuingshan and turned toward the target, staying on the deck. As they neared the airdrome, the 8th FS peeled off as planned and made a strafing pass, with each of its two flights roaring down one of the cross runways with guns blazing. Then the bombers made their runs from west to east across the airdrome, followed by the P-40s of the 23rd, which were carrying rockets. After that it was the 7th FS's turn. Bill arranged his two flights in a single, eight-plane line-abreast formation and led them in, flying from south to north. They topped a small hill and saw the airdrome before them. A fuel dump at the southwest corner of the field was burning furiously, covering the airdrome in smoke, and a parked fighter was aflame in the middle of the field. Antiaircraft fire was sporadic and inaccurate. Bill's fighters shot up some hangars as they crossed the field, then turned left to rejoin the bombers and headed for home. The surprise had been complete.

Capt Hsu was quite honored to have led his flight on the mission, and he gave this account of his actions for an oral history:

As we were entering the target area, a Japanese Oscar fighter just flew above me [at] about 500 feet. At first, I wanted to turn around and attack it, but the altitude difference between us was too great for me to shoot at it. Furthermore, due to the "attack only once" rule, I abandoned the idea. As my division began the attack, I saw a water tower in front of me, on which I fired. After damaging it, I fired at four or five Oscars parked on the south side of the field, causing explosion[s] and thick smoke. I almost flew right into the smoke. In order to avoid an accident, I pulled my aircraft up. At that time, I saw four or five Oscars parked on the west side of the airfield, which I targeted successfully again.

Although the Japanese aircraft mostly were unable to take off to engage us, antiaircraft fire from the airfield was still fierce. A small piece of aluminum plate on the right side of my cockpit was damaged around the time I completed my strafing runs. The strong air currents blew the piece into my cockpit. This damage was probably caused by antiaircraft fire.

By now each of the squadrons had completed its attacks, but the formation was widely dispersed, and we needed to reorganize our formation on the way home. I made an S-turn to avoid antiaircraft fire. The previous wave of B-25 bombers was turning left to return home, and I followed them closely to examine whether the bombers were damaged, and also to seek out my squadron members. After Hancock and Walton joined up, I used the radio to confirm that all the members were safe. Because each aircraft's remaining fuel and degree of damage were different, each aircraft's route for home was different. My aircraft was partially damaged, and I was low on fuel, so I landed at Nanning, refueled and flew back to Kweilin.[1]

All of the aircraft involved in the attack returned safely, although two pilots from the 8th FS nosed up on landing. When the aviators gave their reports, it was determined that 15 enemy aircraft had been destroyed, including three in the air by the 8th FS. Bill did not claim credit for any kills, but several of the pilots with him did. 1Lt Wilbur Walton destroyed three on the ground, while Capt Hsu and Lt Tan Kun were each credited with one ground victory. Hsu and Tan also reported shooting down A6M Zero-sen fighters, but these claims were not included in the squadron records.

A photo-reconnaissance aircraft made a flight over Kuingshan four hours after the attack and reported no fires burning and 25 aircraft parked on the airdrome. The pilots did not know what to think of the report, and expected to make a return visit to Kuingshan in short order. However, the weather closed back in, and by the time it improved five days later, the Fourteenth Air Force had other targets in mind.

Bill was back leading his squadron on March 9 when it escorted B-25s attacking dock and industrial installations in the river town of Shihweiyao, about 350 miles northeast of Kweilin. Despite marginal weather, P-40s from the 7th, 8th and 32nd FSs took off at 0700hrs and headed for Hengyang, where they would refuel before rendezvousing with the bombers over Changsha. The 7th FS's mission description is as follows:

The farther we went, the worse the weather became, and when we got to Lingling and the mountains, the overcast was right down on the peaks. We sneaked over a pass, and about half of the formation went up into the overcast and the other half went down into the valley. The weather was worse there, but we followed the river and finally got to Hengyang. In landing at Hengyang, Capt. Hancock in 667 landed on the wrong runway and hit a roller, damaging both flaps, engine, prop and the center section of the wings. Two 8th Squadron ships also cracked up. After the flights had straggled in, it was found that Lt. Lin S. C. in 662 was missing. The flights were reorganized, making the close cover two six-ship flights, and the fighters took off again and rendezvoused over Changsha.

They then proceeded to the target, where the bombers confused the issue by turning left instead of right. Just east of the target nine Zeros, probably Hamps [more likely Ki-43 "Oscars"], attacked from 3 o'clock. The top cover engaged them, and only three got through to the close cover. Of these, Lt. Burch and Lt. Yang Y. K. claim two shot down, while Capt. Lewis engaged the other with indecisive results. All the bombers got back alright, but one of the 32nd fighters is missing.

The P-40s returned to Hengyang and remained there overnight, before flying back to Kweilin in perfect weather the next day. Later it was learned that Lt Lin had died when his P-40 crashed into the side of a mountain about 50 miles southwest of Lingling. The pride in the 7th FS for having scored its first aerial victories was tempered by the loss of Lt Lin at the hands of an unforgiving Mother Nature.

The only other combat action during March consisted of two night bombing attacks by the Japanese against Erh Tong, resulting in the loss of one 32nd FS P-40 and some lost sleep for everyone on the field. Then, on March 13, came word that the 7th and 32nd FSs were moving across the valley to Li Chia Chen, a new airfield that was in the final stages of construction. This came as a relief, because Erh Tong had become too crowded for efficient operations. At their new home, Bill's men found an excellent 7,000ft runway, which was being lengthened at both ends. Quarters were in Hostel

No. 15, located on the southwest side of the field in a grove of trees. There was just one mess hall, so Chinese and American personnel ate together until a second mess hall was constructed. All agreed that the food was excellent.

American officers and enlisted men lived two to a room in the barracks, and Bill continued to share his quarters with Bill Turner. In a letter home, Bill told Mayme of a humorous encounter when he chanced upon Turner putting Vicks Vapo-Rub on his hair to keep it in place. "His hair laid down nicely, but he reeked, as you can well imagine," he wrote.

Also during this period, Bill's dog "Fubar" came down with pneumonia. With the animal close to death, one of the flight leaders gave him some "high powered sulfa drugs" and he eventually recovered, much to Bill's relief.

During the afternoon on April 5, the two squadrons at Li Chia Chen got word that they should expect to be moving soon. 3rd FG CO Col Al Bennett, his Chinese counterpart Maj Yuan Chin-Han and Lt Col Tom Summers, group executive officer, came from Erh Tong to give them the scoop on an upcoming operation that would send all four squadrons of the group north, where trouble was brewing on a new front.

Since January, Chinese intelligence had been watching the Japanese moving supplies and troops south from Peking (Beijing) and Manchuria via railroad to a staging area in Honan (Henan) Province near the Yellow River Bridge at Chenghsien (Zhengzhou). When the Chinese determined that the Japanese were going to use this buildup for a push south to take the portion of the rail line from the Yellow River to Hsinyang (Xinyang) – the last length of track between Peking and Hankow still held by the Chinese – they conceived an operation to oppose the offensive. They called the plan "Mission A," code name "Fateful." Bill and the others in the room had no way of knowing it at the time, but Mission A would define the rest of their wartime service in China.

Securing control of the rail link to Hankow was in reality a preliminary action that would set the stage for a much larger Imperial Japanese Army effort to follow. With the link in place, the

Japanese would have a supplement to the Yangtze River for moving supplies and troops to the Hankow area. Once sufficient forces were in place, they planned to unleash a ground offensive called Operation *Ichi-Go*, which ultimately would threaten the entire network of Fourteenth Air Force bases in eastern China, and also open a land route from Southeast Asia to Shanghai for shipping war materials to Japan.

Air power was the primary weapon of Mission A. The plan was simple – let the Japanese concentrate their Honan forces, then smash them by air attack before they can start their offensive and continue to strike until the threat subsides. It did not work out that way, however, as bad weather and poor communications conspired against Mission A before it could get off the ground. What might have been a bold countermove against the enemy instead became a defensive struggle, and for all their heroic efforts, the aircrew of the CACW would fail to prevent the Japanese from achieving their goals in Honan Province.

During the meeting at Li Chia Chen, Col Bennett outlined the Mission A objectives as follows to Bill and the others:

1. Defend Chinese-held airfields and cities from Japanese aerial attacks.
2. Destroy the Yellow River bridges.
3. Destroy rail junctions at Sinsiang (Xinxiang) and Kaifeng, the key supply centers for the enemy's drive.
4. Destroy the railroad line from Hankow north to Hsinyang and interdict the Hankow railroad yards.
5. Bomb the railroad bed in the Chinese-held portion of the rail line.
6. Attack Japanese aircraft and airfields, plus boat traffic on the Yangtze and Yellow rivers.
7. Provide close air support for defending Chinese ground forces.

It was a long list of jobs for a force that would total just 84 aircraft during the rare times when all squadrons involved were at full strength. Mission A planners estimated it would take about a month to halt the Japanese. After that, the optimistic planners said, the CACW squadrons would no longer be needed in north China and could transfer to bases in southwest China, where they would fly missions in support of Chinese troops fighting in Burma. It sounded reasonable at the time.

The CACW commander, Col Winslow Morse, had spent a week in late March inspecting the airfields he expected to employ for Mission A and was not impressed with what he found. The bases, noted the CACW official history, were "decidedly inadequate and of a capacity more suited to an air force of World War I." The primary base would be at Liangshan (Liangping) in eastern Szechwan (Sichuan) Province, where the 3rd FG headquarters, one B-25 squadron and two P-40 squadrons would be located. Enshih (Enshi), about 80 miles east of Liangshan, could handle one P-40 squadron, and Hanchung (Hanzhong), about 150 miles north, could support another P-40 squadron and possibly more B-25s. Bill learned that his 7th FS would be going to Liangshan with "Snatch" Cords' 8th FS. That suited him just fine, as Bill and "Snatch" had become close friends over the months since arriving at Malir.

When the meeting wrapped up, Col Bennett led the men outside for a spirited game of touch football. It is likely that Bill did not play, because he was nursing a leg injury suffered in a previous game. He told his mother in a letter that he sustained the injury while trying to "make a big time run." Three days later, Bill wrote a letter to Mayme that touched on a number of subjects, including local farming practices and a list of books he had read recently. Among the books were the novels *Tap Roots* by James Street, *Capricornia* by Xavier Herbert and *The Robe*, the best-seller by Lloyd C. Douglas. Unusually, Bill even touched lightly on the subject of combat near the end:

> The boys have been thinking up pet names for their planes and painting them on the sides of the front cowling. Some of them are pretty rare. We can't quite decide on mine. All of the

boys have been calling me the "boss" so there has been some conjecture as to whether to call my plane "The Boss's Hoss," "Reed's Steed" or "Billy's Filly." Since my crew chief's nickname is "Jug" [Sgt Homer Nunley] I think that on one side I will put "Boss's Hoss" and on the other side "Jug's Plug" [which he did].

Some of the Chinese pilots are playing American records on a phonograph they brought down this morning. Sort of makes me homesick to sit here and listen to them. I bought some records when I got back over here this time, but one of the other outfits has them at the present writing, for at the present I don't have anything to play them on. My records are more on the classical side than these they are playing this morning.

We have been the subject of a few night bombings recently, and I just never have caught up on my sleep. I think the little devils are afraid to come over in the daytime.

On April 19, 1944, Japanese troops crossed the Yellow River in force and headed south toward Hankow. The CACW headquarters had received no advance warning from Chinese intelligence, so the carefully laid Mission A plans for crippling the Japanese by air attacks before they could strike were no longer valid. Overnight, the course of the war in China had changed dramatically.

Bill and the other combat commanders who would be participating in Mission A met at CACW headquarters in Kweilin the next day to receive their final instructions for the move north, along with a revised plan for operations once the squadrons were resettled. The commanders were instructed to prepare their squadrons to deploy to their new bases as soon as the weather permitted.

Late in the afternoon, Bill's friend "Snatch" Cords took off in his P-40 and headed for Lingling, where his 8th FS was now based. It was nearly dark when he reached the base, and in his enthusiasm over his new orders, he buzzed the hostel area before entering the landing pattern. Then, in one of those unexplainable tragedies that occur during wartime, Cords misjudged his landing. As Cords' P-40 lined up on final approach, it faltered and mushed into the top of a tree off the end of the runway. The plane's left wing broke in half, and the aircraft wobbled about another 100 yards before it crashed into the side of a hill and exploded. The blast catapulted Cords out of his cockpit, and he landed about 200ft away, already dead. His stunned squadronmates retrieved his body and shipped it to Kunming for burial.[2] Bill was devastated by the loss of another good friend, and unburdened himself in his next letter to his mother:

> I have been rather blue the last three days. My best friend over here this trip was killed in a crash. We started out together when I first got here, and since we were the leaders of two outfits in the same group, we lived together when we were in India, and were together quite a bit of the time up here. You would think that after all these months, or is it years, I would get hardened to seeing them go, but this was just about like Neil Martin getting it. All one can do is stay in there and try a little harder.

Bad weather closed down attempts to move north for the entire week following the Mission A meeting. Day after day Bill would send out pilots to scout the weather, and each time they would return with news that a solid front was blocking the route to their new base. The delay did have one benefit, however, as it provided time for Bill's 7th FS to be brought back up to the full strength of 12 P-40s. Finally, the weather cleared on May 1, and at 0930hrs the squadron got the word to move out.

Bill led his squadron away from Erh Tong at 0955hrs, leading a flight of four P-40Ns that included one from 3rd FG headquarters flown by Capt Wang. Leading the other two flights were Capts Hsu and Wilbur Walton. The squadron proceeded northeast toward Chungking in company with a flight of B-25s and then turned west for the approach to Liangshan, landing safely after two hours and 45 minutes in the air. All P-40s were carrying drop tanks and rocket launchers under their wings, and these were quickly removed when it was learned that the airfield was under air raid alert. Wasting no time, Bill assigned two of his most trusted enlisted men,

TSgt Rumen and SSgt Nardelli, to man the 0.50-caliber machine guns that had been set up near the alert shack for ground defense. The P-40s were scrambled at 1315hrs with orders to intercept an incoming air attack, but they found no enemy aircraft and soon returned to base. When the all-clear sounded, everyone went to their barracks to get settled.

As the long day ended, Bill and his men had a chance to survey their new home. The air base at Liangshan consisted of an established grass runway and a second one under construction. There were six revetments large enough for B-25s and 15 more being built to shelter P-40s. The base also had a 100,000-gallon-capacity fuel dump and very primitive radio equipment. Hostels and mess halls for the men were under construction, but personnel would be housed and fed in the ramshackle Kuomintang hostel in downtown Liangshan until they were completed. Eventually, Liangshan would have an officers' club on base where the pilots – Chinese and American – could mingle and relax in the evenings. American and Chinese living quarters and dining halls were segregated, however.

The base housed an odd assortment of Russian bombs and Belgian ammunition left over from the early days of the war, as were two rattle-trap gasoline trucks, an American station wagon and seven other well-used vehicles. For aircraft, there were two beat-up, leaky P-43 Lancer fighters of the CAF that apparently had been used for air defense. Bill's squadron would share the alert shack with the 8th FS, now commanded by Capt Harvey Davis.

The nearby town of Liangshan was typical of those in the interior of China. Much less cosmopolitan than even Kweilin, the town had no streetlights, no modern buildings and a single, narrow street that twisted along and sprouted side streets at random intervals. The effects of Japanese bombing were clearly to be seen in Liangshan, where wrecked buildings had been left as piles of rubble by the Chinese inhabitants.[3]

While the squadrons of the 3rd FG were getting settled at their new bases, Japanese troops pushed into Honan Province in several columns. From the soon-to-be-infamous Yellow River Bridge at Chenghsien they moved south down the Peking–Hankow rail line to Saiping (Xiping), with little substantive opposition from Chinese forces. The main drive split off to the west after reaching Hsuchang (Xuchang), then turned back north to Loyang (Luoyang). From there the enemy moved southwest again to Loning (Luoning), eventually pushing all the way to Lushih (Lushi), which was only about 100 miles east of the strategic city of Hsian (Xian). Another drive, meanwhile, pushed across the Yellow River north of Mienchih (Sanmencia) and moved west to Lingpao (Lingbao), also threatening Hsian. Opposing and harassing these efforts by the Japanese would occupy the 3rd FG throughout the rest of the war.

INTO BATTLE

After six long months of training and then waiting for the weather to clear, Bill finally got the opportunity to assert his leadership in battle at the head of his squadron in May 1944. One of the first items on his to-do list was to have a sign installed at the entrance to the squadron's alert shack at Liangshan. Borrowing from the sign that "Oley" Olson had made for the "Hell's Angels" back in the AVG days, Bill instructed that his sign should read:

REED & HSU INC.
EXTERMINATORS
OPEN DAY & NIGHT

By inclination and choice, Bill was a lead-from-the-front commander. He could not, of course, fly every mission, but he flew as many as possible. "Never did like paperwork," he told his mother in a letter written in May. "As my operations officer told me, 'Your idea of running a pursuit (fighter) outfit is to have headquarters in your cockpit and the orderly room in your map compartment.' He's right, too."

Bill's first action of Mission A was a "milk run" escort mission on May 5 with no enemy opposition, but the next day Bill encountered enemy aircraft for the first time in more than two years. The job on May 6 was to escort B-25s attacking Hsiangcheng. After the bombers departed the target area, Bill led his flight of three P-40s down to sweep a road leading out of town and caught a concentration of troops traveling in trucks. The Japanese apparently mistook the P-40s for friendly aircraft and began cheering and waving flags at them. Their joy turned to panic when Bill's fighters returned their greeting with a hail of machine-gun fire. In two swift passes, the P-40s destroyed 25 vehicles and killed an estimated 250 troops. Two Japanese fighters attacked the P-40s as they pulled up from their second pass but did not press the issue after Lt Chang Lo-Min damaged one of them.

For the first time since the start of the war, Bill described a combat mission to his mother when he wrote to her two days after the May 6 action. Writing by candlelight while sitting on a folding cot at the remote air base of Ankang, he told her he had been so busy that he had not combed his hair for five or six days. Then he told her about the scrap:

We were just leaving the target after knocking out a lot of Jap motor vehicles and men (lots of fun) – one of my pilots, just 23 [Capt Walton], got on the radio and said, "They sure are dumb b------s, Boss, not to have air support for such a concentration." It just happened that we hadn't encountered any Zeros, but as I glanced over to look at this pilot's plane, I saw a Jap coming up on his tail but still out of range. So I clicked my microphone button and said, "What do you mean no air cover? There is a Zero behind you just out of range. No, there are two of them!" Well, he darned near did a snap roll, he turned so quickly. We tangled with them for a few moments, and though we were three to two, I think that the Chinese boy with us was the only one to hit one, and we didn't see it go down. I had emptied almost all my "ammo" on trucks etc. I had only one gun firing – felt like I was using a pop gun, but the Jap was still afraid to continue a head-on pass, so it was a moral victory at least.

On May 7 Bill led eight P-40s, including Warhawks flown by the co-commanders of the 3rd FG, Col Bennett and Maj Yuan, north on the one-hour flight to Ankang. There, the P-40s would break into two flights to escort B-25s on two bombing missions that afternoon. The weather was poor and the missions accomplished little. Afterwards, the P-40s refueled at Ankang and flew back to Liangshan. During the landing, Capt John Hancock's plane collided on the runway with the P-40 flown by Lt Wang Kuang-Fu. Hancock's P-40 was destroyed and he suffered a deep laceration to his arm.

This forced Bill to make a decision he surely had been dreading. Hancock was well liked, and he had done an efficient job as squadron operations officer during training. But in the words of the 7th FS history, "He was temperamentally unsuited for combat flying, and he knew it." Hancock had to go. Bill arranged for him to be transferred to a non-flying position in the operations section at Fourteenth Air Force headquarters in Kunming, and he appointed Capt Wilbur Walton as the new operations officer of the "Exterminators." A few weeks later 2Lt Ed Mulholland arrived to bring the complement of American pilots in the 7th FS back up to strength. Lt Wang, meanwhile, went on to become one of the leading aces of the CAF, with a score of 5.5 Japanese aircraft shot down.

The missions continued hot and heavy, with P-40s from the 7th FS heading out on a daily basis to bomb and strafe bridges, railroad facilities and rolling stock, road and river traffic and anything else of military value to the Japanese. One section of road near Loyang yielded so many fruitful targets that the pilots began calling it "Slaughterhouse Alley." And, of course, the P-40 pilots slugged it out with Japanese aircraft whenever they got the chance.

Bill's next encounter with enemy fighters came on May 11, when he led a flight providing top cover for three bomb-carrying P-40s of Bill Turner's 32nd FS. As Turner's planes were completing their runs on a supply dump near the Yellow River, seven Ki-43 "Oscars" jumped the P-40 formation. In the ensuing action, six of the IJAAF fighters were claimed to have been shot down and Bill was credited with damaging the seventh. At one point, according to the 32nd FS history, Turner was climbing up to get at the diving "Oscars" while Bill was chasing them down from above. As a result, the 32nd FS historian noted, "The two Bills almost shot each other's pants off."

Rain shut down flying for several days in the middle of the month, but on May 16 Bill and his men resumed operations with a vengeance. Flying from Ankang, he completed two missions that yielded him a score of three confirmed victories – his most successful day of air-to-air combat in the war. The task for the "Exterminators" on the 16th was to find a P-40 of the CAF that had force-landed behind Japanese lines and destroy the plane before it could be captured. With Capt Lewis as his wingman, Bill took off at 0740hrs and headed to an area southwest of Loyang to look for the downed fighter. Instead, they spotted a lone Japanese dive-bomber (that Bill claimed was a "Val," but which was almost certainly an IJAAF Mitsubishi Ki-51 "Sonia" – the "Val" was an IJNAF aircraft, and there were none in China) and took turns shooting at it until the stricken aircraft went down.

Failing to find the P-40, they returned to Ankang when their fuel supply ran low. Bill took off again at 1415hrs to search for the downed P-40 once more, this time leading fighters flown by Capts Walton and Yieh and Lt Tan Kun. As they approached Loyang, Bill and Walton spotted a Ki-43 "Oscar" and shot it down, sharing credit for the fighter's destruction. Then Bill spotted another "Val" (again, almost certainly a Ki-51) dive-bomber and shot it down by himself. Still later, the flight ran into three Nakajima Ki-44 "Tojo" fighters and attacked. Bill got one confirmed destroyed and damaged another, while Walton shot down a third "Tojo." Lt Tan was shot down, but he managed to elude capture and subsequently return to the squadron. The missing P-40 was never found.

Bill's three aerial victories (two individual kills and two shared) on May 16, added to the three he scored in the AVG, put him over the total of five victories needed to reach the unofficial status of "fighter ace." In his typical low-key way, he failed to mention this when he wrote to his mother about his memorable day:

> Three in one day is the best that I have ever done in one day. Was very pleased yesterday when I got a wire from Chennault with congratulations.

May 18 brought more excitement along "Slaughterhouse Alley" when Bill led a flight of five "Exterminators" escorting CAF P-40s tasked with dive-bombing troops and motor vehicles near Shuichen. After the bombers finished their runs, Bill led his pilots down to strafe targets on the road between Shuichen and Loning. Their gunfire destroyed ten trucks, damaged 20 trucks and eight armored vehicles and killed an estimated 300 Japanese cavalry troops. In appreciation for the success of this mission, Col Wang S. M., commander of the Chinese Third Route Air Force, sent the following letter to Bill:

> Dear Major Reed,
> I am writing to congratulate you upon the great success achieved by your air force while you cooperated with the 3rd and 4th groups of our Air Force and attacked the enemy at Lo-nin and Tsan-swei-tsen. It is reported that the whole regiment of enemy cavalry was killed and numerous trucks were destroyed during this mission. I have reported this achievement of yours to the Generalissimo through phone at 5 o'clock this afternoon, and am glad to tell you that our Generalissimo is very much pleased, and wants me to give his regards to you and to the warriors who participated in this battle.

The deployment of Bill's tiny task force of P-40s to Ankang lasted for another week, and they continued to pound the Japanese around Loning with multiple missions every day the weather allowed. The hectic pace of operations took a toll on aircraft, however. By May 22, the combined strength of the 7th and 8th FSs at Ankang was just nine P-40s, and supplies of fuel and ammunition at the base were getting low. Nevertheless, it appeared their attacks on the Japanese were having the desired effect, as pilots began to report sightings of enemy vehicles heading east away from Loning. At noon on May 24, Bill led his planes back to their permanent base at Liangshan. As the squadron history described the situation, "All planes needed a good inspection and servicing, and the pilots needed a rest, a bath and a change of clothes."

It was a short respite for Bill. The mechanics and armorers swarmed over the P-40s for one day, and then on May 26 Bill led a flight of four P-40s equipped with rocket launchers to Laohokow (Laohekou). The emergency base, about 240 miles northeast of Liangshan, put the P-40s in easy striking distance of the Peking–Hankow railroad line, where the Japanese were steadily advancing to close the gap in the line south of the Yellow River.

After spending the night at Laohokow in a former Norwegian mission house now used as a barracks, Bill and his wingmen – Capt Hsu, 1Lt Don Burch and Lt Hu H. K. – were awakened early for a mission against a barracks area one mile from Hsingyang (Xinyang), a key town on the railroad line. The P-40s, each heavily loaded with two fragmentation-bomb clusters and two triple-tube M-8 rocket launchers under their wings, took off at 0420hrs and headed east for the 140-mile flight to the target.

As the P-40s neared Hsingyang, Bill led them down from 4,000ft to treetop level for their approach to the barracks area from the south. He and Burch lined up on one row of buildings, while Hsu and Hu targeted the other. On their first pass, the pilots dropped their "frag" bombs, and at such a low altitude it would have been difficult to miss. They didn't, as all bombs were seen to explode among the buildings. After passing over the barracks area, Bill led his flight in a tight 180-degree turn so they could attack from north to south, this time using their rockets. Again, they blanketed the target area with hits, although they did not see any fires starting and they could not tell if the barracks had been occupied or not.

Still carrying a full load of 0.50-caliber ammunition, the P-40s overflew the town and reassembled over the nearby airfield, which showed no signs of activity. They encountered some light antiaircraft fire as they passed over the railroad yards at Hsinyang, and then Bill led them south down the rail line for about 15 miles, looking for rolling stock to attack. They found four boxcars parked on a siding and shot them up, before returning directly to Liangshan, where all four P-40s landed safely. It was still only 0745hrs.

By May 30, the Japanese were advancing west again along the Yellow River, so Bill led the "Exterminators" back to Ankang to run some more missions to the north. On his first trip that morning – a sweep in company with Capt Lewis, Bill picked up two bullet holes in his *BOSS'S HOSS* P-40 – one in the wing and one in the tail – while strafing a concentration of horses and men near Loyang. The damage to his fighter was not significant, so later that day Bill flew to Enshih, where the 28th FS was based, to lead an escort mission covering B-25s. The planes had only covered about 100 miles before bad weather forced them to return to base.

That night, Japanese bombers raided Liangshan in the dark. Bomb damage was slight – one aircraft destroyed and two damaged, plus one man killed. TSgt McAdams of the "Exterminators," who had been manning a 0.50-caliber machine gun mounted near the squadron's engineering hut, was knocked unconscious by the concussion of a bomb that went off about 50ft from him, but he was otherwise unhurt. Lt Tsen, the squadron's Chinese engineering officer, was injured after the raid when he tried to remove the booster charge from an unexploded anti-personnel bomb – the ordnance exploded and mangled his hand.

After several days of bad weather, Bill returned to the action on June 2 when he led a 12-plane dive-bombing mission from Ankang against the marshalling yard at Cheng-hsein. The P-40s of the 7th and 8th FSs took off at 0515hrs and headed east in good weather until they picked up the tracks of the Peking–Hankow railroad. A turn to the north sent them straight to the target, some eight miles away. There they found boxcars parked in the yard but no locomotives.

The P-40s were organized into three flights of four. Bill led his flight down first, while the other two provided top cover. The second and third flights attacked in turn, and all bombs were seen to hit in the target area, although the results were only rated as "fair." As he pulled off the target, Bill spotted a Japanese bomber parked on a nearby airstrip. With Capt Lewis on his wing, Bill strafed the aircraft and set it on fire, while Lewis shot up several trucks parked near the runway. Then Bill reformed the flights and swept north following the railroad until he spotted a train traveling in the same direction. Bill went down to strafe and blew up the engine, which stopped the train. Then the other P-40 pilots destroyed the 12 cars that the engine had been pulling. Soon they found a second train and destroyed it as well.

The P-40s continued northward, and as they neared a large railroad yard filled with boxcars near the Yellow River bridge they were jumped by a mixed formation of enemy Ki-43 "Oscars" and Ki-44 "Tojos." Fortunately, the Japanese pilots did not prove particularly skillful, and Bill's boys claimed four victories and one damaged for the loss of Lt Chang L. M. Bill described the action in a letter to home, and remarked on the high morale of his "Exterminator" pilots:

My flight was caught down low, as we had been strafing [shooting ground targets] and I couldn't get up into the fight – each time I'd start up, a Zero would come down at me and I would have to hit the deck again. They were lousy shots, though. I got two locomotives (both blew up) and one Jap bomber on the ground before the Zeros' attack came. That's the way it has been going almost every day. Shooting them up whenever and wherever we can find them. Once in a while a boy will come back sick from watching the slaughter when we catch horses and troops on the roads. The horses are the only thing that bothers my conscience.

The time seems to pass very quickly now that we have plenty to keep us occupied. The boys in the outfit, both American and Chinese, are in high spirits. The only time they get downhearted is when I have to leave them behind when scheduling missions. And we are getting a reputation in this part of China – on three occasions now delegations from various cities have visited us at various fields and made speeches and presented us with banners, etc. Naturally, I have been called upon to respond with acceptance speeches – some fun!

Bill further explored his own attitude toward combat in his next letter:

I'm not a bloodthirsty individual at heart, but it does me a lot of good to see them [the enemy] mowed down by the hundreds, and that is just what my outfit has been doing. And I've certainly no qualms of conscience because I've done my share of it.

"Just one of those Goddamned nights"

In the early afternoon of June 7, 1944, after Bill had crash-landed his battle-damaged P-40 in a river valley behind Japanese lines (see Chapter 1 for details), two of his 7th FS pilots took off from Ankang to reconnoiter the area and see if they could find out what had happened to "The Boss." Capt Bill Lewis, with 1Lt Ed Mulholland flying his wing, found the burned-out remains of Bill's P-40 and then thoroughly searched the surrounding area until their fuel supplies began to run low. But they found no sign of their CO.

Bill had landed at about 0700hrs, and he immediately set out on foot with the intention of putting as much distance as possible between himself and the wreckage of *BOSS'S HOSS*. He had a vague notion of his location in the Funei Mountains (Fuiu Shan), but not much else to help him in his quest to avoid capture by the Japanese. He carried a pistol and a compass and was wearing sturdy G.I. boots, but the most valuable tool he had was a silk banner known as a "blood chit" sewn onto the back of his flight jacket. The chit displayed US and Chinese Nationalist flags. Below them, Chinese characters read, "This foreign person has come to China to help in the war effort. Soldiers and civilians, one and all, should rescue, protect and provide him with medical care." Apparently, the blood chit served its purpose when Bill reached a small settlement after several hours of walking.

Another item Bill carried in his flightsuit was a USAAF "Jungle and Desert Emergencies" booklet, which contained tips for escaping the enemy and had blank pages to be used for a diary. Fortunately, Bill chose to make entries in the diary during the first days of his adventure. His account follows, lightly edited for clarity and style:

June 7
Hid out all day in little farm community nearby. Found from them that Japs were all around. At 10 [pm] an army man came from the nearest Chinese troops and we started walking to Iyang. One of the most beautiful nights I've ever seen, and the scenery was terrific. Reminded me of some scenes in "Lost Horizon." The walking would tax a mountain goat, however, and I'm sure that if it had been daytime I would have been scared to death of some of those trails. Walked until 3 a.m. and then roused some farmer out of his bed so I can turn in. I offered to sleep on the floor, but nothing doing. Most hospitable people in the world. Would have been my dad's 77th.

June 8
Up at 7 a.m. and started again at 0900. My Chinese guide is Li Whu Ozi and doesn't understand any English. He is taking me to the 15th Army. He stopped after I was just about out on my feet and apologized for the stop, explaining that some of the men with us had tuberculosis. They were carrying loads, and we weren't! At noon we were in sight of Iyang and I was relishing thoughts of a long rest. But we encountered the 15th Army on the march and after I met four generals (Wu, Chang, Li and Liu) we took up the march with them. My feet were killing me. The Chinese people are very poor in this district. There is no rice, strangely enough, but wheat is the staple. They make a gruel that I just can't go, and they eat steamed bread. Garlic is also much in evidence – looks as if I may come out of this a hell of a lot thinner. The generals all agree that the enemy is all around us,

but it doesn't worry them. General Wu lets me borrow his horse to cross the rivers. He is General of the 15th Army, composed of the 64th and 65th divisions. They are 15 days out of Loyang and lost two-thirds of their men and all clothing and equipment. We walked until I was practically out on my feet. At one place we came across a half-decomposed body of a Chinese farmer along the trail. We are following a beautiful stream. One of the generals, Liu Hiau Tsii, speaks a little English. He studied [for] 10 years. We marched until 7 p.m. and at last reached our goal for the day. I startled everyone by stripping down and jumping in the river. I asked to be excused – I was too tired.

June 9
Began the day's trek at 0800. Saw six P-40s and they seemed headed for Lushan. I was praying they would not spot our column and strafe us. Stopped at 1100 and they decided not to travel again until 3 p.m. when it wasn't so hot. Naturally I am the center of attraction in these little villages. The people have never seen an American before. Most of the farms and small communes are deserted because the Japs have been through here recently. Began our march again and for a while the going was pretty smooth. We stayed along the bed of the river. It's an awful temptation to get down and drink some of the clear sparkling water. The Generals say no, however, and they should know. About 5 p.m. the going started to get up and down, and it wasn't long before I was completely petered out again. I wasn't the only one though. About 7:15 p.m. we reached our day's mark and found the place almost deserted. No food and we found we had to sleep in a straw stack. All of the people are up in the mountains until the Japs are gone from the district. The straw pile suits me all right. Don't think there are as many fleas as in some of these farmers' homes. I took another refreshing dip in the stream and turned in.

June 10
On the trail one hour, and it's hotter than blazes. We've stopped under a big tree and in a valley that's really scenic.

I've been thinking sometimes when I get so tired and thirsty of how I used to drink three quarts of milk every day and how Mom used to beg me to eat something. She'll never have to do that again, believe me. We stopped at noon and ate and tried to get some rest. Too noisy with everyone in the village wandering in to give me the once over. I get a big kick out of General Liu, whom I stay with when we stop. He is from a very great Chinese family and has studied in Germany and Austria for 12 years. Visited the U.S. for two months. He is stocky, round-faced, slightly deaf and wears his haircut like a European or American. He shakes his head sadly when we can't find anything to eat or a good place to sleep. He instructed in military school [for] six years and was a student [for] two years. They made him attend school because they were afraid he was too Europeanized. He has a Ph.D. in engineering. Yesterday he shook his head and smiled that sad smile as he was putting on his socks, then he confessed they were his No. 1 boy's. About 7 p.m. we reached an old temple where we were to spend the night. A huge white tree stood in the courtyard, and they said it was 10,000 years old. A very picturesque place. Buddhas and all. Quiet, restful, and I'm sorry to say, full of fleas and rats. Noon at Salping.

June 11
The struggle of "500 men and a horse" began at 0815 and we followed the river (Yi He?). Hotter than blazes with the sand reflecting the heat right up into one's face. Notwithstanding we marched a little over two hours. As I write this, I don't know what the plan is. The Generals are talking it over. I would give anything for a drink of cold water for a change. We spent the middle part of the day [resting] anyway, and it was cool at 0400 when we set out. At 0530 we were met by a party from the 23rd Division, and they had horses for the four generals and one for me, too. I'm not much of a horseman, and think I will probably spend half of my time walking anyway. Met General Whang, commander of the 23rd, and his chief of staff, General Li, and

they had received a wire from Chungking to look for me. They had the best meal I've had in five days, and we probably startled them by the way we fell to. I can hold my own with the chopsticks artists now. Bathed in a cold mountain stream, watched over by my guard. Turned in thinking long, long thoughts of home and strawberry shortcake and soft beds, etc. Wonder why fleas hide in the daytime and come out at night. This makes five days and five nights in these khakis.

June 12
General Whang saw us off after a good breakfast and furnished us with five horses and two mules. I took the biggest one, and it was a mule. I'm just not sure I like this better than walking or not. Will know better tonight when I sit down (or stand up as the case may be). Traveled to 85 Army headquarters, and I thought for a while that I was leaving. But later it was decided that I should go on to the Army Group headquarters. I'm gradually going up the chain of command in the Chinese Army. I tried to give General Wu my sunglasses and General Liu my G.I. compass, but they wouldn't listen to me. I wrote them several letters of thanks, etc. Small thanks for all they have done for me, but war is war. Started at 4 p.m. and stayed the night at a little farm. Not much to eat, and General Wu laughed and said I had had a good chance to see how the Chinese army lived – meaning the G.I. soldier. He doesn't speak a word of English. Six days and I really haven't met anyone who can really speak English. We found out that the Japs have advanced past Sunghsien, which puts them not too far away. We are going to start early tomorrow so it's the hay for me – or rather the bamboo mat. I'm getting used to them, hard as they are.

June 13
Away at 0600 and by foot. Our trusty steeds went back to the last stop. Walked 25 [miles] and reached Miadzi, where the headquarters of the 31st is. General Wang is the boss here, and

he tells me that three days by horse, two or three days by car
and an hour or two by plane will put me in Chungking, so I'm
rapidly getting back to where I started from. The spot where
I went down was about an hour's flying time from the base
I started from. Had a swell lunch, complete with fried eggs,
and then said goodbye to my army and its four generals. They
were really swell to me, and I wish I could have thanked them
properly. I just finished a hot bath in a big earthen urn or vase.
Still no one who can speak English. One boy knew some 10
years ago, but he's more of a hindrance than a help. Kind of a
"drip" to boot. They have had two wires here from Chungking
to find me. The General just called, so I'd better go see what else
is up. Dinner I hope. And how it was! General Wang can really
throw a feed, and all of the time apologizing for the poorness
of it. He's about 40 and extremely nervous. Can't sit still – He
surely seems to have things under control around here. Says
he has 10 children and wants them all to fly – we exchanged
letters, etc. and I finally turned in about 9:30 p.m. Tough road
tomorrow.

June 14
Another big breakfast after a rather mosquito-plagued night.
I wouldn't mind so much if the darn things would park their
wings and line up for their turn cafeteria-style. Got away at
0700 and I find I have 18 soldiers to guard me, one to carry
my lunch and one boy to take care of my horse. Our path lies
through the Funei mountain range. It is a beautiful trip. Most
of the time we follow a mountain stream that is full of clear
water and lots of fish. I have a hard time overcoming the urge
to stop once in a while and catch some. They all look pretty
small, though. The vegetation is about the same as spots I know
in Iowa — ferns, mushrooms, daisies, bridal wreath, mulberry
and wild plum, raspberries, etc. There are plenty of pheasant
through this section. Haven't seen any yet but have heard many.
General Koie and another official met me on the trail, and we
proceeded to Taipingzen. Had some more lunch – General

Whang had packed eight boiled eggs, a chicken, some fried fish, some bread (which I ate on top of a mountain), and General Koie had an interpreter (another dope who knew two English phrases, "Don't mention it" and "As you like"). He was more a hindrance than a help. Learned a little of the war's progress in other theatres. Had an immense meal in the evening and hit the hay. The cleanest "sack" I've encountered, so I took off my clothes to sleep for the first time in eight days. General Wang made me take $5,000.00 [Chinese dollars] more with the $4,000 I had. I [am] weighed down.

June 15

On the trail at high noon. General Kou saw me off and had a "wha gar," a chair slung between two bamboo poles carried by three men. I rode it out of sight and had two or three more short rides when my guides insisted, but I would rather walk. We have only five miles more. The trail has been very rugged all morning.

Bill's account of walking out from behind enemy lines ends here, but his trek would last another nine days before he reached the airfield at Laohokow. He hitched a ride on a B-25 and arrived back at Liangshan to a rousing welcome on June 24. The "Exterminators" had learned on June 10 that Bill was in safe hands, and now they were happy to have their "Boss" back in town. Two days later, Bill was back in the cockpit of a P-40, leading an uneventful eight-plane escort of B-25s to Shayang. That night, he wrote his first letter to Mayme since reaching safety:

I've been walking for the last three weeks. Finally got back to civilization. Hope you haven't been too worried and hope no discouraging rumors have reached you. I never felt better in my life, and everything is going along first rate. Looking forward to a ferry trip ["vacation"] to India.

I have a very beautiful souvenir to bring home this time, Mom. It is a "Samurai" sword captured from a Japanese general and presented to me by one of China's most famous generals. It's really a wonderful piece of work, and it sure was a thrill to receive it. It was presented to this Jap by old Hirohito himself – according to the story, and that is their custom. I would mail it to you, but I'm afraid it might be lost.

Bill closed by mentioning that his hair was beginning to go gray and then returned to a common theme in his letters – a desire for Mayme to spend some of the money he was spending home on herself:

Have your eyes fitted with the best glasses obtainable if they cost a thousand dollars. And I want you to go to the best dentist in Cedar Rapids and have your teeth taken care of – hang the expense!

PASSAGE TO INDIA

On June 28, 1944, a C-47 transport plane lifted off from Liangshan, bound for Kunming. On board were three very happy officers – Bill and his friends Capt Lewis of the 7th FS and Maj Turner of the 32nd FS. By coincidence, all three men answered to the name "Bill." Their orders were to proceed to India and pick up three new P-40Ns for delivery to the 3rd FG, which was running low on aircraft as a natural result of the active pace of operations required by Mission A.

When the C-47 reached Kunming, Bill had to time to visit Fourteenth Air Force headquarters for a meeting with Gen Chennault, before proceeding over "The Hump" to India. During Bill's brief time with Chennault, the general complimented him on the work he and the "Exterminators" had been doing recently. Chennault also had a bit of bad news too. Because of the press of operations and the need for experienced, talented leadership, Bill should not expect to be sent back to the US for another six months or so. Then it was back into a C-47 for the flight to India. The plane stopped at Dinjan, in the Indian jungle province of Assam, and "the Bills" proceeded from there to Calcutta, where they would pick up their new P-40s.

The pilots had a week to kill before the new planes would be ready, so Bill somehow contacted Helen Pyle, a young woman who had attended MHS with Bill and graduated a year behind him in 1936. They had several dates in Calcutta, according to a letter Bill sent to Mayme, before the time came for the "three Bills" to return to China. They did not get far, however. The monsoon season was now in full force over Assam and Burma, and heavy rains delayed their ferry flight at Dinjan until the end of July.

Finally, on July 31, Capt Lewis flew in to Liangshan from Chengkung with two 28th FS pilots in three new P-40s. Bill arrived the next day in another new P-40. He had loaded his plane with canned goods – cheese, sardines, fruit juice etc. – to be used for a party celebrating the "Exterminators'" 100th mission, which had occurred on July 29. The squadron gave him a very warm welcome when they discovered what he had packed in the ammunition bays of his plane's wings. Congratulations also were in order, because on August 1 Bill was promoted to lieutenant colonel.

By the time Bill returned to the 7th FS, the Mission A focus had shifted from the Yellow River to the Yangtze. The Japanese had advanced as far west on the Yellow River as they needed, and they had completed the last link on the Peking–Hankow Railroad. Trains had begun pouring troops and supplies into Hankow in support of the main *Ichi-Go* offensive southward to threaten the Fourteenth Air Force bases in the Hsiang (Xiang) River Valley. Now the Mission A effort was directed at disrupting the Japanese in the area around Hankow, especially targeting traffic on the Yangtze River.

Bill only stayed at Liangshan for a day before leading his P-40s to the forward base at Enshih, which placed them about 60 miles closer to their targets in the Hankow area. Despite the arrival of several new P-40s, the 3rd FG was still so low on aircraft that the 7th, 8th and 28th FSs often had to pool their fighters so as to put together a mission force of sufficient size to make the effort worthwhile. This would remain the case for most of August.

Bill took off at noon on August 3 from Enshih, leading six P-40s on a sweep of highways, airfields and the Hsiang and Yangtze rivers from Ichang (Yichang), to Anli (Jianli), Shasi (Shashi), and Shihshow (Shishou). His first mission after returning from India was a relatively quiet one. No enemy planes were observed at Ichang, Tangyang (Changyang), Kingmen (Jingmen) or Anli airfields, and there was no activity on the Hsiang River. They saw only three small boats on the Yangtze River from Shasi to Shihshow and strafed them. One sampan sank and one 60ft boat caught fire. An oil tanker at Shasi smoked but did not burn. All P-40s returned undamaged.

There was barely time to refuel and rearm the P-40s before a second mission of the day left Enshih at 1505hrs. Bill again led six P-40s (two each from the 7th, 8th and 28th FSs) to strafe trucks and other targets of opportunity around Kingmen Field. Their route was similar to the morning mission, but this time they encountered antiaircraft fire at Kingmen, Tangyang and Ichang. Bill was hit in the right wing and wing rack, while his wingman Bill Lewis took a hit in the engine of his plane but was able to complete the mission. They failed to locate a truck concentration reported earlier but shot up the administration building, control tower, barracks area and alert shack at Kingmen airfield. Only one Japanese plane was spotted on the field, and Capt Tsang of the 8th FS destroyed it by strafing.

Later, the P-40 pilots shot up a storage building, barracks and a large tent believed to be a supply dump, plus one truck with three soldiers. Combined, Bill Reed and Bill Lewis expended 1,200 rounds of ammunition. Their first day back in action had been a productive one.

The flying weather remained good, and Bill flew his next mission, strafing boats on the Yangtze, the following day. That evening, he told his mother in a letter that it was so hot at Enshih that "crawling into a plane is like stuffing yourself in an oven, and everything in the cockpit is burning to the touch. Doesn't take long to cool down once you're in the air, though."

Then on August 8 he flew two missions that earned him his highest decoration, the Silver Star. The morning mission that day departed from Enshih at 0555hrs, with Bill in the lead of 12 P-40s for a sweep of shipping on Yangtze between Hankow and Sinti. They carried no bombs but shot up a large number of boats on the river, and all planes returned safely.

Bill had just two "Exterminator" pilots (Lts Ed Mulholland and Tang C. C.) among the nine P-40s with him when he took off at 1300hrs for a return strike to the area he had covered in the morning. They encountered cumulus clouds on their way to the target, but the sky was clear when they dove to attack altitude at 1415hrs. The P-40 pilots got the action started when they strafed a 70ft boat in a canal at Kayu. Then they spotted 20 to 30 sampans on the west bank of the river and strafed them too. Bill set the largest one on fire. Their next target was an 80ft boat at Sinti, which they shot up, and also killed several people who were running down the gangplank to escape the hail of bullets. Proceeding eastward, they had nearly reached Hankow when 12 to 16 "Oscar" and "Tojo" fighters jumped them. In an instant, Bill and his two wingmen were fighting for their lives against a rain of enemy fighters pelting them from above. The 7th FS history describes the ensuing dogfight:

> Lt. Col. Reed got on the tail of an Oscar just after it had pulled off from a pass on a P-40 and gave him a good burst. Lt. Mulholland saw [the Oscar] in an uncontrolled glide at less than 500 feet. Claimed one destroyed. Lt. Mulholland got a good 40-degree deflection shot on an Oscar and gave him three good bursts. [The Oscar] flipped on his back and started down in a glide with black smoke pouring from his engine in a steady stream. Claimed one destroyed. Lt. Mulholland also got hits on two other Oscars in head-on passes. Claims two damaged. Lt. Tang became lost on the return trip and landed at Kaifeng.

On return to Enshih, Bill's plane displayed the only damage suffered by the P-40s in the wild melee – a hit from a heavy caliber slug in its right aileron. Lt Tang later claimed to have shot down a third "Oscar" when he returned to Enshih for debriefing.

The citation for Bill's Silver Star award, dated October 27, 1944, recounted the action as follows:

> He distinguished himself while leading his fighter squadron in two actions against enemy river shipping on 8 August 1944 in a heavily defended area in China. In the morning attack four vessels were sunk and four were damaged. When the squadron returned in the afternoon, sixteen enemy fighters were protecting the area and in the engagement that followed Lt Colonel Reed's aircraft was struck by a 16-millimeter shell and was seriously damaged. Despite the damage to his aircraft, he continued to lead the attack and personally shot down one of the enemy fighters. A total of eight enemy aircraft were shot down and six were damaged by the squadron. He then continued the attack on the river vessels, which resulted in the sinking of three larger steamers.[1]

Bill's combat score now stood at seven enemy aircraft shot down, including AVG and CACW claims. Typically for him, however, he chose to display only four victory flags, signifying his score with the "Exterminator" squadron, on his new *BOSS'S HOSS* P-40N. It was another example of his understated approach to leadership, which kept him focused on the task at hand rather than glorifying past exploits. Still, his reputation as the "Boss" of the "Exterminators," both in the air and on the ground, was growing. In describing Bill long after the war, more than one of his pilots claimed that he could "smell out" Japanese aircraft in the sky. He was a legend in the making.

Bill's next "sniff" at air combat came on August 12 when he led another sweep of the Yangtze to the Hankow area, but this time he came up empty. He was leading "Tampa Red" flight near Sintankao, strafing shipping, when he became separated from the covering flights. "Oscars" jumped the top and medium covers, and the P-40 pilots shot down three of them. However, as the 7th FS history explained, Bill was unable to join the dogfight:

> When Tampa Red leader became aware of what was taking place, he was several miles and several thousand feet away from the point of contact; he attempted to get his planes into the scrap but the Japs did not wait around for a full scale battle.[2]

Bill flew two more sweeps against Yangtze shipping on August 12 and 17, and then he returned to Liangshan to take a break. His visit to the "Exterminators'" home base coincided with a much-anticipated visit from a USO troupe, which was scheduled to perform there on August 20. When the troupe, headlined by movie actress Ann Sheridan and comedian Ben Blue, arrived by C-47 that morning, Col Al Bennett and Bill led them on a tour of the base. They spent some time on the flightline posing for photographs next to Bill's plane, *BOSS'S HOSS*, and Sheridan even climbed into the cockpit for a picture. Bill, as might be expected, turned on the charm, and before the performers left they all autographed the nose of his fighter. The performers started their show in the evening, but then had to beat a hasty retreat from Liangshan, as Bill described in his next letter:

> They were supposed to put on a show here, but we had an air raid while the show was going on, and they left rather precipitously. It was quite a change of scenery for the boys, though, and everyone got a tremendous kick out of seeing a white girl for a change.

The fresh autographs brought bad luck for *BOSS'S HOSS* the following day. The plane was on loan to the 8th FS for a mission when its Chinese pilot crashed on takeoff.[3] It is not known if the plane was destroyed or merely suffered repairable damage, but Bill definitely was not flying it on his next mission, on August 22 – another shipping sweep on the Yangtze. About eight "Oscars" intercepted the P-40s near Hankow, and Bill was able to fire a burst into the forward fuselage of one plane before it dived away, apparently under control. He was credited with one damaged.

Unfortunately, Bill's wingman, 1Lt Robert Guthrie, was shot down by the Ki-43s. Guthrie, who was a replacement pilot who had only joined the "Exterminators" a week earlier, was on his first mission. Not long thereafter word was received from the Chinese that Guthrie had survived a crash landing behind enemy lines and that guerrillas were bringing him out. He never arrived, however, and subsequently was listed as killed in action.

Guthrie had replaced Capt Wilbur Walton, the squadron operations officer, who was the first of the "Exterminator" pilots to complete his combat tour and return to the US. As Bill put it to "Nephie" Dick (who was now safely home and enjoying married life) in a letter at about that time, "I'm beginning to send some of my boys home. Most of them have over 50 missions, and they have been overseas about a year to 14 months, and I think a pilot's efficiency is affected after that length of time. Especially do I think this of the pilots that are married. Of course, a lot depends on the temperament, too."

In that same letter, he took a different view of his own situation. "It appears I may be home sometime around Christmas, but I am not placing too much stock in anything until those old going home orders are in my hand. It would be nice in a way, but then it would be nice to be in on the kill over here, too."

Back at Enshih, on August 29, Bill led 14 P-40s on yet another shipping sweep of the Yangtze River. The pilots on this mission scored six confirmed kills, giving the 3rd FG its 100th aerial victory of the war. Bill got one of them. The mission had a familiar profile – fly the Yangtze from Hankow to Sinti, attacking river traffic and shore installations. After dive-bombing a storage area and sinking a river steamer, the P-40s were attacked from above by Ki-43s near Yuenti. The "Oscars" hit the medium cover first and then the top cover, which had been trailing by several miles.

Down low, Bill fired a good burst into an "Oscar" during a quartering turn head-on attack. The stricken Ki-43 went into a steep, turning dive and continued straight down to crash into the river. His wingman, 1Lt Ed Mulholland, spotted another "Oscar" lining up on Bill's P-40 and fired a 90-degree deflection shot that hit the Japanese plane in the fuselage. The IJAAF pilot broke off his attack, but Mulholland resumed his position on Bill's wing and did not follow the damaged enemy fighter. Lt Tan Kun, also in Bill's flight, put a long burst into an "Oscar" that was about to attack a P-40. The Japanese pilot flipped his plane over and went into a dive, but he never pulled out, and he crashed into the ground.

Pilots of the 28th FS scored three kills on the mission, and the 8th FS also got one.[4] It was, therefore, impossible to say which pilot actually scored the 3rd FG's 100th victory, since all of the action took place within a short space of time. All P-40s returned safely to Enshih.

Then it started to rain. Bill and his pilots were stuck on the ground at Enshih for the first two weeks of September with little to do but play poker to pass the time. Bill got on a losing streak and remarked in a letter, "If the weather doesn't break soon, I'll be flying back to my home base without my britches." He also bemoaned the death of another close friend, George Parker, who had been his operations officer in the 320th FS at Westover Field. Parker died in a takeoff accident while serving with the 5th FG, CACW. "He was my best friend there. I used to double date with him and his wife a lot, and had to write her a letter about it."

Since his P-40 was not being used, Bill sent his faithful crew chief Homer "Jug" Nunley to the recently opened rest camp near Kunming to relax after the strains of summer operations. The "Exterminators" were cut off from regular mail deliveries, which arrived by plane, so a truck was sent to CACW headquarters in Chungking to pick it up. That scheme failed when a key bridge collapsed on the route between Liangshan and Chungking and the truck had to return empty.

The rain eased in the latter part of the month, and the "Exterminators" managed to fly six missions, with Bill leading two of them. The only encounter with enemy fighters occurred on September 21, as the squadron was escorting B-25s attacking the Yellow River Bridge. It proved to be a costly engagement. Eight to ten "Tojos" jumped the formation, and Capt Don Burch, the longest serving American flight commander in the 7th FS, was shot down. Bill's friend belly-landed his P-40 not far from the river and was captured by Japanese troops. Burch spent the rest of the war as a PoW but survived the tortuous experience.[5] 1Lt Heyward Paxton, a former flying instructor, joined the "Exterminators" shortly after Burch went down, to assume command of C Flight.

October brought more rain, but the "Exterminators" were still able to complete 23 missions during ten days of flying. One high spot for Bill came on October 27 when he was awarded the Silver Star for leading the successful missions of August 8. By far the most productive mission of the month took place during the afternoon of that same day, October 27, when Bill led 16 P-40s drawn from all four squadrons of the 3rd FG on a sweep of the railroad between Hankow and Puchi. Alternate targets were the airfields at Ichang, Kingmen and Tangyang.

Bill led four planes in the strafing flight, with one at intermediate cover and two flying top cover. They flew to a point about 20 miles south of Hankow and turned south above the railroad. Just beyond Tutitang, they found a train of 12 to 15 cars heading south at about 25mph. Bill swooped down and fired a burst of 0.50-caliber slugs into the engine, which was hit in the boiler and spouted steam in all directions as the train slowly rolled to a stop. The strafers then proceeded to make 11 passes over the train, attacking it from 90 degrees to lengthwise. Their gunfire set three or four tank cars afire at the back to the train and killed a considerable number of Japanese troops who were riding in coal cars farther forward. Some of the soldiers jumped off the train and escaped, but many could not. The gasoline fire spilled down the tracks for about half a mile, where it set a single-span wooden bridge on fire.

Leaving the train, Bill led the formation farther down the tracks but saw no further targets and turned the P-40s northwest toward Kingmen. There is no way of knowing if it was Bill's long experience in air combat over China or just plain luck that led him to Kingmen, but when the pilots arrived over the enemy air base they found a sight that must have made their hearts leap with anticipation. Nine twin-engined Ki-48 "Lily" bombers and eight to ten "Oscar" fighters were in the landing pattern, and several bombers were already on the ground. Apparently, they were planning to stage through Kingmen for a bombing raid that night.

Bill again led the attack, firing the last of his ammunition into a "Lily" that caught fire and crashed into the ground. Then he circled up to provide top cover while the rest of the P-40s pounced on the enemy. When the smoked cleared, 16 Japanese aircraft were confirmed shot down and four more destroyed on the ground by the P-40 pilots. The only loss was Capt Lewis, whose plane developed engine trouble while strafing the train. He broke off from the attack and headed for Enshih, but the engine failed near Lienyang and he bailed out.

Bill, who was now the leading ace of the CACW with nine confirmed victories, briefly described the mission in a letter:

> We really caught the Japs napping, and it was like shooting fish in a rain barrel. I only got one, but he was a bomber and really made a most merry blaze when he hit. All in all we got 15 or 20 of them, and my old boss [Gen Chennault] wrote us a swell wire of commendation. The very next day, a change of tactics and targets got us four locomotives.

Despite the jaunty tone of that description, the strain on Bill caused by his long months in combat was now beginning to show in his letters. In one, he listed old friends from high school and college who had been killed in action, and in another he asked Mayme to write to letters of condolence to the mothers of his pilots Burch, Guthrie and Lewis, who had all been listed as Missing in Action in the past few months. Bill Lewis, the most recent to go down, was in fact on his way back to the "Exterminators," although Bill did not know it at the time. He told Mayme that Lewis, his roommate, had completed 75 missions, and that he was his "best pilot and right-hand man." Bill closed a third letter with the sad observation, "If this war isn't over soon, I won't have any friends left."

REUNION WITH JINX

Bill's outlook must have brightened quite a bit on November 2 when a C-47 landed at Liangshan and who should emerge from the cargo door but Jinx Falkenburg, his traveling partner from the bond tour of 1942. Jinx was a member of USO Camp Tour 374, which had been making appearances at air bases in China for about two weeks. It is likely Bill knew Jinx was coming, and it is possible he had spent time with her in Kunming after she arrived there on October 19. However, he may have been the only guy at Liangshan who was happy to see the troupe arrive – the hasty departure of the Ann Sheridan show in August had given the Americans there a low opinion of the USO. They would soon learn that this troupe was different.

The leader of the troupe was veteran Hollywood actor Pat O'Brien, who often played Irish and Irish-American characters in his movies. O'Brien had recruited Jinx for the tour in September, hinting broadly that their destination was the CBI theater. Joining them was piano player Harry Brown, dancer Betty Yeaton (known for her ability to contort her body into amazing positions) and the husband and wife musical team of Ruth Carrell and Jimmy Dodd. A guitar player, Dodd had a vast repertoire of songs that allowed him to play just about any tune his audiences requested. A decade later, the boyish redhead would gain fame on television as "Jimmy" on *The Mickey Mouse Club*. O'Brien served as master of ceremonies at their shows, telling jokes, singing, dancing and giving patriotic pep talks to the G.I.s. Jinx, who still was not much of a singer or dancer, mostly did skits with O'Brien. "I just prattled, played straight to Pat and tried to behave just as I would if the G.I.s were all old friends," she said in her book, *Jinx*.[6]

This combination worked perfectly. While some previous USO performers had left the impression that they considered it a big sacrifice to spend a few weeks in a war zone, Camp Tour 374 gave off no such vibrations during the 84 shows the troupe performed. Richard Watts, ex-drama critic for the *New York Herald Tribune* then serving in the Office of War Information, saw their show in Chungking and wrote a review for the *CBI Roundup* newspaper. He said this:

> The fine thing about the O'Brien–Falkenburg company was that there was no suggestion of martyrdom about it. The players gave every indication of having a good time, as well as providing one, and that adds decidedly to any audience's fun. They also gave the impression that they liked, not only their audience, but each other, and that, too, is not the impression created by all the previous visitors to our citadel. All of this adds distinctly to the pleasure of an entertainment that depends for a considerable part of its success on building up an air of pleasant and likeable informality.
>
> As for Miss Falkenburg, she was, to put it in terms of understatement, wonderful. It might ordinarily seem a harsh statement to make of any girl to say that she is "wholesome," but with anyone as beautiful as Jinx Falkenburg it can be said without fear of being an insult. It is in fact one of her greatest virtues that she looks not only lovely and alluring but combines those not unimportant qualities with the rare additional one of being direct and unaffected and utterly, to put it frankly, wholesome. You know that she is delightfully seductive without bothering to work at it – and that is rather an unusual tribute.
>
> I suppose she is no great mistress at the art of song or acting. It is probably true that she sometimes misses the proper stress on a comedy line. It happens, though, that she manages her comedy scenes with such serene and humorous good nature and has in addition so much the quality of being the person you look at on stage – or elsewhere – that she is invariably a delight. I fear it is stuffy to say so, but the boys not only loved her but had deep regard for her.[7]

Bill had a similar assessment of Camp Tour 374's show at Liangshan, which he reported in a letter to his mother on November 4:

I also had a couple of visits with Jinx Falkenburg and Pat O'Brien. They were over here getting their pictures taken all over the place and entertaining the boys. Really put on a good show, and do a lot for morale.

A little bit of old-fashioned serviceman cynicism comes through in Bill's crack about the performers "getting their pictures taken," but he also confirms that he visited them more than once during their China tour. This adds to a mystery that has been part of the Bill Reed story since 1944 and likely will never be solved – were Bill and Jinx romantically involved? The first source that might be expected to shed some light is the autobiography that Jinx wrote after the war. But her 36-page account of the USO tour never mentions Bill. Instead, she goes into excruciating detail about her longing to marry "Tex" McCrary, the newspaper reporter she met shortly before the 1942 Bond Tour, who was now serving in the military in Europe.

Why didn't she mention Bill? It would have made an interesting addition to the story if Jinx had mentioned reuniting with her old friend Bill from the Bond Tour of 1942, especially since he had become a bona fide war hero by this time. Was this omission an oversight on her part, or was it intentional? Jinx did, in fact, marry McCrary, and they went on to become pioneers in television broadcasting. In 1947, they premiered their first network show, *Jinx and Tex at Home*, broadcast Sunday nights on NBC. The program combined film and live interviews of celebrities in their residences. It was a big hit and set the stage for future endeavors together.

By 1951, when Jinx's book came out, she and "Tex" were at the height of their celebrity. Perhaps Jinx had a reason for not mentioning Bill. On the other hand, she did not hesitate to discuss Bill on the air with Gen Chennault when he appeared on her show three years later.[8]

Two further accounts add more substance to the speculation. The first comes from no less an authority than Gen Chennault himself. Bill's close friend R. T. Smith, who named one of his

sons William Reed Smith when he was born in 1949, contacted
the general in 1952 to seek his assistance in writing a book about
Bill. The book never came to pass, but Chennault's return letter to
Smith contains the following paragraph:

> I suppose you know that Jinx Falkenburg and Bill thought quite a
> bit of each other and there was a rumor about their engagement.
> Bill saw quite a bit of her while she was on tour in China with
> Pat O'Brien and company.[9]

We get more specific information from a story written by Earl
Ashworth, a pilot in the 528th FS, for the *Jing Bao Journal*, a
publication of the Fourteenth Air Force Association. Ashworth was
in a flight of P-51s on temporary duty at "a small base in Northern
China" (likely Laohokow) in late 1944 when he met Bill, who
shared a room with Ashworth during an overnight stop at the base.
Ashworth, an inexperienced second lieutenant at the time, took
the opportunity to have a private conversation with the legendary
fighter ace. He wrote:

> It was seventh heaven to spend this time with a real veteran with
> so much combat experience. I had brought some Scotch over
> with me (Vat 69) and still had some left that I was saving for
> a special occasion. Well, how special can an occasion get? How
> often does a real, live hero walk into one's life and want to talk –
> to a lonely second lieutenant no less?
>
> As the evening wore on and the Scotch loosened our
> tongues, we were telling each other all kinds of personal
> history. It was then that I suspected that this man was under
> a lot of stress with lots on his mind. After a few probing
> questions, he finally told me that he was trying to resolve a
> very serious question. He was in love with this very wonderful
> and beautiful girl, and he wanted to go home. However, he
> had this powerful urge to continue his duty in China until all
> the Japs were gone. He had seen the Chinese people suffer so
> much and had heard so many awful tales of torture that he felt

an obligation to stay and do as much as possible to put an end to all that suffering.

He was, indeed, in great pain. What to do? When he told me that the girl was Jinx Falkenburg, the movie star, I couldn't believe that any man alive would give it a second thought. I would be on the first boat homeward-bound, but not Colonel Reed. There was no question that he was deeply in love, but Colonel Reed was a very mature person. He cared about the mission – about the war and the Chinese. He felt a deep sense of duty and reasoned that the war would not last much longer, and then there would be plenty of time to go home and pursue a career with Jinx.

We heard rumors in Ankang that Jinx came to China because of a boyfriend. We later heard he was a lieutenant colonel and some thought his name might be Reed. I did not disclose the rumor to Colonel Reed that night. I listened and tried to be a good and understanding friend. He left the next morning and I never saw him again.[10]

Jinx Falkenburg left China with USO Camp Tour 374 around mid-November. After a final performance in Myitkyina, Burma, the troupers headed home. As reported in Jinx's book, she stopped in Cairo for a rendezvous with "Tex" McCrary. Six months later they would marry, a union that lasted 35 years.[11]

Whatever feelings Jinx had for Bill remain a mystery. Did she travel to China to test her affection for him or, perhaps, to let him know face-to-face that she was in love with another man? Or was her joining USO Camp Tour 374 merely a coincidence that placed her in Bill's war by chance? At this late date, some 75 years later, we can only speculate.

DECORATION AND PROMOTION

Bad weather and low supplies of fuel kept Bill's "Exterminator" squadron on the ground for most of November, with just 18 missions completed. Bill got some welcome news on November 16 when he learned that he had been awarded an Oak Leaf Cluster to his DFC in recognition of "destroying five enemy aircraft in aerial combat" between May 16 and August 29, 1944. Gen Chennault also called him to Kunming at about this time to present him with a commendation for leading the successful October 27 mission.

Bill's star was continuing to rise, and on December 6 it took the next step. On that day, the command of the CACW changed hands when Brig Gen Morse was sent to Europe to check out ways and means of redeploying air units there to China after the German surrender. Col Al Bennett, formerly CO of the 3rd FG, moved up to become acting wing commander, and Bill took over command of the 3rd FG, bringing his buddy Bill Turner along as group operations officer. Capt Bill Lewis, recently returned from his unplanned visit behind Japanese lines, replaced Bill as CO of the "Exterminator" squadron.

Now, instead of leading a single squadron, Bill would have four squadron commanders reporting to him. Since the group headquarters was co-located at Liangshan with the 7th and 8th FSs, Bill did not need to move his living quarters. He simply worked in a different office on the days he was not flying. The administrative and planning workloads would be quite a bit heavier, taking up a lot of his time. Nevertheless, Bill still intended to continue leading from the front. He had this to say about his promotion in a letter to his mother:

> Today I was put in command of the group – a brand new c.o., and it should prove interesting. I won't be able to fly as much anymore, and I know that will make you happy. But I guarantee you they won't make a desk pilot out of me. Until I get a little better acquainted with the new machinery and people, I'm going to have to work overtime. I don't mind though, for I'd much rather be busy as long as I'm over here.

The monthly history report of the 3rd FG was written by Maj Kenneth E. Kay, who wore several hats as the group's armament and chemical warfare officer, public relations officer, historical officer and adjutant. His report for December 1944 began with this note of optimism:

> To replace Colonel Bennett as our Group Commanding Officer came Lt. Colonel William N. Reed, long-time commanding officer of the 7th Fighter Squadron, a young fireball with one of the most heavily decorated torsos in China, priceless experience in combat, and an almost unique record in this theater since he first fought under General Chennault as a member of the widely publicized A.V.G. We were well content with the selection of Colonel Reed as a commanding officer, having, naturally, dreaded the possibility of the employment of outside talent with "notions" and innovation.[12]

One of the last chores Bill completed before leaving the "Exterminators" was to write a Christmas letter to the parents of each of the 30 American members of the squadron. Here is a sample, written to the parents of Cpl Lonnie Neal, a radio technician, in Washington state:

> Once again the holiday season is almost at hand, and though it finds us still engaged in the awful struggle that its costing us so many lives and keeping so many away from their loved ones, yet we are much nearer the victory which ultimately must be ours.
>
> Doing his share, and doing it in an exemplary manner, is your son, Lonnie. Although he has been a member of my command for only the past seven months, he has been doing his job faithfully and well, often working long hours and under trying conditions. Any measure of success we, as a unit, may achieve reflects on him for his cooperation and spirit. Working as we are in a strange land, our group has become closely knit both in work and at play. Lonnie has been, and is, a well-behaved and well-liked member of our little family.
>
> So to you, his parents, I wish to extend the Season's Greetings. Joining me in this wish are all the other officers of the squadron.

Be of good cheer in the New Year to come, and may victory
be ours. With best wishes for your wellbeing and happiness,
I remain – Sincerely, W. N. Reed.

While Bill was busy writing the holiday letters in early
December, Gen Chennault was putting the finishing touches on his
plans for a major air attack on the Hankow area. He had been
lobbying the War Department for months to get permission to use
B-29 heavy bombers, which had been operating out of Chengtu
against targets in Japan, in his effort to blunt the Japanese *Ichi-Go*
land offensive. By mid-November, the Japanese had swallowed
up Chennault's key airfields at Hengyang, Lingling and Kweilin.
The Chinese Army had been ineffective, and the enemy was
close to reaching its goal of completing a rail link through China
to Southeast Asia. Chennault believed that disabling the supply
facilities at Hankow would choke off the Japanese offensive long
enough for the Chinese to prop up their defensive forces.

Finally, Chennault got the go-ahead to use the B-29s against
Hankow, but only for a single mission. The date was set for
December 18, 1944. This would be a maximum effort involving
the Fourteenth Air Force's fighter and bomber units and the
Twentieth Air Force B-29s. The plan called for Chennault's
fighters to attack the enemy air bases in the region in the morning,
disabling the Japanese interceptor force before American B-24,
B-25 and B-29 bombers swarmed over the area to destroy
enemy warehouses, dock facilities, ammunition dumps and
other targets. Bill's 3rd FG P-40s would move up to the forward
base at Laohokow in preparation for flying two of the morning
air strikes.

Bill's part in the Hankow mega-mission was minimal at best.
He led 16 P-40s of the 7th and 8th FSs off from Laohokow at
1125hrs, with instructions to search out and destroy Japanese
aircraft on airfields near Hankow. Their alternate target was to
strafe trains on the Peking–Hankow Railroad from Chowshintien
north to Hsinyang. An hour's flight brought them to Mancheng
airdrome, where it was reported the Japanese had dispersed some

planes from Hankow. Having found no aircraft on the field, Bill turned west to search the railroad. The P-40s proceeded north as far as Hsinyang, finding just one locomotive, which was strafed and destroyed. They also attacked the barracks area there, although results were unobserved. Light antiaircraft fire, moderate to intense, and accurate, was encountered from positions around Hsinyang, resulting in the rudder cable and tail wheel of one P-40K being shot out and slight damage to three other planes. Finding no further targets, they returned to Laohokow, where all landed safely at 1425 hrs.

Bill and his pilots spent the night at Laohokow to be in position for another mission the following day. Their job on December 19 was to escort B-25s assigned to bomb railroad yards and storage areas north of the Yellow River at Pengpu (Pengcheng). It turned out to be another milk run, with no enemy aircraft seen and minimal antiaircraft fire at Pengpu. When the bombers dropped their loads on the railroad at Pengpu, only two of the bombs fell outside of the target area, and a large fire erupted. Three small white bursts and one larger black burst of ground fire were encountered from positions at Pengpu, but all were low and trailing, and none of the aircraft sustained damage.

Bill led the top cover flight, and after the bombers left the target area he decided to do a little hunting along the railroad before heading for home. He found a train just north of Pengpu and led his P-40s down to strafe. Their gunfire blew up the locomotive, stopping the train, and then they made several firing passes at the idle railroad cars. By then fuel supplies were becoming an issue, so Bill turned his flight south for the two-hour flight back to Laohokow, where they landed at 1545 hrs. The "Exterminator" squadron's 187th combat mission was in the books. It would be Bill's last.

Several days before he had left for Laohokow, Bill had sat down in his room at Liangshan to write his mother a Christmas letter. He enclosed $400 in money orders and instructed Mayme to give each member of the family $20 from him for Christmas. It was a generous gesture, considering $20 in 1944 was the equivalent of nearly $300 today. Then he closed with his standard assurance to his mother:

All is well, and I'm working pretty hard these days. Looks as if I wouldn't make it home for several more months at least, but don't you worry, 'cause I'll be all right.

Those were the last words he ever wrote to Mayme Reed.

FINAL FLIGHT

It already had been a long day for three pilots of the 3rd FG when they took off from the advanced air base at Laohokow just before dusk on December 19, 1944. Led by the unit's commanding officer, Lt Col William N. Reed, in P-40N-20 43-23642, the three flyers were bound for their home field at Liangshan, about 250 miles to the southwest in Szechwan Province. Flying with Bill were his second-in-command and close friend, Major Bill Turner, and 2Lt Van Moad, a new pilot who had just arrived in China the previous month.

It would take a little over an hour for the flight to reach Liangshan, and as Bill watched the sun setting off the starboard side of his plane's nose, he had time to reflect on the combat mission he had led earlier that day. As missions went, it was not particularly remarkable except for its four-hour duration, which was somewhat longer than the normal P-40 sortie. Reed was qualified to make that assessment – after two tours of duty in China, it had been his 141st trip into enemy territory. Still, the mission had produced enough excitement to leave him weary and eager to sleep in his own bed in the quarters at Liangshan that night.

Darkness had fallen by the time Bill's flight arrived at Liangshan, but the three P-40s were not the only aircraft in the sky over the airfield. Japanese bombers were reported in the area. There was no chance that the Americans might attack the enemy planes in the darkness because Liangshan lacked a radar installation that could have directed the P-40s toward the intruders. In fact, the only defense that airfields in free China had against night bombing was to shut off all the lights and black out the facilities. Unfortunately, the blackout also meant that Bill and his wingmen would be unable to see the runway. They would have to find somewhere else to land.

With plenty of fuel remaining, Bill decided to lead his flight to the airfield at Peishiyi, some 130 miles southwest near Chungking. He adjusted his radio compass for the Peishiyi frequency and set out for the new destination. The three P-40s did not get far before clouds began thickening. Soon they found themselves on top of a solid overcast, and it revealed no breaks when Bill estimated he had reached the vicinity of Peishiyi. The flight made a few circles, but the pilots knew it would be suicidal to attempt letting down through the clouds with the mountainous terrain that awaited them below. Resignedly, Bill reversed course and headed back toward Liangshan.

Bill called Liangshan on his radio and got bad news. The weather at the air base was deteriorating and the Japanese bombers might still be in the vicinity. Until the CAF base commander received an all-clear message from the air raid warning system, he was refusing to turn on the runway lights for the returning P-40s.

The pale illumination of the gauges in his instrument panel revealed to Bill that his fuel supply was dwindling. With no other alternate airfields within flying distance, the three American pilots were out of options. In a quick radio discussion, they decided to circle near Liangshan until either the runway lights came on or their planes ran out of gas, in which case they would to take to their parachutes. Bill did not relish the prospect of bailing out. In numerous "bull sessions" with fellow pilots over the years, he had expressed his preference to fly his plane down to a forced landing if it became disabled. In fact, he had done exactly that six months earlier after his P-40 was badly damaged by ground fire on a strafing mission.

Time ticked away, but still the lights did not come on at Liangshan. Eventually the engines of the three P-40s sputtered and died as the fighters' fuel tanks ran dry. One by one, the pilots

294 FLYING TIGER ACE

rolled back the canopies over their cockpits, unhooked their safety harnesses and bailed out into inky darkness. Moad was most fortunate, landing uninjured and returning to Liangshan the following day (sadly, he was killed in action not long afterward). Turner hit the ground at a bad angle and broke his leg – villagers soon found him, and they carried him into Liangshan the next morning.

Maj Ken Kay, writing in the 3rd FG history, recalled the frustration felt by the men at Liangshan when they realized their esteemed commander was in trouble:

We watched their navigation lights sink below the hills toward Peishiyi. It was just one of those Goddamned nights. Later on we realized they might have safely landed here at the time, but the Japs were bombing Wahnsien, ten minutes away, at the time, and we were blacked out. When, realizing they could not get into Peishiyi and that they were circling overhead again, their gas perilously low, we finally turned on the field lights. At that moment a Jap "Lily," which had been hovering nervously in the vicinity, dived in, scattering small incendiary and fragmentation bombs to the south of the field. We suffered no damage from the bombing, but our fighters were by that time completely out of fuel and all three pilots were forced to bail out.

Bill's engine went silent when he was about 20 miles from Liangshan. Despite what misgivings he may have had, Bill bailed out as well. What happened next is open to some conjecture. But the stark fact is that he did not survive the jump. His body was found the next morning about a mile west of Lao-Yen-Cheng village. Capt Chuck Lovett, the "Exterminators'" intelligence officer at Liangshan and a great admirer of Bill, led the detail that went out to find their commander's body. Lovett gave this account to the author many years later:

He bailed out, and we don't know what he did, but we speculate he turned the P-40 upside down and dropped out. The pilots used to talk about what they were going to do if they had to bail out. What they were supposed to do was throttle way back and put the nose in an up position a little bit and roll the canopy back, then step out on the wing and dive off. That was the approved procedure, but we don't know what Bill Reed did.

Whatever he did, he must have hit the tail plane with the back of his head, because his body wasn't damaged at all other than there was a flap of hair loose on the back of his head that was scalped there. The chute did not open. His hand was on the rip cord.

"Flying Tiger" Bill Reed, legendary leading ace of the CACW and beloved group commander whose men called him "Boss," was dead. He was three weeks shy of his 28th birthday.

15

"The most staggering blow"

First thing in the morning on December 20, 1944, Capt Chuck Lovett set out from Liangshan in a Jeep to look for the three pilots who had bailed out of their P-40s the night before. With him was flight surgeon Jim Kinder, another friend of Bill. The two men knew that one pilot had escaped unhurt, another was injured and the third was dead, but they did not know which fate had befallen each of them. They had not gone far before they got their first answer when they located 2Lt Moad being escorted back to base by some Chinese villagers. He joined the Americans in the Jeep, and they continued on until they found Bill.[1] Another group of Chinese people was carrying Bill's body. "They had covered him with flowers and reverently cared for him," Maj Bill Turner wrote to Mayme Reed the following month.

Lovett, Kinder and Moad returned to Liangshan with the sad news that Bill had been the pilot who perished. By the time his body arrived at the base, word had spread throughout the 3rd FG, and the grieving had begun. Maj J. T. Bull, 8th FS CO, described it thus:

There was no more respected nor better loved member of our armed forces in all of China. His loss was the most staggering blow we could have received. Every officer and every man, American and Chinese, who worked, flew, fought and lived with him has personally suffered.[2]

Gen Chennault took the loss as hard as anyone. He ordered Bill's body flown to Kunming immediately for burial. The sun was shining when Bill's casket and five others were draped with American flags and positioned for burial at the American Military Cemetery on December 23, 1944, three years to the day since Bill's first combat mission over Rangoon. With Gen Chennault, members of his staff, plus officers and men of the 3rd FG in attendance, Bill was buried with full military honors. His resting place was in an above-ground enclosure – plot 14, row 2, grave 19.

Sheppard Bryan, Protestant chaplain of the 1340th AAF Base Unit, Kunming, conducted the funeral. He described the service in a letter to Mayme Reed:

> You may be interested in the passages of scripture I used. They are as follows: Psalm 23; John 14: 1-6; 1 Thessalonians 4:13-18; 1 Corinthians 15: 20-26 and 51-58. We have an ATC Flower Fund at this station with which we provide flowers for all funerals. In addition to the religious service, Military Honors are given. As you doubtless know, these consist of an Honor Guard, the firing of volleys by a firing squad and taps by the bugler. During the entire service all military personnel stand at attention uncovered, holding the cap over the left breast. You may rest assured that your husband [sic] had a properly conducted funeral, both from a Christian and Military point of view.

Unfortunately, the good chaplain used the word "husband" where it should have said "son" throughout the letter.[3]

While Bill's comrades in China were honoring him at his funeral, the bureaucracy in Washington, D.C., was grinding at its normal pace and efficiency. No one in Marion knew of Bill's death yet. In fact, people there were enjoying a story about their hometown hero's latest exploits that ran in the *Cedar Rapids Gazette* on nearly the same day as his funeral.

A news release issued by the USAAF on December 21, 1944, had listed Bill among 34 USAAF fighter aces who were credited with shooting down 15 or more enemy aircraft as of mid-December. It was a good-news story except for one shortcoming: Bill's name was included in error. In the release, Bill was credited with 16.5 aerial victories when, in fact, his actual score stood at nine confirmed destroyed and three damaged. Apparently, someone had mistaken the 7.5 ground kills credited to Bill in the AVG for aerial victories. The error persisted for decades after the war, as books published as late as 1977 listed the inflated score with Bill's name.[4]

On New Year's morning, 1945, Mayme Reed answered the telephone at 1314 5th Avenue in Marion. On the other end of the line was a friend of hers, offering condolence for the sad news that just came over the radio. News, what news? Why, the news about Bill; haven't you heard? With that, Mayme began to cry. Her grandson Ed Reed, not yet eight years old at the time, remembers that she spent the remainder of the day "on the couch, crying." In the afternoon, official word from the USAAF finally arrived. Somehow, the news of Bill's death had been released to the news media before his family was notified. This went against USAAF policy, but it happened to the Reed family nevertheless. And it did not change the essential truth. Their beloved Bill would not be coming home from the war.

Misfortune seemed to be stalking the Reeds. First, baby Josephine died in 1908, then George in 1919 and Kenneth in 1937 – now Bill. By the time Mayme Reed died in 1961, she had outlived her husband and all but three of her nine children.

Newspapers in eastern Iowa, from Dubuque to Des Moines, gave big coverage to the death of their state's top war hero, but an anonymous writer for the *Marion Sentinel* topped them all. The un-bylined story opened with a line borrowed from "Night-Thoughts" by 18th-century English poet Edward Young, "Death loves a shining mark," and went on to recount not only Bill's life history but also the shoddy handling by the USAAF of Mayme's notification of his death.

Mayme still did not know the circumstances surrounding the tragedy, but these soon came to light when she began receiving letters from Bill's friends in China a few days later. The most detailed of these came from Bill Turner, as might be expected. Two of the most emotion-filled letters follow. The first was signed by all 19 Chinese pilots in the "Exterminators":

We, members of the 7th Fighter SQ., humbly express our sympathy and comfort to you from the depths of our hearts. We also wish to express our appreciation for the great deeds Col. Reed has accomplished, for both his country and our own, to the devotion of our common cause. The loss of your beloved son is as well the loss of one of our fighting comrades and our best friend.

To our country, Col. Reed has nobly offered his best voluntarily. To us, he was our ablest leader in combat both in skill and courage. He has won the admiration of all his Chinese brothers-in-arms.

Although bodily he has gone from us, yet spiritually he will live in our hearts forever.

The second came later from Bill's good friend Capt Chuck Lovett, 7th FS intelligence officer. He wrote on May 27, 1945:

Just a note from one of the boys in Bill's squadron to tell you that we are carrying on in the spirit he instilled when he was here with us, and as we know he would have us do. The awful business of waging war on a cruel and ruthless enemy must continue, but with God's help the end is now in sight.

We who lived and worked with Bill, and who knew him best, will always cherish his memory. He was truly a great man. Of all his attributes, perhaps the most outstanding was that of respecting the feeling of the other man, a quality indeed rare in the army and in the world in general. He made the lowliest of us feel as a man and an equal. His courage, gentleness and kindness have inspired us all to great efforts to establish a combat record, which we are still maintaining, and is as yet unequalled in our organization.

Let us thank you, Mrs. Reed, for giving us such a man. He will live with us throughout our lives. And every time our planes take off, he is with them, leading them, and giving them courage and the will to win.

Others from the 3rd FG who wrote to Mayme included Al Bennett, J. T. Bull and Bill Lewis. From further up the command chain came letters from Maj Gen J. A. Ulio, the adjutant general; Maj Gen Chennault, Fourteenth Air Force commander; and Gen H. H. Arnold, USAAF commanding general. Bill's friend from the Loras College faculty Father George Stemm and the school's president, the Reverend M. J. Martin, wrote condolence letters, too.

As would be expected, Mayme received many letters from family and friends as well, and more messages came from another group – the show-business friends Bill had made during the war. Among these writers were Ralph Bellamy, Walter Abel, Pat O'Brien and the Ritz Brothers. Another letter, from Paramount Theater owner G. Ralph Branton in Des Moines, broached the subject of what Bill might have done after the war if he had survived:

You did not know it, and as a matter of fact, Bill didn't, but I had him all set to go in movies. We were going to screen test him in Hollywood. I don't know that he would have gone for it because Bill never wanted to be a glamor boy, but I guess that's why he was so glamorous. He had it without trying, without knowing it. He never took himself seriously and I know it was going to be quite a job to ever get him before the cameras. He, as you know, didn't like the hero stuff. I guess that is why he was a great hero.

In one of my last letters to him I was trying to tell him about his future in motion pictures. In all of his letters to me he talked about it, but he never talked very seriously and he kidded me a great deal about the motion pictures, but I think he liked them. All of us in the business who met him wanted his future for our own.

MEMORIAL SERVICE

The Presbyterian Church in Marion was filled to overflowing at 1500hrs on Sunday, January 7, 1945, when a memorial service for the town's fallen hero got under way. Sitting with his grandmother in the front of the church was Maj Dick Reed, who had arrived at the last minute from his duty station in Mission, Texas. Dick had intended to fly directly to his home town, but bad weather forced him down in Wichita, Kansas, and he was fortunate to catch a train for the remainder of his journey. Mayme's daughters Leota and Isabelle traveled from out of state to attend the service for their little brother.

Also in attendance was SSgt "Mick" Forbes, US Marine Corps, who received emergency leave from her post in Washington, D.C., in order to comfort Mayme and say her goodbyes to Bill. After waiting ten years for Bill to marry her, it must have been heartbreaking for "Mick" to sit through the service. The future she dreamed of had died with Bill on that tragic night in China.[5]

The service opened with an advance of colors by members of the Marion Post 298 American Legion, and several local veterans of the Spanish–American War added to the military flavor of the event. The Reverend C. V. R. De Jong delivered the scripture reading and invocation, before turning over his pulpit to Bill's friend from Loras College Father George Stemm for the memorial address. As one reporter covering the event observed, Father Stemm "left all his theology at home, and spoke only as a friend." Here, in part, is what he said:

There was something about Bill Reed – seldom has God endowed one man with so many gifts and talents as he did this one man. He was one of the greatest men I ever knew. He was superb in body and mind and had a great quality of soul and character.

It was nothing less than a deep sense of personal duty that caused him to turn his face again toward China after he came home in 1942. With his whole heart and mind crying out to stay with his family and friends, he was compelled by an innate sense of duty to go where he could make the greatest contribution toward perfecting the kind of civilization we are fighting for.

There was no room in Bill for pettiness, intolerance or bigotry. Let us too, cast out pettiness, intolerance and bigotry from our lives that we may keep faith with those who fought and died for us.

After a rousing rendition of "Faith of Our Fathers," accompanied by the pianist, Mrs. I. L. Ford, Reverend De Jong returned to the pulpit to lead the meditation and deliver the benediction. Then the service was over, and the crowd dispersed, each person to consider privately the tragedy of losing Bill Reed in his or her personal life.

Mayme continued to receive messages of condolence for a few weeks following the memorial service, but eventually they stopped coming and she was left to cope with her grief alone. Just as she was becoming adjusted to the reality of life without Bill in the late summer of 1945, a package arrived from Gen Chennault that must have revived her feelings of loss. Chennault had returned to the US after being relieved of his command in China, and he brought with him the samurai sword that Bill had been presented with by his Chinese admirers the previous year. Not trusting normal channels to deliver the valuable sword from overseas, Chennault hand-carried it home before seeing to its delivery to Mayme.[6]

CONTINUING TROUBLE IN CHINA

In nearly every letter Bill Reed wrote to his mother from the war, he implored Mayme to take care of herself and not to worry about his wellbeing. Time after time he assured her that he was perfectly safe and feeling fine. Mayme, of course, knew better than to believe that anyone flying fighter planes in combat, including her son, was not facing danger on an almost daily basis. But Bill was a loving son and did his best to assuage her fears for his safety.

Mayme's worries might have ended when she received the terrible news of Bill's death, but it was not that simple. With the end of World War II in the late summer of 1945, China fell into a new conflict almost immediately. Chiang's fragile and corrupt Kuomintang government now faced a foe in the Chinese Communists, who in a short time would grow even more formidable and determined than the Japanese had been. As news reports in the United States told of the growing conflict in China, Mayme had to face a new reality – her son was buried in a cemetery halfway around the world, and that cemetery sat in the middle of a country mired in a brutal civil war. Who knew what might become of Bill's grave under those circumstances?

Fortunately, the US government shared the concerns of Mayme and other mothers whose sons were buried in the American Military Cemetery in Kunming. On October 10, 1947, a ship arrived in San Francisco carrying the remains of Americans who had been in the Kunming cemetery for re-interment in the United States. Lt Col William T. Hull, an Iowan who had served briefly under Bill before assuming command of his own fighter squadron in the CACW, escorted Bill's casket on the long train ride from the West Coast to eastern Iowa.

The eastbound Hiawatha train from Kansas City arrived on Tuesday afternoon, October 21, and Lt Col Hull turned over his charge to the Yocom Funeral Home. At the request of Mayor M. H. Biddick, flags flew at half-staff in Marion on Wednesday when the funeral procession passed through town on its way to Riverside Cemetery in Anamosa, Iowa. On arrival at 1430hrs on October 22, the Reverend C. V. R. De Jong presided over a brief religious ceremony, and then an honor guard from Marion Post

298 of the American Legion conducted military rites. With that, Bill's casket was lowered into his grave at Block 1, 2nd Addition, Lot 14.

Bill Reed had come home from the war. Now Mayme and her family could visit him whenever they wished. She would not have to worry about her son ever again.

Appendix

CHINESE PLACE NAMES

The Chinese government adopted a new phonetic system in 1958 for Romanizing Chinese language sounds. That system, called "Pinyin," replaced the Wade Giles spellings of place names that were created by the British colonial postal service during the 19th century and still used by Americans in China during World War II. For the purposes of consistency and familiarity, this book uses the traditional spelling for Chinese place names in the 1940s. Wherever possible, the Pinyin spelling follows in parentheses behind the first appearance of a place name in the text. However, this was not possible to do for some locations that are too small or remote to appear on contemporary maps.

Endnotes

CHAPTER 1

1 Carl Molesworth, *Wing to Wing – Air Combat in China 1943–45* (Orion Books, New York, 1990), p. 61
2 R. M. Corbitt, *History of Jones County, Iowa* (S. J. Clarke Publishing Co., Chicago, 1910), p. 590. Will Dearborn would lose most of his fortune in the stock market crash of 1929
3 Bureau of Labor Statistics, *Monthly Labor Review Vol. X No. 6* (US Government, Washington, D.C., June 1920)
4 Ed Ferreter, "Decades Later, Old Friend is Hard to Picture," *The Marion Times*, March 3, 1944, p. 4A
5 Goodyear, like Bill and Dick Reed, would become a military pilot. He lost his life when the aircraft carrier USS *Langley* (CV-1) was attacked by Japanese aircraft and then scuttled off the Dutch East Indies on February 27, 1942

CHAPTER 2

1 Columbia College changed its name to Loras College in the spring of 1939, just as Bill Reed was preparing to graduate
2 William Ray, *The Forgotten Brother* (unpublished manuscript, 2015), p. 3
3 Ibid., p. 4
4 Michael Dennis, *Blood on Steel, Chicago Steelworkers and The Strike of 1937* (Johns Hopkins University Press, Baltimore, 2014), p. 31
5 Ibid., p. 43

6 The newsreel footage of the Memorial Day encounter is included in the film *The Memorial Day Massacre of 1937*, produced by the Illinois Labor History Society. The film is available online at: https://www.youtube.com/watch?v=-Q3RUGLfFvo

7 The transcript of the LaFollette Committee hearings is available online at: http://usw1010.org/lafollette.html

8 Front-page story in the *Chicago Tribune*, July 21, 1937

CHAPTER 3

1 F. F. Liu, *A Military History of Modern China, 1924-1949* (Princeton University Press, Princeton, 1956), p. 197

2 Stephen G. Craft, "Laying the Foundation of a Mighty Air Force: Civilian Schools and Primary Flight Training During World War II," *Air Power History*, Fall 2012, pp. 7–8

3 Enzo Angeluzzi, *Rand McNally Encyclopedia of Military Aircraft, 1914-1980* (The Military Press, New York, 1980), pp. 340–41

4 "Training Program of Air Corps Expansion," *Air Corps Newsletter*, Vol XXIII, No. 12, June 15, 1940

5 Lt John H. Cheatwood, "Barksdale – Never a Dull Moment," *Air Corps Newsletter*, Vol XXV, No. 2, March–April 1942, p. 39

6 Selma information from usafunithistory.com

7 Duane Schultz, *The Maverick War, Chennault and the Flying Tigers* (St. Martin's Press, New York, 1987), pp. 56–78

8 Wanda Cornelius and Thayne Short, *Ding Hao – America's Air War in China, 1937-1945* (Pelican Publishing Co., Gretna, 1980), pp. 101–103

9 Daniel Ford, *Flying Tigers, Claire Chennault and the American Volunteer Group* (Smithsonian Institution Press, Washington, D.C., 1991), p. 48

10 William N. Reed, letter to Mayme Reed, July 17, 1941

11 Robert T. Smith, *Tale of a Tiger* (Tiger Originals, Van Nuys, 1986), p. 33

12 Ibid., pp. 37–39

CHAPTER 4

1 Robert T. Smith recalled the ship sailing from San Francisco on July 24

2 ww2gravestone.com
3 Robert T. Smith said the ship's name was the *Penang Trader*
4 Two AVG recruits had jumped ship in Batavia
5 Father George Stemm was one of Bill's professors at Columbia College

CHAPTER 5

1 William N. Reed, letter to Mayme Reed, September 17, 1941
2 Ibid., October 16, 1941
3 Robert M. Smith, *With Chennault in China, A Flying Triger's Diary* (Tab Books Inc., Blue Ridge Summit, 1984), pp. 138–41
4 Robert T. Smith, *Tale of a Tiger* (Tiger Originals, Van Nuys, 1986), p. 71
5 Martha Byrd, *Chennault, Giving Wings to the Tiger* (The University of Alabama Press, Tuscaloosa, 1987), p. 57
6 Malcolm Rosholt, *Claire L. Chennault, A Tribute* (The Flying Tigers of the Fourteenth Air Force Association, Silver Bay), p. 42
7 Robert T. Smith, *Tale of a Tiger* (Tiger Originals, Van Nuys, 1986), p. 99
8 Operations Memorandum No. 1, Headquarters, First American Volunteer Group, October 22, 1941

CHAPTER 6

1 Frank S. Losonsky and Terry M. Losonsky, *Flying Tiger, A Crew Chief's Diary* (Schiffer Publishing Ltd., Atglen, 1996), p. 70
2 Daniel Ford, *Flying Tigers, Claire Chennault and the American Volunteer Group* (Smithsonian Institution Press, Washington, D.C., 1991), p. 133
3 Frank J. Olynyk, *AVG & USAAF (China-Burma-India Theater) Credits for the Destruction of Enemy Aircraft in Air-to-Air Combat World War II* (Frank J. Olynyk, Aurora, 1986), p. 1
4 Overclaiming of aerial victories is a common phenomenon that dates back to the dawn of air-to-air combat in World War I. In this case, the AVG claims were reasonably accurate
5 Daniel Ford, *Flying Tigers, Claire Chennault and the American Volunteer Group* (Smithsonian Institution Press, Washington, D.C., 1991), p. 136

6 Frank S. Losonsky and Terry M. Losonsky, *Flying Tiger,
   A Crew Chief's Diary* (Schiffer Publishing Ltd., Atglen, 1996),
   p. 72

7 Carl Molesworth, Air Vanguard 8 – *Curtiss P-40 Long-nosed
   Tomahawks* (Osprey Publishing, Oxford, 2013), p. 56

8 Frank J. Olynyk, *AVG & USAAF (China-Burma-India Theater)
   Credits for the Destruction of Enemy Aircraft in Air-to-Air Combat
   World War II* (Frank J. Olynyk, Aurora, 1986), p. 1

9 Robert T. Smith, *Tale of a Tiger* (Tiger Originals, Van Nuys, 1986),
   p. 165

10 A "short snorter" was a banknote signed by people traveling
   together on an aircraft to convey good luck. When the "short
   snorter" was signed, the collector would have to produce it upon
   request. If not, he was bound to buy the signer a drink

CHAPTER 7

1 Robert T. Smith, *Tale of a Tiger* (Tiger Originals, Van Nuys, 1986),
   pp. 174–75 and Daniel Ford, *Flying Tigers, Claire Chennault and
   the American Volunteer Group* (Smithsonian Institution Press,
   Washington, D.C., 1991), p. 154

2 William N. Reed, letter to Mayme Reed, January 8, 1942

3 Erik Shilling, *Destiny – A Flying Tiger's Rendezvous with Fate*
   (Erik Shilling, Alta Loma, 1997), p. 132

4 Raines did, in fact, get better. He scored 3.2 confirmed aerial
   victories from April through June 1942

CHAPTER 8

1 Daniel Ford, *Flying Tigers, Claire Chennault and the American
   Volunteer Group* (Smithsonian Institution Press, Washington, D.C.,
   1991), p. 252

2 Loyal Meek, "Fighting Zeros While Blinded by Oil – Reed's
   Tightest Tight Spot," *Cedar Rapids Gazette*, sixth of seven articles,
   September 1942, p. 1

3 Chennault recently had been promoted to brigadier general in the
   USAAF

4 Albert "Ajax" Baumler had been an instructor with Bill at Selma,
   and he flew in the Spanish Civil War before that. He was now part

of the initial contingent of 23rd FG officers beginning to arrive
in China

5 Robert T. Smith, *Tale of a Tiger* (Tiger Originals, Van Nuys, 1986),
pp. 207, 321 and 323

6 Ibid., pp. 336, 338 and 347

7 Ibid., p. 352

8 Ibid., pp. 356–58

CHAPTER 9

1 http://www.u-s-history.com

2 Laurence M. Olney, *The War Bond Story* (unpublished manuscript)

3 http://www.joebaugher.com/usaf_serials/usafserials.html

CHAPTER 10

1 http://www.pressofatlanticcity.com, February 26, 2017

2 Frank J. Olynyk, *AVG & USAAF (China-Burma-India Theater)
Credits for the Destruction of Enemy Aircraft in Air-to-Air Combat
World War II* (Frank J. Olynyk, Aurora, 1986), p. 321

3 Robert G. Riley, letter to the author, September 29, 1987

4 Geoff Duvall, *Republic P-47 Thunderbolt Described, Part 1*
(Kookaburra Technical Publications, Victoria, 1969), pp. 1–2

5 When William R. "Dick" Reed joined the USAAF, his Army
friends began calling him "Bill." This account will refer to him
as "Dick" throughout, however, to avoid confusing him with his
uncle, William N. "Bill" Reed

6 Ernest R. McDowell, *Checkertails – The 325th Fighter Group in
World War II* (Squadron/Signal Publications Inc., Carrollton,
1994), p. 6

7 Herschel R. Green, *Herky – The Memoirs of a Checkertail Ace*
(Squadron/Signal Publications Inc., Atglen, 1996), p. 17

8 Ibid., p. 21

9 Ibid., p. 26

10 Ibid., p. 32

11 Thomas G. Ivie, Aircraft of the Aces 117 – *Aces of the 325th Fighter
Group* (Osprey Publishing, Oxford, 2014), pp. 22–23

12 Dick returned to Marion after the war and established a successful
business career in real estate and insurance. He also earned a
reputation as one of the top amateur golfers in the region

CHAPTER 11

1 Robert T. Smith, *Tale of a Tiger* (Tiger Originals, Van Nuys, 1986), p. 218

2 Laurence Martin did not become a pilot, but he fought in Europe with the 71st Infantry Division

3 The parent unit of Bill's squadron was the 326th FG

4 William N. Reed, letter to Mayme Reed, July 6, 1943

5 Carl Molesworth, *Wing to Wing – Air Combat in China 1943–45* (Orion Books, New York, 1990), p. 74

6 Air Commodore Henry Probert, *The Forgotten Air Force – the Royal Air Force at War Against Japan 1941–1945* (Brassey's, London, 1995), pp. 116–18

7 Kenn C. Rust and Stephen Muth, *Fourteenth Air Force Story* (Historical Aviation Album, Temple City, 1977), p. 4

8 Warren Bodie, "Skybolt Part IX," *Airpower*, Vol. 7, No. 4, July 1977, p. 51

9 Rebecca Hancock Cameron, *Training to Fly* (Air Force History and Museums Program, 1999), p. 543

CHAPTER 12

1 Lt Harry Kebric was the 3rd FG's intelligence officer

2 Military History and Translation Office, *The Immortal Flying Tigers – An Oral History of the Chinese-American Composite Wing* (Ministry of National Defense, Taipei, 2009), pp. 103–38

3 Seventh Fighter Squadron unit history, October 20, 1943

4 Military History and Translation Office, *The Immortal Flying Tigers – An Oral History of the Chinese-American Composite Wing* (Ministry of National Defense, Taipei, 2009), p. 119

5 28th Fighter Squadron unit history, October 9, 1943

6 *Union City Times-Gazette*, January 4, 1944

CHAPTER 13

1 Military History and Translation Office, *The Immortal Flying Tigers, An Oral History of the Chinese-American Composite Wing* (Ministry of National Defense, Taipei, 2009), pp. 128–30

2 Carl Molesworth, *Wing to Wing, Air Combat in China 1943–45* (Orion Books, New York, 1990), p. 52
3 Ibid., p. 50

CHAPTER 14

1 7th Fighter Squadron unit history, August 8, 1944
2 Ibid., August 12, 1944
3 Ibid., August 21, 1944
4 Frank J. Olynyk, *AVG & USAAF (China-Burma-India Theater) Credits for the Destruction of Enemy Aircraft in Air-to-Air Combat World War II*, (Frank J. Olynyk, Aurora, 1986), pp. 48–49
5 Carl Molesworth, *Sharks Over China – the 23rd Fighter Group in World War II* (Brassey's Inc., Washington, D.C., 1994), pp. 220–21
6 Jinx Falkenburg, *Jinx* (Duell, Sloan and Pearce, New York, 1951), pp. 125–61
7 Richard Watts, Jr., "New York Drama Critic Surveys the China Scene And Reports the Travels of Pat, Jinx & Company," *CBI Journal*, November 16, 1944
8 NBC Interdepartmental Correspondence, May 14, 1954. This author requested an interview with Jinx Falkenburg in 2000 but never received a reply. She died in 2003
9 Claire L. Chennault, letter to Robert T. Smith, February 27, 1952
10 Earl Ashworth, "A Love Story," *Jing Bao Journal*, August–September 1993, pp. 30–31
11 Jinx Falkenburg, *Jinx* (Duell, Sloan and Pearce, New York, 1951), p. 170
12 3rd Fighter Group unit history, December 1944

CHAPTER 15

1 Charles Lovett, interview with author, September 12, 1981
2 James T. Bull, letter to Mrs. Mayme Reed, December 24, 1944
3 The Reverend Sheppard Bryan, letter to Mrs. Mayme Reed, January 15, 1945
4 Gene B. Stafford, *Aces of the Southwest Pacific* (Squadron/Signal Publications, Carrollton, 1977), p. 59

5 "Mick" Forbes moved to Los Angeles after the war and had a
   long career with the Carnation Milk Company. She died in 1980,
   having never married
6 Bill's samurai sword, along with other items of memorabilia and
   a full-scale replica of his AVG P-40, are proudly displayed at the
   Iowa Gold Star Military Museum near Des Moines

Bibliography

BOOKS

Baisden, Chuck, *Flying Tiger to Air Commando*, Schiffer Publishing Ltd, Atglen, 1999

Bond, Charles R., Jr. with Anderson, Terry H., *A Flying Tiger's Diary*, Texas A&M University Press, College Station, 1984

Byrd, Martha, *Chennault: Giving Wings to the Tiger*, The University of Alabama Press, Tuscaloosa, 1987

Cheung, Raymond, Aircraft of the Aces 126 – *Aces of the Republic of China Air Force*, Osprey Publishing, Oxford, 2015

Clements, Terrill, Aircraft of the Aces 41 – *American Volunteer Group Colours and Markings*, Osprey Publishing, Oxford, 2001

Cornelius, Wanda and Short, Thayne, *Ding Hao – America's Air War in China 1937–1945*, Pelican Publishing Company, Gretna, 1980

Dennis, Michael. *Blood on Steel – Chicago Steelworkers & the Strike of 1937*, Johns Hopkins University Press, Baltimore, 2014

Dorr, Robert F. and Jones, Thomas D., *Hell Hawks! The Untold Story of the American Fliers Who Savaged Hitler's Wehrmacht*, Zenith Press, Minneapolis, 2008

Duval, Geoff, *Thunderbolt Described Part 1*, Kookaburra Technical Publications, Victoria, 1969

Falkenburg, Jinx, *Jinx*, Duell, Sloan and Pearce, New York, 1951

Ford, Daniel, *Flying Tigers – Claire Chennault and the American Volunteer Group*, Smithsonian Institution Press, Washington, D.C., 1991

314

Green, Herschel H., *Herky! The Memoirs of a Checkertail Ace*, Schiffer Publishing Ltd., Atglen, 1996

Heiferman, Ron, *Flying Tigers – Chennault in China*, Ballantine Books Inc., New York, 1971

Hill, David Lee with Schaupp, Reagan, *Tex Hill – Flying Tiger*, Honoribus Press, Spartanburg, 2003

Holik-Urban, Jennifer, *To Soar with the Tigers*, Generations, Woodridge, 2011

Ivie, Thomas G., Aircraft of the Aces 117 – *Aces of the 325th Fighter Group*, Osprey Publishing, Oxford, 2014

Jimison, Susan Clotfelter, *Through the Eyes of a Tiger*, Deeds Publishing, Athens, 2015

Johnson, Earnest D., *In Search of Ghosts – China Perspective Past and Present*, Jet Publishing Company, Boise, 1989

Kellams, Dan, *Mistaken for a King*, FAIT Accompli Publishing, Phoenix, 2016

Liu, F. F., *A Military History of Modern China – 1924–1949*, Princeton University Press, New Jersey, 1956

Liu Lee-hsuan and Wang Chien-chi, editors, *The Immortal Flying Tigers – an Oral History of the Chinese-American Composite Wing*, Military History and Translation Office, Ministry of Defense, Taipei, 2009

Losonsky, Frank S. and Lasonsky, Terry M., *Flying Tiger – A Crew Chief's Story*, Schiffer Publishing Ltd., Atglen, 1996

McDowell, Ernest R., *Checkertails – The 325th Fighter Group in the Second World War*, Squadron/Signal Publications, Carrolton, 1994

Molesworth, Carl, *Wing to Wing – Air Combat in China, 1943–45*, Orion Books, New York, 1990

Molesworth, Carl, *Sharks Over China – the 23rd Fighter Group in World War II*, Brassey's Inc., Washington, D.C., 1994

Molesworth, Carl, Aircraft of the Aces 43 – *P-40 Warhawk Aces of the MTO*, Osprey Publishing, Oxford, 2002

Molesworth, Carl, Duel 8 – *P-40 Warhawk vs Ki-43 Oscar*, Osprey Publishing, Oxford, 2008

Molesworth, Carl, Air Vanguard 8 – *Curtiss P-40 Long-nosed Tomahawks* Osprey Publishing, Oxford, 2013

Nalty, Bernard C., *Tigers Over Asia*, Elsevier-Dutton, New York, 1978

Olynyk, Frank J., *AVG & USAAF (China-Burma-India Theater) Credits for the Destruction of Enemy Aircraft in Air-to-Air Combat World War II*, Frank J. Olynyk, Aurora, 1986

Pearson, Michael, *The Burma Air Campaign, 1941–1945*, Pen & Sword Military, Barnsley, 2006

Probert, Henry, *The Forgotten Air Force – the Royal Air Force in the War Against Japan, 1941–1945*, Brassey's, London, 1995

Rosholt, Malcolm, *Days of the Ching Pao*, Palmer Publications Inc., Amherst, 1978

Rosholt, Malcolm, *Claire L. Chennault – A Tribute*, The Flying Tigers of the Fourteenth Air Force Association, Silver Bay, 1983

Rosholt, Malcolm, *Flight in the China Air Space 1910–1950*, Rosholt House, Wisconsin, 1984

Rust, Kenn C. and Hess, William N., *The Slybird Group*, Aero Publishers Inc., Fallbrook, 1969

Rust, Kenn C. and Muth, Stephen, *Fourteenth Air Force Story*, Historical Aviation Album, Temple City, 1977

Schultz, Duane, *The Maverick War – Chennault and the Flying Tigers*, St. Martin's Press, New York, 1987

Shilling, Erik, *Destiny, A Flying Tiger's Rendezvous with Fate*, Erik Shilling, Alta Loma, 1993

Shores, Christopher and Cull, Brian, *Bloody Shambles, Volume Two*, Grub Street, London, 1993

Smith, Robert M., *With Chennault in China – a Flying Tiger's Diary*, Tab Books Inc., New York, 1984

Smith, R. T., *Tale of a Tiger*, Tiger Originals, Van Nuys, 1986

Snyder, Louis L., *The War – A Concise History 1939–1945*, Simon and Schuster, New York, 1960

Stafford, Gene B., *Aces of the Southwest Pacific*, Squadron/Signal Publications, 1977

Stilwell, Joseph W., *The Stilwell Papers*, Sloan Associates, New York, 1948

Toland, John, *The Flying Tigers*, Random House Inc., New York, 1963

Tuchman, Barbara W., *Stillwell and the American Experience in China, 1911–45*, The Macmillan Company, New York, 1970

Whelan, Russell, *The Flying Tigers*, The Viking Press Inc., New York, 1942

Wilson, Dick, *When Tigers Fight – The Story of the Sino-Japanese War, 1937–1945*, The Viking Press, New York, 1982

YEARBOOKS

Purgold, Loras College – 1936, 1937, 1938, 1939
The Quill, Marion High School – 1930, 1934, 1935, 1936

MAGAZINES

Air Power magazine, "Skybolt, Part IX," Warren Bodie, July 1977
Jing Bao Journal, "The Young Commanders," Ken Kay, August–
    September 1981
Jing Bao Journal, "A Love Story," Earl Ashworth, August–September 1993
Time, "Battle of Asia – So Sorry," March 9, 1942

NEWSPAPERS

Air Corps Newsletter
Air Power History
CBI Roundup
Cedar Rapids Gazette
Des Moines Register
Marion Sentinel
The Cedar Centurian
The Lorian

UNPUBLISHED UNIT HISTORIES

3rd Fighter Group, Chinese-American Composite Wing
3rd Pursuit Squadron, First American Volunteer Group
7th, 8th, 28th and 32nd Fighter Squadrons, Chinese-American
    Composite Wing

List of Illustrations

but was bothered by the heat, the food, and the bugs. (*From the Reed family collection, © Ed Reed*)

19   Claire Lee Chennault, a retired USAAC pilot from Louisiana, would become famous for his success as the commander of the AVG. Bill formed a close bond with Chennault during their many months of serving together. (*Photograph by R. T. Smith, © Brad Smith*)

20   Bill took his first AVG flight in P-40 "No. 12" on September 18, 1941, and quickly developed a reputation as one of the top pilots in his squadron, the 3rd PS "Hell's Angels." (*From the Reed family collection, © Ed Reed*)

21   Bill's roommate and best friend during AVG training was Neil Martin, who, like Bill, had been a college athlete before the war. Martin would be killed over Rangoon on his first combat mission on December 23, 1941. (*From the Reed family collection, © Ed Reed*)

22   Bill takes a rickshaw ride in the fall of 1941 during one of his infrequent visits to Rangoon. Pilots would take the train to Rangoon to pick up new P-40s and fly them to Kyedaw. (*From the Reed family collection, © Ed Reed*)

23   Bill's P-40 "No. 75" sits at readiness at Mingaladon airdrome, Rangoon, shortly after the 3rd PS arrived there on December 12, 1941. Bill flew his first mission from Mingaladon – an airfield patrol – on December 16. (*From the Reed family collection, © Ed Reed*)

24   P-40 "No. 75's" twin portside wing guns are the focus of this photograph. Also visible is the "Hell's Angel" cartoon and Bill's name on the fuselage, plus the aircraft number painted out below the cockpit. (*From the Reed family collection, © Ed Reed*)

25   Bill was still sporting his short-lived mustache when he posed for this photograph with his trusty P-40 "No. 75." Bill scored two victories in this plane on December 25, 1941, while defending Rangoon from an IJAAF air raid. (*Molesworth collection*)

26   The "Hell's Angels" pilots pose in Kunming with Squadron Leader "Oley" Olson's P-40 "No. 99" on January 27, 1942. Bill is kneeling at far left, wearing his coveralls, helmet, and goggles. (*From the Reed family collection, © Ed Reed*)

27   Three victory flags had been applied to Bill's P-40 "No. 75" by the time this photograph was taken in early 1942. Note Bill has shaved off his mustache, and the plane is showing signs of wear. (*From the Reed family collection, © Ed Reed*)

28   Bill's closest call in aerial combat came on April 10, 1942, when his vision was obscured as the cap on the oil tank of P-40 "No. 59" blew

They would meet again two years later when Jinx came to China on a USO tour. (*Molesworth collection*)

39   Bill returns to the Quaker Oats plant in Cedar Rapids, Iowa, where he and his father worked before the war, to sell war bonds and boost the morale of workers. A US Navy combat veteran joined him. (*From the Reed family collection, © Ed Reed*)

40   Dick, left, and Bill took places of honor at the head of the table when the Reed family got together for a picnic shortly after Bill returned from China. Mayme Reed is next to Bill. (*From the Reed family collection, © Ed Reed*)

41   Bill used part of his AVG earnings to buy a late-model Plymouth convertible. With him in the front seat are Mayme and his older brother Edward. He sold the car in 1943. (*From the Reed family collection, © Ed Reed*)

42   Bill and fellow AVG veteran R. T. Smith drove to California in November 1942 and stopped to visit friends at Randolph and Kelly fields. Here, they attend a party at the home of Lou and Joan Van Mullen. (*Photograph by R. T. Smith, © Brad Smith*)

43   Dick Reed, seated third from left, and his fellow pilots of the 317th FS/325th FG pose with their P-40s on the flight deck of the aircraft carrier USS *Ranger* (CV-4) while on their way to North Africa in January 1943. (*Porter Reed*)

44   Dick Reed takes a smoke break while seated on the cockpit rim of his first P-40F, 41-19496 "No. 10" "*Queen Mary.*" By this time he had been promoted to captain and given command of the 317th FS. (*Porter Reed*)

45   Maj Gen Jimmy Doolittle, commander of the Twelfth Air Force, pins the DFC on Dick Reed. The medal was awarded in recognition of Dick's heroism during the July 10, 1943 mission to Sicily. (*Porter Reed*)

46   Bill was not impressed by the early models of the Republic P-47 Thunderbolt he flew at Millville, complaining of unreliability and lackluster performance. This P-47B was wrecked by 2Lt Frank Emory at Millville, New Jersey, on April 2, 1943. (*Molesworth collection*)

47   Bill made friends with two fellow combat veterans, Capts Bill Turner (left) and Gerald Dix, while training P-47 pilots at Millville in 1943. Turner would later serve with Bill in China. (*From the Reed family collection, © Ed Reed*)

48   Lt Col Irving "Twig" Branch was Bill's closest traveling companion on his long trip by air back to China in 1943. Branch became the commanding officer of the 1st BG of the CACW. (*Molesworth collection*)

49   Appointed CO of the 320th FS – a P-47 training outfit – in June 1943 at Westover Field, Massachusetts, Bill had his hands full

60   Col Al Bennett congratulates Bill during a party in August 1944 to celebrate the 7th FS completing its 100th mission. Next to Bennett are 8th FS CO Capt Harvey Davis and Capt Wilbur Walton. (*Molesworth collection*)

61   Bill prepares to take off in a P-40N fitted with fragmentation clusters and triple-tube M-8 rocket launchers for ground attack under the wings. The rockets were not particularly accurate but did serious damage when they hit their targets. (*Molesworth collection*)

62   When Ann Sheridan's USO troupe visited Liangshan in August 1944, its members autographed Bill's P-40N *BOSS'S HOSS*. Posing with Bill, from left to right, are Mary Landa, Ruth Dennis, and Jackie Myles. (*From the Reed family collection, © Ed Reed*)

63   Capt Armit W. "Bill" Lewis kept a detailed scoreboard of his combat claims on the fuselage of his P-40N "No. 664." Lewis, a good friend of Bill, took command of the 7th FS when the latter became group commander. (*Molesworth collection*)

64   Crew Chief Homer "Jug" Nunley helps Capt Hsu strap into Bill's P-40N *BOSS'S HOSS* prior to a mission. SSgt Nunley named the plane *JUG'S PLUG* on the starboard side of the nose. (*Molesworth collection*)

65   Capt Don Burch, long-serving flight commander in the 7th FS, scored one victory in his P-40N "No. 665" *RUTH-LESS*. Shot down and captured in September 1944, he spent the rest of the war as a PoW. (*Molesworth collection*)

66   Capt Chuck Lovett, intelligence officer of the 7th FS, plays catch in front of the alert shack at Liangshan. Chuck led the effort to retrieve Bill's body when Bill was killed parachuting from his fuel-starved P-40N on the night of December 19, 1944. (*Molesworth collection*)

67   Gen Chennault and his Fourteenth Air Force staff (far left) listen as Chaplain Sheppard Bryan speaks during Bill's funeral service on December 23, 1944, at the American Military Cemetery in Kunming. (*From the Reed family collection, © Ed Reed*)

68   Lt Col William Dunn, himself a World War II fighter ace, presents Mayme Reed with a set of the medals awarded to Bill by the US government. The ceremony took place in Marion in 1947. (*From the Reed family collection, © Ed Reed*)

69   A simple stone marks the grave of Lt Col William N. Reed at Block 1, 2nd Addition, Lot 14 in Riverside Cemetery at Anamosa, Iowa, where Bill was laid to rest in 1947. (*Molesworth collection*)

Acknowledgments

A lot of pieces had to come together in order for me to write this story of Bill Reed's life, and I appreciate everyone who gave of their time and knowledge to help me complete the job.

My thanks go first to Bill himself. A tireless letter writer, he kept up a steady correspondence with his mother from the time he started college until a week before his death. Bill also kept up a diary during parts of his military service. Which leads me to Mayme Reed, who had the foresight to keep all of her son's letters, diaries and photo albums throughout her life; and to Ed Reed, her grandson, who carried on after her death in 1961. I am supremely grateful for Ed's willingness to share those materials with me. Without him, this book would have been impossible. Porter Reed, Mayme's great-grandson, made an immense contribution by scanning all of Bill's letters and providing them to me.

I gained further insight into the personal qualities of Bill Reed from a number of people who knew him, especially his childhood friend Ed Ferreter, his nephew Larry Martin and military comrades Ken Jernstedt, Bill Lewis and Chuck Lovett. The writing and photographs of Bill's AVG buddy R. T. Smith, provided to me by his son, Brad, added much more. Details about Bill's formative years emerged with the help of fine folks at the public library and the historical society of Marion, Iowa, as well at Loras College.

I also must acknowledge the work of many writers who have covered parts of this story before, especially historians of the AVG. And the staff at the Air Force Historical Research Agency got me started many years ago by providing me historical records of the various units in the CACW.

Finally, my deepest thanks go to my wife, Kris, who never wavered in her belief that I could and would write this book, and to my late mother-in-law, Florence Ekstrand, whose unflagging interest and useful suggestions helped to keep me on task.

Index

Abel, Walter   175, 177, 184, 300
Accra   206–7
Adair, C. B. "Skip"   74–75
aircraft, British:
  Blenheim bomber   152
  Buffalo I   110
aircraft, Chinese   210–12
aircraft, Japanese   259–60
  Hayabusa Ki-43
    "Oscar"   118–19, 122,
    149–50
  Kawasaki Ki-48 "Lily"   113
  Mitsubishi A6M2 "Zero"   98
aircraft, US   25–26, 219
  AT-6 Texan   66–67
  B-24 Liberator   123
  B-29 Superfortress   290
  Curtiss Hawk 81-A-2:   74
  North American BC-1:   66
  North American BT-9:   63–64
  P-40 Warhawk   15–19, 70,
    93, 94, 95–96, 98, 150,
    151–52, 188–89, 234
  P-47 Thunderbolt   185–86,
    197

Republic AT-12
  Guardsman   70
Seversky P-35:   70
Stearman PT-13:   61, 63
alert system   105–6
American Volunteer Group
    (AVG)   74–78, 81–84,
    151–52, 161–62
  1st PS   133
  2nd PS   130
  3rd PS ("Hell's
    Angels")   106–7, 108–9
  and Burma   92–97
  and Kunming   113–14,
    126–28
  and Rangoon   109–14,
    114–22
  and training   99–101
  and USA   131–32
  and USAAF   160
Ankang   15, 16, 258–60,
    261–62
Arnold, Gen H. H. "Hap"   59,
    74, 213–14, 300
Ascension Island   205–6